PUBLISHED BY
The Toronto Prospect Club

First Edition: 2021

ISBN: 9798705653713

TALES FROM THE PROSPECT CLUB
70 Years of Adventures in Mining

Introduction by David Harquail

Edited by Kerry Knoll and Nick Tintor

Cover Illustration by Barbara Blackstein

Photos supplied by the authors

To Diane & John —
With best wishes,

Ross & Joan

There's gold and it's haunting and haunting;
It's luring me on as of old;
Yet it isn't the gold that I'm wanting
So much as just finding the gold.

Robert W. Service
The Spell of the Yukon

Contents

EDITORS' NOTE

Somebody in the Prospect Club once said that our stories could fill a book. Well, now they have.

When Dave Rogers first came up with the idea and we agreed to do the editing, things started off with a slow trickle and we were wondering if it would happen all. But thanks to Ed Thompson's cajoling, that trickle soon turned into a waterfall and before we knew it our bullshit detectors were red-lining.

These stories cover seventy years of adventure, brilliance, discovery, malfeasance, good luck, bad luck, and the plain old laughs that our industry is so famous for. The more than 200 stories are presented in no particular order. We decided to publish everything submitted, and it's not all politically correct. If you are offended blame the author. We didn't have a professional editor, so please do your best to ignore any issues with spelling and grammar. Lastly, bear in mind that these are just stories, told the way we all remember them. If you read about a time and place where you were present, well, don't be too surprised if you recall things a little bit differently.

Kerry Knoll & Nick Tintor

INTRODUCTION, *By David Harquail, Chair, Franco-Nevada Corporation, 1996 Brass Balls Winner*

I have been asked to capture the "essence" of the Prospect Club. For most investment clubs, the objective measure of success is how well the fund performs. Anyone joining the Prospect Club expecting that a committee with some of the most experienced players in geology, mining and the markets would naturally translate into the successful trading of speculative mining stocks, would be sorely disappointed.

For the majority of members, the success of the Prospect Club was found in the spirit of comradeship that came out of the regular biweekly Friday investment lunches and, of course, the infamous Christmas annual dinners.

The Prospect Club's history in Toronto dates back to 1968. Meetings were held initially at the storied Engineers' Club on Victoria Street until 1992 when it closed, and meetings moved to the more modern facilities at the Ontario Club in Commerce Court South. When that too was closed in 2007, the Prospect Club relocated to the National Club on Bay Street.

Membership in the Prospect Club would average about 20 and included many storied names including Canadian Mining Hall of Fame inductees Mort Brown, Bill James, Terry McGibbon, Ed Thompson and Mac Watson.

Probably every discipline related to the mining industry was included from lawyers, engineers, geologists, geophysicists, metallurgists, stockbrokers and even the odd analyst such as myself. My experience of the Prospect Club was limited to the 1990's.

But that decade caught the incredible bull market driven by the Diamet and Voiseys Bay discoveries in the first part of the decade followed by the Bre-X market crash in 1997.

My original investment in the club quadrupled during the bull run only to see it revert back to its original value after Bre-X. But the dividends received during that ride in the form of good friends, laughs and the open bar and cigars at the Christmas dinners made it all worthwhile. A highlight for any member at one of those dinners was to be honoured with a "Brass Balls" award.

Every older member of the Prospect Club had investment wisdom to impart to its newer members. Many of these would be a revelation to any business school curriculum and are worth study. The following are pearls of wisdom that I noted from members of the Prospect Club in the 90's:

1. He who makes money pleases God -- Terry Ortsland
2. Money stays the same. It's just the pockets that change – Will Barbour
3. Never bother about stocks with real assets or earnings – Len Bednarz
4. Any stock trading under $0.05 is an automatic buy, no research needed – Andy Rickaby
5. Who needs research when I have an advance copy of the press release – Not attributed
6. Buy on visual assays but sell before the truth comes out – Gord Fancy
7. Summer stocks are like perennial flowers. They blossom every summer – Dale Hendrick
8. Buy anything recommended by Leon La Prairie except Darnley Bay – Dave Rogers
9. If Dave Rogers is not attending, sell whatever he had us buy – Leon La Prairie

These quotes capture the true "essence" of the Prospect Club. Thank you for the education.

THE BACKSTORY

A Geologist's Mantra from "The Ore Finders" *by Siegfried Muessig, 1957*

1. "The odds are best in the shadow of the head frame."
2. "Go for the jugular." If you have faith in your geology and judgment of the potential of the area take the bold strokes that make for discovery.
3. "IQ gets you there, but NQ finds it!"

A Short History of the Prospect Club, *by Ed Thompson*

The Prospect Club was formed in the fall of 1968 at the instigation of Orval Leigh, a geological engineer graduate from the U of T in 1958 and patterned after the Tuesday Club that had been formed a couple years earlier. The idea was to have a social luncheon group to discuss junior mining stocks and to buy a few of them. We merged with the Tuesday Club in 2013.

Original members I believe were Bill Hill, Dave Rogers, David Rea, John Auston, Orval Leigh, Len Bednarz, W. Hutchinson, Bob Van Ingham, Mac Watson, Leon La Prairie, Wilson Barber, Gerry Grant, Jack Tindale, Gord Fancy, Mike Gray, and myself

According to Bill Hill, it was Orv Leigh's idea and proposed to him over lunch and then soon after a meeting with Gord Fancy, a broker and a fellow U of T graduate in Geological Engineering, me and probably Leon La Prairie, who was in the Tuesday Club and involved in all social events and maybe others. Anyhow, we quickly assembled 16 members, made a small financial contribution and started meeting every two weeks and paying $10 per meeting. Fancy did all the trading and knew all the rumors.

We started a Christmas Dinner party that year that has continued ever since. During the evening we all selected a stock pick for the following year and later on metal prices and members donated prizes. usually booze, books or items from mine openings.

At that time most of us were in our mid 30's and had relatively important jobs and full of ourselves. Many of us were solid drinkers and the bar bill was astronomical. We moved around to the various clubs, the Engineers, Albany, Ontario, Granite, which asked us not to come back, the Ontario, and Leon's condo.

Early on we formalized some Awards. The first and most prestigious was the Brass Ball Award that was given each year at the Christmas Dinner to the member that had achieved the most in the previous year. In the early years we had lots of candidates but as we reached retirement, worthy nominees were harder to find.

Another Award was the Mackenzie. This $50 prize was

supposed to be given by each member who had made a profit from buying another member's recommendation. Some people have short memories.

Later on, we added the Big Bull Award and a Dave Rogers carving Award to the member who had made the most profit in their TFSA.

We now have about 34 members and still meet every two or three weeks, recently by video. I don't think that we have really made any serious money over the 50 odd years, but we have had a good time and made many lifetime friends. And this book recounts some of our stories.

Ed Thompson presenting the Brass Ball Award to
Mac Watson, probably in 1990.

The first presentations of the Brass Ball, made at our annual Christmas Dinner, were prestigious and entertaining events. As an example, the 1980 booklet included the agenda for the evening, the dinner menu, and the voting procedure for the Brass Ball Award. Individual and group pictures were taken. The members at that time were Len Bednarz, Wilson Barbour, John Cooke, Art English, Gerry Grant, Bill Hill, Bob Van Ingen, Leon La Prairie, Orval Leigh, David Rae, Ed Thompson, Jack Tindale, David Rogers, and Mac Watson.

Someone, probably Leon La Prairie, had contacted the

presidents of Shell Oil, the TD Bank, Lacana Mining, Noranda Mines and the Northern Miner Press and persuaded them to write in a humorous nomination letter supporting their respective employee - in this case, Bob Van Ingen, Art English, Ed Thompson, Wilson Barbour and John Cooke respectively. These letters were read out at the dinner to great amusement.

The winner that year was David Rogers and there was a congratulatory letter from the Premier of Ontario, Bill Davis. It was a fun evening and we felt that we were on top of the world.

The Tuesday Club: A Short History, *by Ross Lawrence*

Don't gamble; take all your savings and buy some good stock and hold it till it goes up, then sell it. If it don't go up, don't buy it – Will Rogers

In the beginning there were several investment clubs with members connected to the mining industry. They were mostly formed in the early 1960s among folks who were members of the Engineers' Club. Two of them are the subject of this note. Both were composed of members from the mining industry – broadly defined. One club is the Prospect Club. The other was called The Tuesday Club and was originated by Leon La Prairie and Lionel York according to a memo penned by Leon La Prairie dated 29 October 1964. The first meeting was held in early October 1964 and by-laws were formulated and the following officers elected: President, Lionel York; Vice President, J.A.L. White (a.k.a. Giacomo Capobianco); Secretary-Treasurer, John K.L. Crawford.

The memo goes on to say that the members will meet every other Tuesday at the Engineers' Club. An interesting procedure was described, namely: Investment ideas will be proposed at each meeting, and these ideas will be turned over to the Selection Committee for consideration. The committee was composed of John Crawford (ex-officio), Lionel York, Jim White and Wil Barbour. The committee will decide on what to buy and sell, and any one of York, White or Barbour are authorized to enter orders.

John Crawford was a stockbroker at Crawford & Company and seems to have been the club's broker (hence his ex-officio status on the committee). Funding began with a small down payment and then a procedure for monthly contributions was described. Eventually the total contribution was capped at $620 for each of the original members.

There was a limit of 20 members and the original members were: Dave Asbury, Charlie Pegg, Wil Barbour, Al Storey, John Crawford, Doug Sullivan, George Disler, Linc   Torrence, Peter Howe, Andy Troop, Bill James, Jim White, Tom Kerr, Lionel York, and Leon La Prairie

The initial investments were: 1000 shares of Anglo Rouyn, 200 shares of Versatile Manufacturing Limited, and 1000 shares of Zenmac. Orders had been placed for United Keno Hill, and the committee was considering Opemiska Copper, Patino and Blackhawk Mining.

Records are sparse for the following years, although there was a motion made by Hamish McGregor, seconded by Tor Jensen, on 31 January 1996, that a distribution be made to each member of $5,000. The rationale was that (1) because the portfolio was so large, the meetings were becoming too long, and (2) it was hard to recruit new members because the tab was so large. The motion was put to a mail-in ballot and was duly defeated. (Must have been fraudulent?) Meetings were held at the Engineers' Club.

Fast forward to November 2011 and Leon La Prairie did a little calculation as follows:

Funds received: $192,192
Payouts – cash to former members: $217,060
Payout Opawica 300,000 shs @ $0.65: $195,000
Cost of Lunches: 24 meals x 30 years x $300: $216,000
Christmas lunches $3000 x 25 years: $75,000
Invited guests $2000 x 5 years: $10,000
Portfolio value @ 22 November 2011: $322,965
Total: $1,036,026
Net gain: $943,834
ROI: $439.06%
Annual return: 4.65%

After the Engineers' Club was liquidated and merged with the Ontario Club in 1992, the Tuesday Club met regularly at the Ontario Club – usually in the President's Room. Sandwiches and refreshments were served up buffet-style. This was a pleasant way to meet until the Ontario Club found itself in trouble with a new landlord and was forced to depart the premises. For a while we met in various venues, until eventually the Ontario Club merged with the National Club.

In October 2012, The Tuesday Club merged with the Prospect Club. The portfolio of The Tuesday Club was the bigger of the two clubs and it was decided that a distribution of $7,715.28 would be made to The Tuesday Club members to equalize the two portfolios. It was also agreed that the name of the merged club would be The Prospect Club and in return we would meet on Tuesdays.

Since then, the members have met regularly, usually every fortnight, originally at the National Club after the merger with the Ontario Club. In recent years, meetings have been held in the boardroom of the club's stockbroker, Durham Sims of RBC Dominion Securities. This has been quite satisfactory as Durham orders in a sandwich lunch from a local restaurant while at the same time allowing us to observe stock charts or other information as a group on a large projection screen.

Members have tried very hard to follow Mark Twain's advice – with varying success. My records show that the value of one share of the new Prospect Club was about $5,700 at the time of the merger in October 2012. Over the next three years the value per unit steadily fell until reaching its nadir in November 2015 at $1,650. This was not a merger made in heaven – but we have jolly meetings, and it has really become a social club. From that point the value has gradually risen until, at our virtual Christmas lunch in December 2020, the value had reached $4,500.

With the advent of the COVID-19 virus in March 2020, meetings have been held over ZOOM. We don't get to socialize the way we did before, but turnout has been better, and we hear from folks who are not in Toronto.

The History of the Brass Balls Award, *by Dave Rogers*

The Brass Ball award originated with Wil and Elsebeth Barbour. They were throwing out an old brass bed when Elsebeth detached the two Brass Balls and said what a shame to throw these out. They had another drink and then she had an 'eureka' moment and said why not mount them and propose to the club that they have a "Brass Ball Award" to be won annually for a secular performance in the past year by one of the members. Wil brought the mounted Brass Balls to a club Christmas party and made the proposal which was seconded and voted in 100%.

As you can see the Brass Ball Award has fallen on tough times in the maintenance department over the past 40 years

The Brass Balls Award is given annually at the Christmas Dinner to the individual member who has successfully executed a large project or undertaking either personally or through their company and deserves to be recognized.

1978-Leon La Prairie	1987-Gord Fancy	1997-Leon La Prairie	2006-P. Huba-check	2014-Mac Watson
1979-Wil Barbour	1988-Jack Tin-dale	1998-John Cooke	2007-Tom Toth	2015-Ed Thompson
1980-Dave Rogers	1990-Mac Watson	1999-Pot-vin & Hen-dricks	2008-Mac Wat-son	2017-Terry MacGib-bon
1981-Wil-liam Hill	1991-Or-val Leigh	2000-J.C. Potvin	2009-Mac Wat-son	2019-J.C. Potvin
1982-Ed Thompson	1993-J.C. Potvin	2002-P. Huba-check	2010-J.C. Potvin	2020–Kerry Knoll
1983-Mac Watson	1994-Da-vid Hut-ton	2003-Kent & Bojtos	2011-Fen-ton Scott	
1984-Jack McAdam	1995-John Pat-erson	2004-George Kent	2012-Kerry Knoll	
1986-Dave Rogers	1996-Da-vid Har-quail	2005-Terry MacGib-bon	2013-Pat-rick Reid	

Winners of the Brass Balls Award over the years – it was not awarded every year

Speaking of Brass Balls, I remember having a meeting with Peggy Witte and a number of respective company officials in our Duration board room. The discussion had gotten a bit heated and there was silence around the table. I spoke up and said, "Peggy! You have to possess the biggest set of balls on Bay St." Dead silence then she smiled and said, "David. I already know that." No, we did not come to a meeting of the minds.

THE LURE OF MINING

Forks in the Road of Life, *by Ed Thompson*

I am sure that most readers will sometimes reflect on the forks in the road of life. How one seemingly insignificant happening sends one in a completely different direction. I know this happened to me on several occasions and this is one of my stories.

I am now 84 years old and have been in the exploration/mining business for about 60 years. These were some of the forks in my road.

I was born in August 1936 in the middle of the depression. We were as the saying goes "dirt poor." My father was uneducated and cut wood for $1 a day. My mother died in early 1944 during a flu epidemic. From the time I was about 13, I worked at hard summer jobs, including three summers at McNallys lumber mill in Utterson, south of Huntsville, Ontario and two summers river driving on the Nipigon.

I was in high school in Bracebridge in 1954 and had obtained a cushy summer job pumping gas at the Muskoka airport when the first fork appeared. I had a friend, John Ellis, with whom I played on several sports teams. His mother had obtained a summer job for John and a friend to work on the Nipigon River for Abitibi Power and Paper. The friend was careless and had to get married, and, at the last minute, John asked me to join him. River driving sounded more adventurous then pumping gas so off I went to the Nipigon.

Now the next fork wasn't until August, the next summer, when we were both again river driving at Pine Portage, a camp where the Nipigon River leaves Lake Nipigon. I had finished high school and had little idea of what to do. There was essentially no guidance at Bracebridge High School.

So, in late September, 1955, I enrolled in Geological Engineering at Toronto. I was good at math and had applied to U of T Engineering but had limited funds. Then bingo - two forks in the road. In late August I was notified that I had a bursary that would cover my tuition fees and secondly, there was a staking rush around Lake Nipigon. The metal was lithium which wouldn't come back into favor for another 50 years. The supervisors were staking claims and carrying around samples of spodumene. I thought this seems interesting and it's an outdoor job. Little did

I know!

The next major fork occurred within a month. Of course, you don't recognize it at the time. A lab partner, John May, was being 'rushed' by Kappa Sigma fraternity where his two older brothers had been. This fraternity had many members from the Haileybury area and quite a few in mining, including the Smith brothers, George and Bob, the three Cunningham Dunlop brothers, and Clarke and Ron Campbell, mining lawyers with Day, Wilson & Campbell. Clarke was the voluntary legal counsel for the PDA and would be very helpful to me as a director and later VP and President. Little did I know at the time.

The fraternity would be a great benefit to me, a hick from the sticks, and I made a number of lifelong friends.

In 1958, the University expropriated our frat house, and we couldn't replace it. I had no place to stay so I decided to marry my long-time girlfriend Marie Taylor. Best decision I ever made, and we had 50 great years and four lovely kids before Marie died of gall bladder cancer in 2009.

Graduating in 1959 I had a job offer with Longpoint Gas & Oil drilling for gas around Lake Erie. A fairly easy job and heading for the oil and gas industry. However, another fork. My classmate and fraternity brother, Norm Keevil, said to me, "Why don't you go in and see Joe Frantz at my dad's company? They are looking for someone to run an exploration program out of Pickle Crow."

And stupid old me, not knowing anything about this dismal asshole of the world, hired on. Keevil had acquired control of Pickle Crow the previous winter and was planning an exploration program around the mine and a regional program with a hundred-mile radius east and north of the mine. The area is mainly water and swamp. Five months of misery and I considered leaving the business. So, I went back to U of T for my Masters in Science. And the following year hired on again and had a great ten years with Keevil, spending about half my time in exploration and half on acquisitions.

In 1961, a major turning point in my life occurred when Jim Walker left Keevil and I was asked to look after the grubstakes. A word of explanation: Grubstaking was the method that prospectors used to raise funds for their summer programs. The 1960s was the last decade of grubstaking. A prospector might raise between $10,000-$25,000 to cover his season's prospecting activities from up to a dozen companies. We usually subscribed for $1,000-$2,000. If a showing was found, one of the subscribers would send out a geologist to examine. I continued this practice at Lacana, and our most successful example was the Musselwhite Grubstake that after about 20 years became the Musselwhite Gold Mine.

But I digress. When Jim left, someone said, "Ed, can you represent us on the grubstakes?" So, I got to know a number of prospectors who were PDA directors and they encouraged me to get involved, especially after Viola MacMillan left in 1965. However, they were always suspicious of engineers and PDA had a policy prohibiting engineers from becoming a director.

But times were changing, the old prospectors were dying out and in 1970, under the guidance of my fraternity brother, Clarke Campbell, the rules were amended, and I was elected and became active on committees and the convention.

In 1975, Jim Walker was elected president of the PDA, and Fred Jowsey and I were tied at seven votes each for VP. Fred was from the famous Jowsey family and his dad had been a PDA President. I liked him but didn't think that he would do a good job running the association, then a strictly volunteer organization. So, I decided to let my name stand and the following morning Fred didn't show up, so I became VP.

Jim was a geophysical contractor and in the bush for months at a time. Our part time helper, Claude Taylor, an old newspaper man, died a couple months later and I was left to run the organization. We made major changes, increasing the board to 48 directors with representation across Canada and instituting monthly meetings. Lots of help at convention time from Keevil, Art White, Andy Troop and Noranda.

I'm coming to a couple of major forks in the road of life. In 1977, as president of the PDA, I was invited to the CIM Annual Dinner in Montreal where they gave out their awards during a long and tedious evening. I debated about going as I was busy, but I went and, as I sat at the head table twiddling my thumbs, I had the inspiration for the PDA to have awards.

So, at the next directors meeting I proposed establishing a Prospector of the Year Award, naming it after Bill Dennis who had just died. We now have six or seven awards, and I chaired the

Awards Committee for the next forty years. And because of my chairing of the Awards Committee, when Mort Brown, the Editor of The Northern Miner, called about starting the Canadian Mining Hall of Fame, I committed the PDA and helped run that organization for the next 30 years until I was myself inducted. I made many lifelong friends at both associations and all because I went to that boring CIM dinner in 1977.

Back to 1970. I had been with Keevil for ten years and was looking for a change. I had four different career paths and I decided to join up with my old professor, Bill Gross, who was still teaching at the U of T and doing some consulting work including some research with me at Keevil's.

One of the companies he was consulting for was Pure Silver Mines. He wanted to leave teaching and move to Mexico, so I agreed to look after the Canadian side. Keevil wanted out of Mexico so we vended in our properties and formed Tormex Mining Developers for Mexico and Lacanex Mining for Canada and the US.

Most of the 1970s was a lousy period for mineral exploration and we were broke most of the time. We merged the three companies in 1976 into Lacana Mining. Wood Grundy financed us for $7 million, the largest junior company financing at the time. We persevered and developed in joint ventures, six mines in Mexico and four in Nevada.

In 1985, a friend from the 1950's emerged, John Ellis. John now held a senior position with Inspiration Copper, controlled by Anglo American, and he wanted me to join him. I didn't relish working for a big international company but finally in 1986 they made me an offer I couldn't refuse.

So, John and I ran things for AA for five years. We had big programs in Canada and the US with offices in Denver, Reno, Missoula in the US and Toronto, Vancouver and Flin Flon in Canada. We didn't have much success, so the work was shut down in 1991.

Not getting an offer I couldn't refuse, I then went on my own, running several junior companies and sitting on the boards of many others. One day I ran into Bill Roscoe and John Postle who ran a small consulting company and had rented space from us when I was with Anglo. They invited me to rent an office from them, which I did on a month-to -month basis for 25 years.

The last major fork in my road of life occurred in 2011. I had written a book encompassing my career, my ancestors, and some of the companies I had been involved with, and I was looking for an editor. I had worked with Saley Lawton at the PDAC for many years, mainly with the Awards Committee and the CMHF, and knew that she was a superb grammarian. She was retiring and had bought a house in Kingston.

The last fork in my road. My big proposal. Do you think we might be compatible? Surprisingly, we discovered that we have many interests in common, including tennis, swimming, history, investing, and reading. A plus for me was that she knew people in the mining business, so I didn't have to worry about her at mining functions!

We made a few trips together and soon set a marriage date. In the ensuing eight years we have travelled extensively, completing some 50 trips together. My book was finally published in 2016!

So, readers, what were the main forks in your road of life?

My Introduction to Exploration and Mining, *by Mackenzie I. Watson*

In 1960, the Icon Syndicate was created by four well-known mining companies: Gunner Gold, Kerr Addison, Rayrock & Barrymin Exploration. Later, Newmont replaced Barrymin. Andy Troop was hired as the manager and given a budget of $100,000 per year. The game plan was to fly an airborne geophysical survey over volcanic belts in Eastern Canada and follow up on the ground.

I had worked a couple of summers as a student with Andy at Mining Corporation and, with visa in hand as I was about to leave for the southwest U.S. to look for work, Andy called and offered me a job as field geologist.

Not really ready to step into the unknown in the U.S., I accepted the job. We started in Northern Manitoba exploring near Flin Flon, then Wabowden and Knee Lake. In 1962, Andy decided to explore out of the Chibougamau area. The initial programs were south and west of Chibougamau but in 1964, we decided to explore the area north, as a new road was being constructed to Lac Albanel.

One of the reasons we picked this area in which to fly was because of a documented copper lake bottom anomaly at the portage between Waconichi and Mistissini Lakes. This anomaly was found by Stratmet and to our knowledge, never explained.

In the summer of 1965, I sent our prospector, Paul Benard, to check out the anomaly. Paul returned to camp that evening with a sample of quartz dolomite well mineralized with chalcopyrite, which he'd taken from a large quartz boulder found under the root system of a fallen tree. The next day, I returned with him to the site to further examine the find.

Using a grub hoe, I pulled back the moss in the area around the boulder and found massive chalcopyrite boulders, each the size of a softball. "Eureka," maybe we were onto something.

The next day, we traveled to Chibougamau and bought licenses and tags to stake twenty claims. As we drove through Chibougamau with a canoe on top of our panel wagon, Jack McAdam saw us go by his office and said to Terry Flannigan, his partner,

"I wonder what the Icon boys are doing? They seem to be in a hurry!"

After the staking, we cut lines and did some horizontal loop geophysics over the immediate area and found a broad anomaly. Later, we discovered it was caused by a flat-laying graphitic horizon adjacent to the quartz dolomite horizon. This area of interest was located on the west side of the Waconichi River and three drill setups by Stratmet were discovered there.

Because the zone was sub-horizontal, the holes all missed the copper ore zone. It was apparent the holes were drilled in wintertime with heavy snow, as under one of the setups large quartz boulders with copper were found.

Another factor in our favour was that the main portage from Lake Waconichi to Lake Mistissini was on the east side of the river and all of the quartz float was on the west side. This portage was probably used for hundreds or maybe thousands of years as it was the main portage from Lake Mistissini south.

The portage was about 100 feet east of the west shore and obviously no one would be going in that direction. Two lessons I learned there, when prospecting always look under the roots of overturned trees and don't walk away from an anomaly if you cannot explain it. There has to be a reason for it.

Our next exploration method after outlining this broad anomaly, was to bring in a Winkie drill and drill a few short holes. We hit on the first hole, 3.5% copper over 12 feet. Andy now had to convince the Syndicate that we should bring in a large drill to further explore the discovery. Why should we chase what looked like a flat lying quartz vein with copper? How many copper mines have been found in quartz veins?

On January 30, 1966, we drilled the first hole on the east side of the river beside the portage and intersected 22 feet of quartz dolomite with good copper mineralization. After drilling for about eighteen months and spending $350,000 in exploration and development, a production decision was reached. At that time reserves were calculated at 756,400 tons grading 3.58% copper.

A deal was made with Merrill Island Mining to treat the ore. Their mine was coming to an end, so it was a good fit. Merrill was paid 50 cents a ton plus 10% of the operating profits after amortization of capital costs. The Merrill Mill was 44 miles away and they also operated the new Icon Sullivan mine. The cost of putting the deposit into production was exceptionally low—they did not have to build a mill and the physical nature of the deposit area was accessible, lying close to the surface the ore was extracted by open pit, then by decline and trackless vehicles. As a result, the capital expenditures including roads, buildings and equipment totaled just over $1,000,000.

Later on, they built a heavy media plant to upgrade the lower grade zones. One zone, the No.3, 160,000 tons, did not need upgrading as it graded 7.4% copper. I remember when we hit this zone, the young geologist said we drilled twenty feet of massive pyrite but when I asked the drillers, they said, "Non, c'est la cop." The hole assayed 15.9% copper over twenty feet.

I also called Kerr Addison's office late afternoon that day as Andy was away on holidays. I got Paul Kavanagh on the phone as it was after hours, and told him we had intersected a zone that should run 15% over 20 feet, then asked him if he would like me to call the other companies. "No," he said, "I will look after them." Rayrock was up 30% the next trading day—no worries of insider trading.

Jack Botsford from Gunnex was the original manager and built the mine. Great guy. I always remembered when we returned from the mine site each evening to our apartment in Chibougamau, he would get out a bottle of Scotch. I really developed a taste for Scotch that year.

The mine lasted about seven years and produced approximately 100 million lbs. of copper. Because we were working for a Syndicate, Andy had a deal whereby he would have a 5% profit interest in anything found and developed. Consequently, I ended up with a bonus over a few years of $75,000; not bad for the late 60s, with which Rena and I partially used to buy our home in Westmount in 1970 for $25,000, an excellent investment.

Because of this great start in Chibougamau, I am in the process of giving back $100,000 to the EXCEL Foundation which provides bursaries to deserving students in the Chibougamau area. This copper deposit, if found today, would never have been developed. The river was diverted without environmental studies and no consulting with the Crees at Mistissini ever took place.

Basically, in those days, all that was needed to obtain permissions to develop a mine was to submit to the government an outline as to how a mine would be planned and developed, and in most cases, agreement permits came through.

I met Pat Sheridan, from whom we'd bought the horizontal loop, for the first time at PDAC in 1966. "Mac, you found the deposit with my equipment, so, I have a 10% interest." I actually believed him. I never made it to the mine opening in 1968 but I believe Len Bednarz was there with Rayrock.

How I Got Involved In Mining, *by Kerry Knoll*

I look at life as a series of hinges. You apply for a job and wind up pursuing a new career. You meet a woman at a party who might become your wife. Leon La Prairie was the architect of one of my hinges.

I met Leon in 1978, when he was dating the mother of one of my closest friends, Marc Hannigan. His mother Anne had gone from living a life of dreams to one of tragedy. She had been Queen of the Ice Capades in her hometown of Pittsburgh in the early 1950s, where she met her husband Gord. After playing a year in Pittsburgh, he and his roommate Tim Horton were both brought up to the Maple Leafs in 1952, and Gord lost by one vote to Gump Worsley as Rookie of the Year. After hockey he started a very successful burger chain in Alberta.

Being good Catholics, Anne and Gord had nine children in about 12 years before Gord, at 36, keeled over from a heart attack and died, making Anne, in her mid-30s, a single mother. Beautiful and smart as any woman I have ever met, I watched as she struggled with all those kids and managed the business, which declined over time. To this day I try to stop by and see her every time I'm through Edmonton, where she lives in the same house where she and Gord raised those children. She just celebrated her 91st birthday.

A dozen years after Gord died, the newly single Leon was coming through Edmonton all the time on his way to Uranium City, where he was opening up the ill-fated Cenex mine. The two started dating and our paths crossed several times. I thought Leon was brilliant and hilarious, and for some reason he took a shine to me and said if I was ever in Toronto, I had a place to stay.

That spring, I had applied to go to Ryerson for a graduate degree in journalism. There were only 25 slots for over a hundred applicants, but I was writing a column for the Edmonton Journal, so I thought my odds were good. My horrible marks in my undergrad degree did me in, and I only made it as far as the waiting list.

I called my Aunt Frances who was a professor at the University of Toronto and asked her for advice. She said, "Just show up on the first day of classes with a cheque. Somebody won't show up and if you're there, they won't bother going down the waiting list. They will be busy as hell and they need to fill the class to get full government funding."

I hitched a ride with my sister's friend who was a student at Ryerson, arrived in Toronto after three days and three nights with a single stop, and went straight to the journalism department. They were happy to take my cheque. I was in!

But I had nowhere to stay and called my friend Marc who was by then working for Leon as some kind of apprentice. Leon said c'mon by. He invited me to stay and to top things off, he lived a block from Ryerson at Bay and Gerrard. In a penthouse apartment no less. He told me he was living there because "you've got to live it up when you're "in the chips"". He was apparently in the chips at that time with Cenex, which had just been listed on the Toronto Stock Exchange and was trading around three bucks. He lived across the street from a fitness place called the Bay Street Racket Club, and he told me that the Toronto Stock Exchange was suing them for stealing their name.

Leon's penthouse was like Grand Central Station. One night he'd be hosting a big party. The next entertaining his brother and family. The next would be some other function with his mining pals, and the next week his kids would be visiting. I was the official bartender. I remember one night when a good-sized party was going on, there was a knock on the door. I opened it and there was a guy with longish hair, a cravat around his neck, dandruff on his shoulders, a soup-stain on his shirt, and a shit-eating grin on his face. You guessed it, Patrick Sheridan. He put his hands in the air and suddenly a crowd formed around him as if he was some kind of rock star. In a way, I guess he was. Patrick and I would do many deals over the years, and once or twice I even came out ahead.

I eventually got an apartment with Marc in the same building, and Leon and I kept in touch over the next few years. He'd call me with some free Leaf tickets, or invite me to his famous St. Patrick's Day party. During my years at Ryerson, I was at one point elected editor of the campus newspaper, which put me in charge ultimately of advertising, editorial, production and babysitting a bunch of drunk students on production night (okay, I was one of them).

When I graduated, I had my heart set on a job at the Globe

and Mail, which I landed in early 1981. I hated it. The shit hit the fan when I was told to interview the family of some poor bastard who had died in a plane crash. When I got to their house, they slammed the door in my face. The City Editor told me to go back to their house and "don't leave until you get the damn interview."

I toyed with starting an alternative newspaper in Toronto. I had a business partner, we raised some funds, then I got a very short letter in the mail.

"There's a job opening at The Northern Miner. Go see Mort Brown. Use me as a reference. Leon" My wife at the time, a nurse who had been paying the bills, said in no uncertain terms that I was going to apply for that job. Mort Brown hired me on the spot, apparently amazed that someone working at the Globe and Mail would apply to the Miner. A few months later, when we were in Hy's and he'd had quite a lot to drink, Mort told me that the real reason he hired me was because I looked just like the star reporter who had just quit.

After six eventful years at the Miner, including doing most of the reporting about the Hemlo discovery, I was going through a divorce and decided it was time to start making my own news rather than reporting on what other people were doing. I had written a long article about heap leaching, which was then turning the gold industry on its head. There were no heap leach mines in Canada, for reasons I couldn't really figure out. I decided that there must be some low grade deposits that would fit the bill, and that I would build the first one.

Meanwhile, I had a few interesting properties around Kirkland Lake to get me started. I went to my broker, Ian McDonald, and asked him if he'd take my little company public.

"Sure," he said. "But under one condition."

"What's that," I asked.

"In a year, I'm going to quit my job and join you."

We had a deal. Twenty years later we had five operating mines and 2000 employees in four countries. Ian and I went on to raise $1.5 billion for our mining deals, are still partnering on some projects to this day. We didn't build the first heap leach mine in Canada, but we did build the second one, and to this day, the only one that has made any money.

I spent six months going though all of the ridiculous paperwork needed to prepare a prospectus, and finally one Monday morning my lawyer called and said, "you have your final receipt from the Ontario Securities Commission. You can go public now." I called Ian with the good news.

"Have you looked at the market?" he groaned, clearly not very pleased to hear the news. It was October 19, 1987, and the stock market was having a hissy fit, the worst one-day crash in history, later to be known as Black Monday. Why black and not red I never figured out, but after a few weeks of delay, Glencairn Exploration was trading on the over-the-counter market.

From Mining to Politics and Back, *by Patrick Reid*

One of the ironies of my life, is that the last place I ever wanted to be was in the mining business. I grew up in Atikokan, with Steep Rock Iron Mines, and Caland Ore, a subsidiary of Inland Steel of the U.S. We moved to Atikokan in 1947 from Fort Frances where my father was a businessman.

The only way in and out in those days, until 1952-was by the "local" train from Fort Frances, which was often shunted to a siding so the freight trains could go through. When we moved as a family to Atikokan in 1947, it took 12 hours to get from Fort Frances to Atikokan, a distance of 90 miles! As a result, we were very isolated and from an early age I wanted to get out and see the rest of the world.

However, one of the best things that happened in regard to the mine was it sponsored a "Speak of Safety", a course in public speaking by the safety supervisor, Roger Thew. It gave me confidence and experience which stood me well in University and politics.

I was elected to the Ontario Legislature in 1967 for the Riding of Rainy River, which included a number of mines, including Noranda's Mattabi copper-zinc mine north and east of Ignace, which was at the far northeast corner of my electoral district. They also had a long history of mining and very active exploration projects. Amongst other ministries of the government, I was the opposition critic for the Liberals for the Ministry of Mines and subsequently the Ministry Of Northern Development and Mines as well as the revenue critic, which gave me a background in the wider mining world and the Mining Tax Act, one of the most complex acts of the government of Ontario.

After 17 years in opposition and a lot of travelling back and forth from Toronto to the Rainy River District, I wanted to do something different, but I wanted to somehow keep my northern roots. I was approached by a senior vice president of Inco who told me that the then Executive Director of the Ontario Mining Association was retiring, and I should apply for the job, which I did, and was hired, in October of 1984.

I learned afterwards there had been over 40 other applicants, almost all mining personnel. I was hired because the Board of the OMA decided that they didn't need someone who knew how to mine. They needed someone who knew how the government worked. They realized and had been frustrated for years because they felt that the government wasn't listening to or acting on any of their concerns. I believe the PDAC felt the same way. There was, amongst the mining fraternity, a feeling that government was all bad and incompetent and didn't understand them.

Since I was a newcomer and didn't have a mining background, I reached out to anyone I could, including the then executive director of the PDAC, Bill Griffiths. I had lunch with him, and I remember he told me that this was the first time he had spoken to anyone from the OMA. I resolved to get everyone I could across the mining industry together, so we were speaking with the same voice and not just trashing the government.

I learned later as well that the Executive of the OMA asked the Premier, Bill Davis, if I would be acceptable to his government, as I had been an opposition member for 17 years. Davis said yes, Reid was a good man. Those words are mine, not Davis', but that was the gist. I had been strong in opposition, but never overly partisan or personal in my remarks in the legislature. In the first couple of years I was successful in some to the OMA's initiatives, particularly in getting the mining tax reduced from 30%, can you believe it? to 20% and then a few years later, to 10%.

I joined the PDAC, and the CIMM and the Northwestern Prospectors Association amongst other mining organizations. One of my earliest memories was having a lunch at the old Engineers Club where I met Ed Thompson for the first time. My recollection of Ed's reaction to me was one of being very suspicious and not overly impressed!

In 1998, Leon La Prairie invited me to become a member of the Prospect Club. Harry Hodge had asked me to be on his Moss Resources Board and then on Canstar's and then on Probe Mines which he and Dennis Peterson resurrected and bought from Agnico Eagle. Harry Hodges' two brothers, Joe and Jack, who were both prospectors, lived in my riding and we had become great friends.

I thought when I joined the Prospect Club, I would become rich. All mining engineers and geologists knew what stocks to buy with their mining backgrounds. The first shower came when I bought $10,000 worth of Newfoundland Gold Bar from Dale Hendrick and lost it all.

That put things into better perspective after that dose of reality and I laid back and enjoyed the camaraderie and fun of the Club. I enjoyed the Christmas dinners and all the members. I remember the one Christmas dinner at the National Club when some of the members, including myself, got food poisoning from some of the appetizers.

It has been an enjoyable trip and I have enjoyed every minute of it. I look forward to many more years of the Prospect Club, and the camaraderie.

A Mining Career, *by Len Bednarz*

Unlike most of the members , past and present , my contribution to the industry provided little in the way of excitement. Following graduation in the early 1960's from the University of Toronto and Engineering Geology, I became employed by the following - James Richardson & Sons , The Byrne Group (Rayrock & Discovery Mines) CSA Management and Goldcorp.

CSA Management managed two gold funds before launching Goldcorp inspired by its founder Don McEwen. Some $175 million was raised; at that time South African gold issuers were very much part of the portfolio. The financing was a noteworthy achievement at that time .

While at Rayrock we became involved in a joint venture development of The Icon Sullivan Joint Venture copper mine in northern Quebec. Jack Botsford was Mine Manager. The capital investment was recouped in just under one year. Rayrock was an original participant in the Cordex Syndicate that operated successfully for many years in Nevada. Managing the exploration projects was the incomparable John Livermore. The syndicate had become known for its longevity.

Nearing the end of my mining career I developed an interest in horticulture and subsequently earned a degree from The University of Guelph , and then became employed for over a dozen years by Ontario's largest garden centre . It is amazing how much there is to learn in that business. Back to mining I am most grateful for having developed rewarding relationships with many of the industries finest individuals. I must say that the mining industry is without question exciting, always challenging, and rewarding.

The Path to a Life in Mining, *by Howard Stockford*

I attended Worthing High School for Boys in Sussex from 1952 to 1959 (aged 11 to 18), having passed the "11Plus" exams. This was a method of streaming students into either academic or trades-oriented secondary schools, according to the students' strengths. Our futures were therefore decided for us at 11 years old, having completed 6 years of primary school tuition. Then we were streamed into the subjects we were good at (8 to 10 basic subjects from 11 to 16 years old and then down to three or four subjects in the last two years (GCE "A level") for entrance to a British University). County Scholarships were available to cover tuition and living expenses, subject to a parent's means test.

My geography teacher was actually a geologist who was unable to get a job in that field after WW2 and he had introduced geology into the A Level curriculum. He was dedicated to his students and took us on many field trips during our vacations to locations in England, Scotland and Wales. The school was well equipped with microscopes, fossil and mineral collections. Ray Band and I were in the same class and then we both went to RSM (Imperial College) to study Mining Geology. Subsequently we both ended up working for Falconbridge in later years.

I was fortunate to work for a number of bosses that subsequently became inductees into the Canadian Mining Hall of Fame (Michael Knuckey, James E Gill, consultant to Lac, Jim Boylen at Coniagas, Ab Moss at Bechtel, Bob Smith and Art Stollery at Morrison/Argor, indirectly, Marsh Cooper at Falconbridge, and James W Gill at Aur Resources. These people had a huge influence on my career, as well as Stan Charteris and Chris Jennings at Falconbridge.

My first employer was Little Long Lac Gold Mines's Barnat Mine in Malartic, Quebec. Mike Knuckey met me at the Val d'Or airport after a 14-hour flight from London to Montreal via Manchester, Prestwick and Gander on an old Britannia and then the milk run on a Viscount via Earlton and Rouyn/Noranda. I arrived in Canada on July 25th, 1962. Jeannie paid for my airfare and then I sent her a passage ticket on the Empress of Canada three months later. Malartic was a culture shock for her having left the beautiful scenery of the Isle of Arran in Scotland! We were married in Kirkland Lake four days after she arrived, with the help of many of the staff at Barnat/East Malartic. We were provided with a yellow company house for 50 dollars a month. We only had $8 (enough for the red roses) so we had to go into debt to buy basic second hand furniture for the house. The people of Malartic were very welcoming, and I was given Saturday October 20th, 1962 off to get married! Our honeymoon was a weekend in Malartic! Blair Morton, who later had his own mine contracting business (Ross Findlay) tried to hassle us on our wedding night by climbing up to our bedroom window so we dumped water down on him to get some peace!

Barnat was a 1700 tpd underground operation with 1200 tpd of ore coming from large open porphyry stopes running 0.09 oz/ton Au and 500tpd from high grade cut and fill diorite stopes running 0.3 to 0.4 oz/ton Au. I started out with a daily routine of marking up the face in the diorite stopes where it was essential to move the ore quickly because of bad ground conditions, with weak slippery wall rocks (talc chlorite schists) along the Cadillac Break. The diorite was brittle and crackled almost continuously and rock falls were common. Operating costs averaged $3.50/ton in those days and with EGMA (Emergency Gold Mining Assistance) we were getting $47/oz so we were able to make $0.5million net profit/year.

The miners went on strike in the summer of 1963 and closure seemed imminent so Mike Knuckey and I left Lac to take up positions at the Coniagas Mine in Desmaraisville, a small (VMS) zinc-lead -silver operation which was discovered by Dome Mines but operated as a three-year "salvage operation" by the Boylen Group.

Ironically, years later, the Barnat is now part of the Canadian Malartic Mine, a large, 65,000 tpd open pit operated by Agnico Eagle and Yamana and our original yellow house is in the location of a large berm which separates the open pit from the town of Malartic. I was on the Board of Agnico Eagle from 2005 to 2018. What goes around comes around!

Mining: The Long and Short of It, *by Ross D. Lawrence*

Bloom Lake

My story begins during the year when, as a greenhorn student who had just completed first year engineering, I took to the bush for the first time. I was hired by geologist Robert C. "Bob" Cunningham to join his field party for the summer of 1953. Cunningham was working for Quebec Metallurgical Industries (a Thayer Lindsley company) and a sister company called Quebec Cobalt and Exploration Limited (QCE), which was financed in part by the Hoffman brothers – Robert and Arnold – and by Thayer Lindsley.

The Hoffmans were the sons of Jacob and Minnie Hoffman, Russian immigrants who settled in Boston. The eldest, David, was killed in WWI. Robert D. the next-born was a Harvard graduate mining engineer (1919) who began prospecting in Canada in 1921 and worked principally around Kirkland Lake and Noranda. His brother Arnold graduated as a mining engineer in 1920 also from Harvard. He joined his brother while still a student and together they were important contributors to Canada's mining industry. Arnold is best known for his book Free Gold: The Story of Canadian Mining published in 1946. The fourth brother, Irwin, who was an artist, provided beautiful illustrations for Free Gold, including the wonderful sketch shown below.

Thayer Lindsley is considered to have been one of the great mine finders and company builders in the world. A true international mine executive, he was best known by the nickname "TL". He found or was involved with the development of many well-known companies, including Sherritt-Gordon, Giant Yellowknife, Canadian Malartic, and United Keno Hill as well as developments in Africa and Australia.

However, it was Falconbridge Ltd., which he built into an international powerhouse, for which he was best known. In 1928, TL along with a group of investors founded Ventures Ltd. as a holding company for a variety of properties that included Falconbridge. The original owner of the Falconbridge claims was Thomas Edison.

During 1951, brothers James and Michael Walsh were prospecting north of Sept-Iles. They were on a trek south from Quartz Lake and came across an exposure of cobalt bloom. Cobalt bloom is a pink mineral called erythrite, a secondary mineral that forms on exposed cobalt arsenide minerals. Crystals are rare; it usually forms as crusts or small reniform aggregates. It is a good indicator of potentially economic cobalt mineralization. The Walsh brothers staked 10 claims in the early spring of 1951, and named the nearby lake Bloom Lake.

Arnold   Robert

As was often the case in those days, they sought a financial backer, who would typically form a new company, give the prospectors a few dollars and a wad of "vendor's shares". Then the new company would sell more shares to raise funds for the first phase of exploration work. Such was the case here, when they did a deal with the Hoffmans and TL. In February 1952 Quebec Cobalt and Exploration Limited (QCE) was incorporated to acquire the claims staked by the Walsh brothers.

That year, a small program was carried out that included drilling six small-diameter drill holes for a total of 475 feet on the cobalt showing. The drilling was negative, and so iron ore became the focus.

There were extensive showings of iron formation, typically specularite, to the west of Bloom Lake. It was felt that this could be a mirror situation to the Mount Wright property being drilled by United States Steel ten kilometres to the south .

In 1953, the team consisted of Bob Cunningham, party chief, Robert J. Roach, J. Cherny, as senior assistants and R.J. Stirling, Douglas G. Bice and me as junior assistants plus a cook.

We did line cutting, staked claims, made pace and compass surveys and did reconnaissance mapping. I learned how to paddle a canoe big-time, how to use an axe, and all of the other elements of bush craft that are important to success working in the bush.

In late August, Bob Roach and I were flown to an unnamed lake west of Boulder Lake, which we named Lawrence Lake, and established our fly camp. Our main target was iron formation that was reported by the Iron Ore Co. in the general area. A large hill to the southwest caught our interest. The hill is about 750 feet high and we climbed to the top. Eureka! We were rewarded with the discovery of an important exposure of iron formation. None of the skimpy geological maps that we had showed any indication of iron formation here, and it was obvious that no one had bothered to climb the hill before. We staked 15 claims to solidify our discovery. The hill has subsequently been named Roach Hill. Detailed work has now shown a mineral resource at Roach Hill, which will undoubtedly become feed to the concentrator at Bloom Lake.

Robert D. Hoffman arrived at our camp Sep 2nd to inspect our work on the property and stayed with us until we packed up on September 15th. He was a remarkable man who had worked in the bush around the early mining camps of northern Quebec and Ontario starting in 1922 . He was still a strong man and pitched right in as we cut lines and staked claims.

Work continued for another few years with various steel companies taking up options. These included Jones & Laughlin (1955), Cleveland-Cliffs (1956-57) but ultimately petered out as iron ore exploration fell into disfavour with markets being well supplied.

In 1971-72, Buzz Neal (H. E. Neal & Associates Ltd.) did some more work for QCE including 21 drill holes.

From 1973-76, Republic Steel Corporation optioned the property and Buzz Neal prepared a preliminary evaluation of the property. This included a mineral resource estimate, mine design by Dames & Moore and metallurgical testing at Lakefield Research.

In 1985, several companies controlled by the Hoffman family were merged, including QCE being acquired by Consolidated Thompson-Lundmark Gold Mines Limited (CLM), which became the owner of the Bloom Lake property.

In 1991, Ed Thompson took control of CLM and the company carried out exploration in other areas of Canada and the USA.

In 1998, a major exploration program was conducted by Watts, Griffis and McOuat (WGM) for Quebec Cartier Mining. QCM was operating the Mont Wright Mine 10 km south, and had optioned the Bloom Lake property from CLM. QCM dropped the option in 2001.

Over the ensuing five years, Ed Thompson approached at least 50 groups seeking to sell or finance CLM. Finally, in 2005, and with the help of Tor Jensen, our unsung hero, Ed Thompson, was able to reach a deal with Gerry McCarvill which led to major financing of CLM. Fifteen years of patience was finally rewarded.

In 2005, CLM retained WGM to conduct a technical review in compliance with NI 43-101. In 2006, CLM changed its name to Consolidated Thompson Iron Mines Limited (Consolidated Thompson). From 2006 to 2007, Consolidated Thompson drilled 17 drill holes to get a sample for metallurgical test work. The Lakefield laboratory performed these tests.

Overall, 243 holes were drilled from 1957 to 2009 (45,386 m) and 273 holes were drilled in 2010, 2012 and 2013 (89,197 m).

Construction of the Bloom Lake mine started in 2008 and the plant was commissioned by Consolidated Thompson in December 2009. Almost immediately, Consolidated Thompson started a study to double production by adding a second concentrator. The feasibility study was completed in June 2010.

Construction of the expansion started in Q4 of 2010 and continued after the acquisition of Consolidated Thompson by Cliffs in May 2011 for $4.7 billion. Cliffs was already the owner of the nearby Scully mine.

Cleveland-Cliffs was known in the early 2000s as Cliffs Resources as its hot-shot new CEO went hog wild on an acquisition spree. Cliffs expanded into coal and other industries and took a leading position in Ontario's Ring of Fire. This all collapsed in 2014, as a new board took over, and a new CEO was appointed.

Construction at Bloom Lake was halted in November 2012 as iron ore prices fell, and mining ceased in December 2014. Ultimately protection was sought under the CCAA. On 12 April 2016, Champion Iron Mines Limited acquired the Bloom Lake Assets out of bankruptcy for $10.5 million. Yes, $10.5 million with an "m" just five years after Cliffs paid $4.7 billion with a "b".

Champion resumed operations at Bloom Lake in February 2018 after completing a new 3.5-kilometre conveyor connecting the mine and plant, major upgrades to the concentrator plant and acquiring access to a new multi-user berth on the St. Lawrence River at Pointe-Noire. Nearly $4 billion was invested in the complex. The mine achieved iron concentrate production of almost 7 million tonnes for its first full year of operation (fiscal year ending 31 March 2019) and reported a nice profit.

To conclude, exploration of the iron formation at Bloom Lake began in June 1953. A mine was not brought into production until 2010 – a period of 57 years. But it was not until Champion took on the property that a working profit was finally achieved in 2018 - 65 years since exploration was initiated.

George Jamieson

Watts, Griffis & McOuat was formed in 1962. Tom Griffis had just completed a three-year stint during which he studied the McIntyre Mine in Timmins. This involved re-logging all the drill core, extensive geological mapping underground and reviewing lots of reports and maps. The happy result was that Tom was able to outline a copper mine within the gold mine.

Tom's next adventure was to join the happy gang in forming WGM. One of his first assignments was to assist the Royal Trust Company, executor of the Estate of George Jamieson. Tom's task was to establish a value for the Jamieson property to assist the executors in administering the estate. During his work in Timmins, Tom made many friends in the community. A group of business people had talked to Tom about initiating some exploration/development activity in order to invigorate the economy of the city, which was in decline.

Once he had completed his work for the Royal Trust Co. Tom made a pitch to his friends: why not take on the Jamieson property where there was sufficient data available to enable a drilling program to be initiated straight away. And so a deal was struck with the trust company and a new company was formed in April 1964: Canadian Jamieson Mines Limited (CJML). Coincidently, Texas Gulf Sulphur struck it rich at Kidd Creek, and announced the discovery on 16 April 1964. A huge staking rush ensued, as well as the acquisition of the many small plots around the discovery that had been grants of 160 acres given to veterans of the Boer War, and whose descendants were now widely scattered.

The directors of CJML were Tom Griffis (president), Ned Bragagnolo (VP), Reg Pope CA (treasurer), Rino Bragagnolo QC (secretary), Gerry Killeen and me. Reg, Gerry, Rino and brother Ned were all Timmins residents.

I can remember that Tom and I were booked into the Empire Hotel in Timmins in April or May 1964. The place was going crazy. Don McKinnon, John Larche and Fred Rousseau had staked huge numbers of claims north of the city. They set up in a suite at the Empire Hotel to sell their claims to the highest bidders. Stock brokers were also there in abundance. Our chore was to organize an IPO and raise some money for drilling. We thought we might do the IPO at 25 or 40 cents. But by the end of the evening, and after a number of discussions with underwriters, we struck a deal at $1.00 a share with Doherty Roadhouse, which was the premier stock broker in Timmins, and an important player in the junior mining scene in Toronto. We were off and running. Ultimately, 2,206,000 shares were issued in CJML.

The Canadian Jamieson property, located in northern Godfrey Township, was staked by George Jamieson in 1941. He had done extensive trenching and drilled a few short holes. We were ahead of the pack and were able to secure a drill for immediate work. The drilling was supervised by Ed Neczkar WGM's senior geologist. The drilling went well and within a couple of months Ed was able to estimate a decent resource – sufficient to last four years if we milled at a rate of 450 tpd. Altogether 30 surface diamond drill holes (18,481 feet) and 57 underground holes (3,566 feet) were completed.

We purchased the complete mill and plant of H. G. Young Mines Limited in Red Lake and moved it to Godfrey township, where mining engineer Jim Bates re-built the mill as well as all the required infrastructure.

A vertical three-compartment shaft was collared and sunk to a depth of 639 feet in 1965. The shaft contractor was F. A. McIntyre Limited. The 1st, 2nd, 3rd, and 4th levels were established at depths of 256, 354 feet, 466 feet, and 578 feet. H. R. Fowlie was the mine manager. Mill start-up was on 11 April 1966 and by year-end was treating 350 tons per day.

The mine operated until 1971 and during this six-year period produced 826,000 tonnes at a grade of 2.3% Cu, 3.5% Zn and 24.2 g/t Ag. Concentrates were shipped by rail to Quebec City. Copper concentrates were smelted by Boliden in Sweden, while the zinc concentrates were shipped to Belgium. Metal prices were good, and the company made quite a decent profit, paying dividends to its shareholders.

The remarkable achievement was that it took less than two years from the time the first drill hole was collared until production was initiated in April 1966.

Conclusions

That is my tale of the amount of time needed to open a mine: the long and short of it.

Exploration of the iron formation at Bloom Lake began in June 1953. A mine was not brought into production until 2010 – a period of 57 years. But it was not until Champion took on the property that a working profit was finally achieved in 2018 - 65 years since exploration was initiated.

Conversely, it took less than two years from initial drilling to commercial production at the Canadian Jamieson Mine (albeit at a smaller scale).

I am proud to be able to say that I played a role in both of the mines.

ROUNDERS, REPROBATES AND STRAIGHT SHOOTERS

My Intro to Bob Fasken, *by Dave Rogers*

Dr. Derry phoned Bob Fasken while I sat in his office and said Bob, I am sending a young geologist over to you to listen to. Fasken was president of Camflo Mines. We all bought in on his grubstake and I think you should also.

Wow! I am walking on air over to the Camflo office. I am shown into his office. He is on the phone. Stands up and shakes my hand and indicates I should sit down. Between phone calls I give him my pitch. I was in his office for about 2.5 hours as he was trading stocks with different brokers in Canada and Ireland. He tells me he is in for one unit and his son-in-law is in for the final unit. Stick around I want to chat.

Meanwhile I am mesmerized with the number of different companies he is trading and the dollar amounts. I did not dare to take notes and after about $500,000 of trades I lost track. Wow, what a quick insight to serious trading in the penny stock market in 1971s.

The Irish Base Metals play was in full swing. Dr. Derry was the top consultant in Ireland at the time. Ian Thompson was Derry's man on the ground. Fasken knew all the players both Irish and Canadian. He called his secretary and told her to cut cheques for both the grubstake units he and his son in law signed for. Then looking at me he said that he liked my pitch and ideas. David, I am backing you this time. I will probably back you a second time, but you miss again it will have to have one hell of a story if I decide to cut you a cheque a third time. Yes, we did hit for the grubstake the first time and made some good money, tax free in the marketplace. And yes, Bob Fasken backed me and or made introductions to others in several follow up ventures over the next 20 years or so. To me Bob Fasken Sr. was a solid partner and taught me many good things about deals on the street, people, junior companies etc. I could always phone him for advice if and when I needed another opinion.

"Stop Selling, The Bullshit's True" *by Kerry Knoll*

Mining promoter Charlie Stewart, aka The Fat Man, (because he looked like the character of the same name in the movie The Maltese Falcon), was hustling the Davidson-Tisdale property in Timmins in the mid-1980s. One night he was holding forth in their suite in the Royal York at the PDAC, claiming they had discovered 10 million tonnes grading half an ounce of gold. Which they hadn't.

He told the story of raising some money and starting drilling and promoting the stock. He had put the property in a very tight shell and the share price went through $2, then $5 then $10, with no results yet announced but strong rumours of loads of visible gold. Then they announced an amazing drill hole, 30 or 40 feet of half an ounce of gold.

He said that when news of the discovery came, "I had to call my brokers and say, "Stop selling, the bullshit's true. Start buying the stock back.""

Except the bullshit was bullshit.

He managed to option the property to Getty Mines, an offshoot of the old Getty oil fortune that had been spun off to a group of Canadians. Not long after Getty started preparing the deposit for production, Yorkton mining analyst Mike Pickens and I got an underground tour.

The geologist taking us around was an old friend of Mike's and wasn't going to bullshit him. He told us bluntly that the underground development was showing something very different from the drill holes and the gold was only on the margins of the very impressive looking quartz veins, not throughout, and that it was a very unpleasant surprise. This had been a problem with some of the other deposits at Timmins, which was why geologists had there had the expression, "Drill for structure, drive for grade."

Leon La Prairie, *by Patricia Mannard*

While Patricia Mannard is not a member of the Prospect Club, she spent much of her career working with one of the club's founders, Leon La Prairie. This is the eulogy she gave at his funeral in 2016.

I worked for and with Leon beginning in October, 1987 when he generously offered me a position within his group of companies. I was George Mannard's daughter and that is what you did. We shared the next 27 years rolling with the minor successes and major punches that the junior resource industry threw at us all. Leon was often heard saying 'Poor old Dad'...I would occasionally ask, 'What's wrong with Dad?' and he would sometimes say, 'Nobody loves him'...that was clearly, never the case (as seen here today). I think I still have my 'Honk If You Love Leon' bumper sticker.

I can never throw anything out. Leon was the king of throwing things out, rearranging what was left and purchasing the necessities, all according to his unique standard which was somewhat military in nature. We often disagreed but it was a relationship of mutual respect and very much, as pointed out to me recently, like the familiar cartoon depicting the wolf and the sheepdog; at odds while at work but always friendly when punching out.

With all the comings and goings of old schoolmates, various relatives, friends, sons and daughters of friends, neighbours, industry heroes and scoundrels not to forget the guy from the copy shop or the closest deli, La Prairie Ltd was a combination mining mecca, drop-in centre and orphanage. Leon was the main attraction and the generous patron; everyone was welcome especially if you had little time to hear the latest story and perhaps a little money to invest plus, lunch was always available. If you couldn't drop in, you were surely part of the mailing list and would receive everything from promotional documents to the latest party invitation. Leon consistently offered his expertise and time to many, many great social events...it's a La Prairie thing that we all know well.

I learned countless lessons from Leon: be generous and inclusive, dream big or go home, I know what time to go to the dentist, always talk to people in elevators, you can't spoil a child, if someone says 'you can't do that' ignore them and make it happen, no need to check the weather before heading out onto the lake, eat the chips before the fish and the ice cream before the pie, do not be afraid to call someone up or write that letter, it doesn't matter how you pronounce someone's name, they'll forgive you, anyone can fix a toaster, no one will throw an 80-year old man in jail, you don't need a professional to move a piano, where there's a will there's a way out, there is delight in mischief and 100 is the only percentage worth mentioning.

Finally, Leon had a few little sayings (okay, many) that he used, or sang, in jest and with a particular twinkle in his Irish eye. Maybe you know this one and can join in...We're sad to see you go, we're sad to see you go, we hope to hell you never come back, we're sad to see you go (wink).

On behalf of my family, I would like to acknowledge the generosity that has been shown to us with such kindness by the La Prairies over the years.

Financial Chicanery on Bay Street, *by Dave Rogers*

I was in the process of doing a financing on Aurogin Resources. The shares were trading in the $0.80 range. Out of the blue on a Friday morning someone came into the market and ran the share price up to $1.30 on volume. At 4:15 in the afternoon my phone rang, and a voice asked me if I liked the share price and volume.

I replied that it certainly had taken me by surprise, and I had no idea why it had happened. The voice said we will be in your office at 9:30 Monday morning to discuss your financing and they hung up. I was baffled.

That is when you call Gord Fancy, the most knowledgeable broker in the junior exploration business. I did and he laughed and said yes, I saw the action but was too busy to call you. He proceeded to give me two names of ex brokers on the shady side who had lost their licenses and were freelancing on the street. They were both under investigation. Gord says go ahead and meet with them. See what and how they pitch their scam.

So, I prepared my desk for their visit. Front and right side was a large aerosol can labelled "BullShit Repellant". On a small table beside my right side, I laid my geology hammer in view. No visitor chairs to sit in. Right on time Monday morning they came swaggering into my office trying to look scary and tough. Physically they were anything but, and I would have no problem putting them both on the floor – hurting – if they wanted to get rough.

They gave me their pitch and said how they could keep the share price up in the $1.25 range while I did the financing near that level. They wanted 100,000 free trading share certificates each by Wednesday and not to worry they would keep the share price up. If not, they would run my share price down below $0.30/share. I smiled and said that is an interesting offer—or is it a threat?

I am aware that you are both currently under investigation by both the Ontario Securities Commission and the Toronto Stock Exchange. Your proposal and threat to me have been recorded. I suggest you leave this office now.

I picked up my hammer and proceeded around my desk. They walked quickly out of my office. End of story. The Aurogin share price returned to the $0.80 level by Friday and my financing went through a week or so later @ $0.75/share with no fuss.

Agnico Eagle and the Penna Legacy, *by Peter Hubacheck*

In the summer of 1986, I was managing a drilling program on the Goldex Project in Val D'Or working out of Agnico Eagle's exploration office. At this time, Paul Penna successfully financed two flow-through exploration projects, Goldex and Dumagami, which our firm prepared the technical qualifying reports for TSX approval.

Don LaRonde was the mining engineer hired to commence a virgin exploration underground program near the Dumagami massive sulphide showing. Both properties were recommended by my father, Wencel "Hub" Hubacheck, to Paul Penna in 1971 when he was chief exploration geologist with Ventures Group McIntyre Mines during the 1960's.

Hub with Don LaRonde, namesake of the big Agnico mine

While working in Val D'Or Exploration office, headed by Anton Adamcik, during the summer of 1986, Don LaRonde was gearing up for the shaft sinking program, asked me to assist Marcel Desbien to locate the collar position of the new shaft on the only outcrop near the Dumagami Pit. The following summer of 1987, the shaft captain, Conrad Hache, had advanced the shaft to the 600 level and Don LaRonde instructed his shift boss to drive a sill drift along the massive sulphide zone. Ebe Scherkus was recently hired by Anton to manage the surface and underground drilling program.

I remember being in Cobalt that summer when Ebe made a special trip to visit the Silver Division headed by Gordon Kirk, John Young, Brian Thornily and jumped out his car with great excitement, opened the trunk and lifted out a 100 lb. slab of massive sulphide with visible gold coating the fracture slips. This specimen is on display at Agnico's head office today.

Hub with Paul Penna en route to Rouyn

The drift miner who broke that round the day before was "Cadillac Jack Brooks". This discovery was the first " Aha" moment allowing Paul Penna to raise additional flow-through funds. Ebe had enough budget to collar a deep exploration hole looking for extension of the ore body at depth. This famous drill hole refused to flatten and eventually intersected the massive sulphide zone at a vertical depth of 2500 feet. The assays returned 0.3 oz/ton over 45 feet which indicated that a really significant gold deposit existed below the shaft...the jackpot!

Dumagami went into production in 1988 with the shaft deepened to 2 000 ft. a few years later. At that level, a major exploration drive was driven for 3,000 feet across the property which was proven successfully at their Eagle-Telbel property which was still operating at this time.

Keep in mind that the Eagle Mine in Joutel, a great success in itself due to perseverance and hard work, led by Anton Adamcik, was the only source of income for the juvenile company. During these years, an eclectic technical and financial team under Paul Penna including mining engineers, geologists and metallurgists...the likes of Wencel Hubacheck, Anton Adamcik, Ebe Scherkus, Paul Henri Girard, Yvon Silvestre, Marc Legeau, Daniel Racine, Sean Boyd, Jim Nasso and Jean Robitaille, advanced both the LaRonde and the Goldex underground projects.

Paul loved the local Quebecois team of people, largely hired by Ebe Scherkus, Paul Girard and Anton Adamcik.

Penna Shaft construction 1995; from left, Hub, Penna, Sean Boyd, Marc Legeault and Ebe Scherkus

By 1994, a series of 5,000-foot bore holes discovered multiple stacked lenses of the LaRonde deposit to depths exceeding

7,000 feet. Agnico's technical and financial management now had the confidence to plan a single lift shaft to a depth of 7,500' to realize the potential of this world class deposit.

The Penna shaft was commissioned in 1994, two years before Paul Penna and Don LaRonde passed away. After Paul's passing, my father became president for two years and I resigned my board of director's seat allowing Sean Boyd to join the board, who was later appointed as President by the board in 1999. By 2001, this great shaft was completed and myself and my father along with 50 guests were invited to attend the commissioning ceremony at the bottom of the shaft.

Paul's legacy is still kept alive with his values passed down by Jim Nasso, Ebe Scherkus and Sean Boyd. It's astounding that that the LaRonde Deposit is still expanding after 32 years of continuous production and still the leading gold producer in Quebec with gold reserves to 2035.

A tiny little company from Cobalt in the 1970's is now a powerhouse with global operations in Canada, Mexico and Finland supported by 10,000 employees that affectionately refer to the flagship entity known as "LaRonde University".

If I could make one statement it is that the "Penna legacy" is the cornerstone of outstanding excellence and achievement in our mining industry and a brilliant example of Canadian exceptionalism.

Ice Road Icon, *by Kerry Knoll*

One of the best claim stakers in Canada is a guy by the name of Matt Mason. When news of the Voisey's Bay discovery hit, he and his partner John Robins spent a million bucks and rented every helicopter in Atlantic Canada, shutting down competition, and then staked most of the area, and parceled it off to dozens of junior mining companies, including Cartaway, which was the Windfall scandal of the 1990s.

Matt came to me one day in 1996 with a shell called Arauco and the possibility of buying two million ounces of gold in the high Arctic, a project named Back River owned by Homestake which he heard was for sale. We had bought Golden Bear from them and he thought we had a good shot at getting Back River. I called up Lee Graber, otherwise known as Santa Claus (see my story with that title), but found that he had changed his name to the Grinch. He wanted $35 million for the property, no ifs ands or buts, though he would take $15 million of that in shares. I finally agreed, and Arauco made the announcement.

I had one small problem to deal with, raising $30 million. No junior mining company had ever raised that much before, a fact we luckily didn't realize at the time. Back River was a hard sell then, being near Bathurst Inlet in Nunavut. As one broker told me, "If Yellowknife is the asshole of the earth, then your property is 300 kilometres up that asshole."

Lee Graber suggested to me that while we might be good at raising money (which we weren't, but it was a nice compliment), we could probably use the expertise of somebody who had mining experience in the far north. He suggested we talk to the guy who we outbid, John Zigarlick. I knew of John, since we at The Northern Miner had picked him for Mining Man of the Year for his accomplishments at Echo Bay Mines. The story of John's life could fill a book. Somebody should write it. I called John and asked him if he wanted to get involved.

"Shit," he said. The line went silent. I thought maybe he had hung up. Finally, he went on. "I was hoping to get that." Homestake hadn't told him yet. He had bid $5 million.

"What are you proposing," he asked. I asked him if he would join our board and help us market the story since he believed in it, and maybe there were ways for him to get involved with his ice road. John was a legend for his ice road.

We hit the brokerage circuit. It was hard slogging, though. BMO was about to do a bought deal when their big swinging dick in New York, Michael Vitton, said no. Too far north and too expensive, he thought. We finally found a little firm that would put its shoulder behind the deal. One memorable presentation was at Altamira, the hottest mining fund at the time. The fund manager spent the entire meeting shitting all over the project and insisted that John, who had joined the company two weeks before, put at least $2 million of his own money in. We walked back to the elevators, feeling a little sheepish. When we got back to our office, he had put in a $5 million order. We raised $29 million, the largest raise to that point in Vancouver Stock Exchange history.

We raised the money at $1.75 a share, and analysts were predicting it would go to $5. We drilled and did a pre-feasibility study, but by the time it was finished gold had tanked and was sloshing around $275 and the project just wasn't economic. It didn't help that we closed the deal the month Juan Guzman fell or was pushed out of a plane in Indonesia. Within a year the shares were at 15 pennies and having spent what money we had remaining on exploration, were essentially broke. The company was merged into Wheaton River. That project is now with a company called Sabina. With reserves approaching 10 million ounces, it has a market cap of $850 million. Timing is everything.

Along the way John Zigarlick gave me a clue about what a big thinker he was. He had an idea to build a coal or gas power plant at the bottom of Bathurst Inlet, to power the diamond mines as well as several other possible mines in the area. It would be financed by bondholders and owned by the Inuit. One of the problems was, Bathurst Inlet was the last unmapped shoreline of the North American continent. Nobody knew if ships could even get in there.

Well, it happened that summer that an Arctic cruise ship became grounded not far from the inlet. A Canadian Coast Guard cutter came to the rescue but by the time the cruise ship was freed, the rescued vessel didn't have enough fuel to get back to Alaska. So, the Captain of the government vessel gave the cruise ship its fuel, meaning that it was going to be ice-bound for the coming winter. John got on the phone to his contacts in Ottawa, and somehow managed to convince them to use the ship to map the Bathurst Inlet shoreline in the spring. It was agreed to, and the mapping was done right after breakup the next year.

John wasn't that well known in the mining community, at least outside of the Northwest Territories, partly because he chose to have his head office in Edmonton. He was also a pretty shy guy. Early in his career, John had worked in the various uranium camps in northern Canada, and at one point got a business degree. He eventually landed a post as purchasing manager for Echo Bay's Port Radium silver mine, where his father was the mine manager. At that point it was owned by Utilities International, a company run out of Philadelphia that had bought it for the uranium. By 1977 he became President of Echo Bay, but the mine was nearing the end of its life, and John went looking for something else to mine. He knew about Inco's Lupin gold deposit, located smack dab in the middle of nowhere, 300 kilometres over the tundra north of Yellowknife.

As his biography in the Canadian Mining Hall of Fame says, "It was not an easy sell to Echo Bay's owners, but Zigarlick persevered and built Lupin almost entirely with materials brought in by a Hercules and Convair aircraft, on time and on budget, in 1982. He then took on the challenge of building a winter road to service Lupin, a phenomenal feat that contributed to the mine's profitability and also demonstrated the viability of remote Arctic mines to the world." Rather than hire a Herc to bring in all the equipment, John simply bought one, and sold it for a profit when the mine was built. The long, skinny-looking ball mills at the Lupin mill were a result of being built to fit in the hold of a Hercules with only a few inches clearance on either side.

People scoffed at the idea of developing Lupin. Able bodied people had tried to mine the nearby Tundra in the 1960s, but it was a financial disaster. John didn't invent ice roads, but he knew a lot about them. His ace in the hole was that, as purchasing agent for Port Radium, he paid for and depended heavily upon an ice road built each winter by a guy named John Denison.

Denison was famous in the north for pushing his road from the Yellowknife Highway to Port Radium each winter, with a motley crew of northern loners and a collection of broken-down machinery, most of which fell through the ice at one time or another. Denison was awarded the Order of Canada for his pioneering spirit. The ice roads are very different today, being built 50 metres wide and using specialized equipment like Sonar to determine ice thickness and even speed traps to make sure the truckers aren't in too much of a hurry.

If you look up the word innovation in the dictionary, there is a picture of John beside it. Take the way he financed Lupin. In 1980, the financial world was gaga with gold, which had recently hit an all-time high of $800 per ounce, after having spent most of the last 100 years at $35 or less. Rather than use the traditional route of bank loans and selling shares to the public, John did a deal with the brokerage firm Burns Fry to borrow the money and instead of interest (which was very high that year) hand out three- and five-year gold warrants. People bought the right to purchase an ounce of gold directly from the mine for $500, $600 or $700. His mine would be very profitable at those prices, and he wouldn't have to babysit his share price while building the mine.

His company wasn't even listed on the stock exchange (though the warrants were). With analysts and other touts predicting a gold price of $2000 within a few years, they were an easy sell, and he raised the $200 million needed to build the mine. Of course, the gold price fell into the $300's and $400's for the next several years, and not one of those warrants was exercised. Echo Bay got essentially free money. I'm amazed that nobody else has tried this. The Echo Bay mine became very profitable and was the springboard for Echo Bay to become one of the world's top gold mining companies. By 1992 the now-public company was worth $2 billion, by this time mainly on the riches coming from their Round Mountain mine in Nevada.

One day I asked John how much they had paid for Round Mountain. It had been the company's first venture outside of the Northwest Territories and would turn Echo Bay into a market darling. There isn't much more fun in our business than running a company that has become a market darling.

John heard that a company out of New Orleans named Louisiana Land and Exploration was willing to sell it's 50% interest in Round Mountain, and Echo Bay struck a deal to buy it for $80 million. However, Louisiana Land's partner, Homestake Mining, had a first right of refusal. The president of Louisiana Land suggested they fly out to San Francisco on the company jet and have a sit-down with the Homestake boys. They did just that, sitting in the same cavernous boardroom that a few years later I negotiated the purchase of their Golden Bear mine in B.C.

It was no surprise that Homestake coveted Round Mountain for itself. The group were told by the Homestake president, the notorious Harry Conger that first, Echo Bay was paying far too much, and second, if they tried to do the deal without Homestake's okay, they would be tied up in court for time immemorial, and no, Homestake was not saying okay. And with that they were escorted to the elevators. The Louisiana Land people were rather embarrassed, and they all flew back to New Orleans to figure out if there was a Plan B.

It turned out that Louisiana Land's Round Mountain holding was held through another company, Copper Range, which also owned a large copper mine and smelter in upstate Michigan named White Pine. John asked, why don't you sell us Copper Range, then Homestake's first right doesn't come into play. The Louisiana Land guys shook their heads, saying that was a really bad idea. Copper Range had been closed for a couple of years due to an ongoing strike and would lose money at the prevailing copper prices even if the strike ended. It would probably never reopen, and the cleanup and reclamation costs were at least $25 million. John and his team got to thinking, and made an offer for Copper Range, for $55 million, with the difference between the two proposals being enough money for the cleanup. It relieved Louisiana Land of a massive headache, Echo Bay would get Round Mountain, and everybody was happy, with the exception of Homestake's fuming Harry Conger.

Well, it just so happened that not long after the deal closed, the copper price went up well past the point where White Pine would be able to make a profit again. In the meantime, Echo Bay started hauling away at least $5 million in equipment that could be used at Lupin, which made the striking employees extremely nervous. They now feared a permanent closure which would not only kill their jobs, some of them third generation. That gave Echo Bay an excellent bargaining position, and a sale of White Pine to the employees was negotiated, for $40 million, most of which was borrowed from a bank, no cleanup by Echo Bay was necessary.

"So," John said. "You tell me how much we paid for Round

Mountain." That mine has produced 15 million ounces of gold since Echo Bay bought it and is still going strong as I write.

John had had a falling out with Echo Bay's management in 1993, and eventually the board of directors, and resigned a year later, just in time to sell his shares at the top of the market before the gold price plummeted in 1997. Which was when we met. He had just bought a yacht from Jimmy Pattison and having a blast, using it quite successfully as a chick magnet.

He also had the foresight to make a deal for next to nothing with Echo Bay the buy his beloved ice road, which he told me was enshrined in an Act of Parliament. The nitwits running Echo Bay hadn't figured out that the new diamond discoveries would make the road hugely profitable. Once he secured control of the road, he immediately made a deal with the local First Nations to give them 51%, for free. When I asked him why he did that, he said "because now no government is going to take the ice road from us, ever." The ice road is still servicing the diamond mines to this day, long after his death, and they even made a reality TV show about it. The federal government is finally talking about building an all-weather highway into the area.

One time I asked John what he was doing for Christmas. He was divorced and had recently broken up with a girlfriend, and I was a little worried. "I'll do what I always do at Christmas," John said. "I go to the Boyle Street Community Centre in Edmonton and spend Christmas Eve cooking a turkey dinner for the homeless people. I finish about 10 am in the morning and sleep the rest of the day." I later found out that he also paid for all the food, for several hundred people.

As a postscript, I brought John to one of the Mining Hall of Fame dinners around that time, and he was so bored he left after the first speech. He was much more at home on the tundra than in a Toronto ballroom. Little did he know that I had spearheaded a nomination for him to the Hall the next year. I wondered if, were it successful, would he show up at the ceremony. He wasn't chosen. Years later, he was finally inducted posthumously. I asked Ed Thompson, who led the awards committee, why John hadn't gotten in the first time around, when he was still alive. Ed said that they had called up Echo Bay's president for a reference, and the jerk had nothing good to say about one of Canada's true mining pioneers, so he was dropped from the ballot.

Wine, Women and Gold: Prospectors I Knew and Worked With, *by Mackenzie I. Watson*

The Ceré Brothers: Toussaint "Tous" Ceré was born in Maniwaki, Québec and moved to Val d'Or as a teenager. He had three older brothers: Leo, Gustaf and Romeo, who were all involved in mining. Jacques Duval, also a prospector, told me a story about Tous that happened during the Gaspé Park opening staking rush in the late 60s.

Toussaint Cere

The main base for the staking rush was Sainte-Anne-des-Monts, and each night after a long day of difficult staking, the guys would fill up the bar and discuss their challenges with the mountainous terrain. Tous was telling how his line went straight up the mountain, and, being a foggy day, he actually finished his line above the clouds.

Some smart guy, probably a broker from Toronto, asked Tous, "Did you see any angels up there?" Tous looked at him and said, "No, but I heard them singing."

Another time, Tous was on his way to a summer job in the Labrador Trough with Ray Carson. They stopped over in Montreal overnight to get the weekly plane to Schefferville the next morning. Tous knew he would not be seeing any girls for a while, so he borrowed $100 from Ray who also gave him an extra $25 for a taxi back so Tous would not be late for the early flight. The next morning, Ray waited and waited for Tous, who arrived just in time to catch the flight.

"Why didn't you take a taxi?" asked Ray.

Tous replied, "She was such a nice little girl, I had to give her a tip."

Tous worked for Freewest in the Lebel-sur-Quévillon area. Joe Perkins had told me about finding gold about eight miles east of Quévillon, so we staked some claims. It was not long before Tous made a discovery, but not Joe's—a new one which we called the Verneuil Project, after the name of the township. Unfortunately, the zone is small, about 40,000 ounces but might be mined by a decline if there was a mill close by.

Gustaf "Gus" was a big, barrel-chested man who found many mineral showings but nothing of any size. Leo, his brother, lived east of Val d'Or on a claim with a gold showing. He was a big, good-looking man with a gold tooth. He was also a boxer and apparently went a couple of rounds against Dempsey when he visited Val d'Or. Leo built a house on his claims. In his basement, he had installed a small crusher so that he could mill his own rock from his quartz vein. This was just a front so that he could buy and process high grade from the mines. The cops couldn't stop him as he had his own sources of ore.

Romeo lived in Desmaraisville, east of the Bachelor Lake Mine. He was the businessman of the family and raised money in Montreal for their many ventures.

Prospector Reuben Armstrong: Reuben "Rube" came from

Powassan, Ontario and started prospecting in Red Lake during the 1930s and 40s. He told me his first trip to Red Lake was by dog team. In the late 1930s, he made a discovery and sold it for $35,000—a huge sum back then. Rube also recounted a time in which he went to Montreal for a little R & R. While there he rented a plane and flew his girlfriend around but soon ran of money and had to return to prospecting.

While working for M. J. O'Brien, Rube found the showing that became the Bachelor Lake Mines. Rube said he knew he had gold because he had burned the rock then crushed it with his mortar and pestle so that it could be panned. He sent the samples out to be assayed but before he had even finished his own staking, planeloads of stakers were flying into his lake.

Rube worked the Icon Syndicate during the 60s and always found a showing. I recently shared information with André Tessier of Delta Resources about an area south of Chibougamau where Rube had discovered gold. André sent his team there, and did find gold, announcing the discovery in a news release in October 2020.

Rube never married but sure liked the girls. I recall the char woman at the Waconichi Hotel asking me where Rube was. I said I didn't know. "Why do you ask?"

"Well," she replied, "He laced me three times last night and never paid."

Frank Minoletti of Thunder Bay: Frank Minoletti worked with Icon Syndicate north of the Eastman River in the summer of 1964. After three months in the bush, he and his partner headed to Chibougamau, where they first stopped at the liquor store. Later that evening they decided to give each other a haircut. Having used ordinary dull scissors, the pair looked like members of the Three Stooges. The next day, still liquored up, they boarded Halls Airlines to fly to Val d'Or to catch Air Canada to Montreal and then on to Thunder Bay.

Frank's partner, a big 250-pound Swede, passed out in the aisle of the Viscount plane on the way to Montreal and did not awaken until their arrival at Dorval airport. Air Canada was not happy and would not let him fly on to Thunder Bay until he sobered up.

Later in life, Frank married a much younger woman.

However, it didn't last long—not more than a year. The story goes that after a season in the bush, he returned home to Thunder Bay. Eager as he was to go out on a binge, rather than getting cash from the bank he used cheques, which he could do because he was well known.

A few days later, someone stopped him in the street. "Frank, your cheque bounced." As it turned out, his young wife had spent all of the money Frank had earned that season.

Tom Johnson, Frank Minoletti, and "Swede"
near Beardmore, Ontario in 1975

Charlie "Woodchuck" Simard: Charlie, a guide and prospector lived in a log cabin just south of Chibougamau. One winter, after many heavy snowfalls, the cabin literally was buried in a huge snowbank, save for the smoking stovepipe sticking out of it, which is how Charlie earned his nickname of "Woodchuck."

Charlie also guided for American tourists. Once, when a group didn't want to have a canoe flown in by seaplane to a lake, they were to visit south of Chibougamau, he offered to take the canoe, with their heavy supplies, by water to the lake. Well, that was okay, but not knowing he was an alcoholic, they also sent up cases of beer and many bottles of vodka. Charlie arrived alright to their camp—four days late—booze gone.

"Chibougamau Joe" Mann: Joe I believe came from one of the Ontario mining camps. Though not a big man, he was powerful and strong, and could handle a canoe as well as any Cree could. He made many mineral discoveries in the Chibougamau area, resulting in the Joe Mann Mine named after him. Joe married Helen, a singer from Montreal, whom he'd met at the Chibougamau Inn in the 1950s. However, the marriage didn't last long because Joe died young sometime in the 1960s. Thereafter, Helen would often visit the bar where they'd met, bringing Joe in an urn. She'd plunk him on the bar, raise her glass and toast him with a "Salut mon Joe."

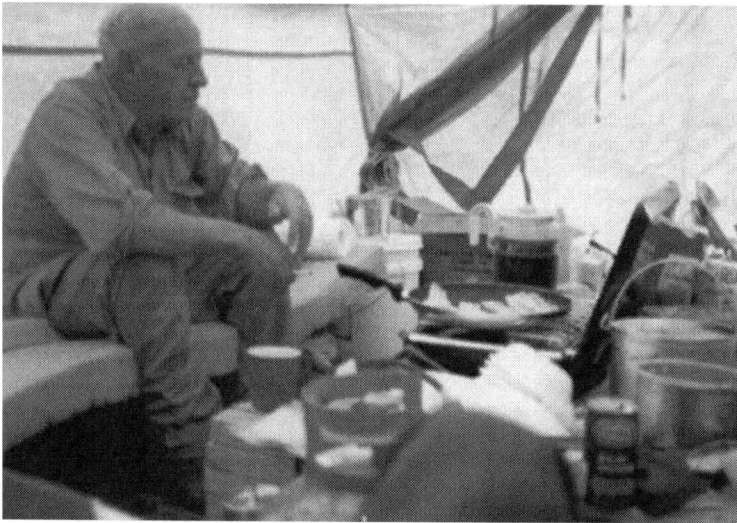

Gerry Bruce near Beardmore, Ontario in 1975

Gerry "The Wolverine" Bruce: Gerry was from Toronto and

served overseas as a fighter pilot during the Second World War. He flew for Austin Airways after the war and pioneered flying with large wheels so that he could land on the beaches in the Arctic.

His nickname was "The Wolverine," for survival instincts. He was shot down over Germany but managed to land his plane between a row of houses. In doing so, the occupants of the house came out to kill him with pitch forks as he had torn up their gardens.

Gerry kept his hands inside his jacket pretending he had guns. He kept them at bay until the police arrived and hauled him off to prison. Another time while flying on a mission, Gerry realized his squadron leader was taking them all on a suicide trip, and apparently, he shot the leader out of the sky.

Dave Thorsteinson and Nolan Cox were prospecting with him one summer and the plane was days late in picking them up. They realized that their grub started to go missing. Gerry, having been a prisoner of war had started to hoard certain foods.

Gerry had a Cessna 180 and I remember flying with him up the Ottawa Valley, and holding the scintillometer while Gerry flew just above the treetops. Once was enough for me.

He often prospected with Dave Thorsteinson, probably one of the best prospectors I ever knew. Dave unfortunately died much too young in a car accident.

Building a Billion Dollar Mining Company – Ned Goodman Style, *by Sethu Raman*

A significant chapter of my life was entwined with that of a great Canadian, Ned Goodman, the founder of Dundee Corporation. It all began back in 1980, on a Friday afternoon, when I was invited to a meeting where Ned Goodman presented his vision and strategy for Campbell Resources Inc.

He said, "We have a solid team here. We can build a billion-dollar mining company in 5 to 7 years... say, to become the next Teck Corporation".

There was silence among those at the meeting - Hugh Mogenson, President, Gordon Strasser, VP Mining, Paul Middleton, VP Finance and Pierre Lassonde, who had recently joined Beutel, Goodman & Company. Ned went on to outline two parallel strategies – the initial focus on filling the underutilized mill in Chibougamau by acquiring and developing all advanced properties in the area.

Second, an aggressive plan to acquire public and private companies with advanced gold projects or small mining operations in Canada. Exploration and development funds would be raised via flow-through financing recently approved by the Canadian Government. He founded the first exploration flow-through partnership, CMP Group, which has raised over $5 billion since 1980.

From that day forward, my career changed, and this included my role in the evaluation and acquisition of projects and turn-around companies including Royex Gold Mining Corp, Meston Lake Resources, the Joe Mann gold mine, Renabie Gold Mines, Cullaton Lake Gold Mines, Shear Lake Mine, Goldlund Mines, International Corona Resources and a start-up project for Mascot Gold Mines.

At that time, I was working as the Regional Exploration Manager-Eastern Canada for Campbell Resources, with a small annual budget of $200,000. Ned asked me to prepare a plan to develop new projects in Chibougamau with a $3 million budget. On the following Monday, I presented a plan to acquire several properties within trucking distance of the Chibougamau mill using that budget.

A few days later, he asked me to increase the budget to $5 million. It was just a few weeks later that I received a phone call from Mogenson saying that Ned had decided to promote me to Assistant VP in charge of all Exploration. At my request, based on my recommendation that all exploration in and outside the mines should be managed and coordinated by one person consistent with growth policies of the company, I was appointed as Vice President Geology of all Operating Companies. This appointment put me in charge of property evaluation as well as exploration programs including grade control at all operating mines.

To back up a bit, I had met Ned in 1977 when he visited Chibougamau as Director of Campbell Chibougamau Mines, which was controlled by Allan & Company, based in New York. He was made aware of my research and compilation work since 1974 that led to multiple Joint Venture projects in the Chibougamau area.

The JV projects were funded by other companies like Petro Canada, Norcen Energy and Union Oil. In 1978, Ned resigned as a Director of the Company when his proposal to expand the operations outside Quebec was rejected by the Board of Directors.

In 1979, Ned Goodman and Myron Gottlieb initiated a proxy battle to take over Campbell. At that time in corporate history, takeover attempts initiated at the annual meeting were almost certain to fail. Nevertheless, Ned and Myron went ahead and won. Surprisingly, they won based on a technicality that a controlling shareholding in a subsidiary company could not be voted in favor of the management, so Ned won and took control of the Company with $10 million in cash.

During the 1980-85 period, a series of acquisitions were negotiated and concluded. The Company grew in large part because of the acquisition of undervalued assets and the subsequent exploration success leading to discovery and development of gold deposits in and around abandoned mines. During the same period, my annual exploration budget increased from $200,000 to over $30 million spent on over 20 projects and six operating mines across Canada.

I introduced innovative exploration management concepts to sustain and expand the Company's gold production. By integrating the mine and surface exploration departments and introducing incentive bonuses for geologists, the Company's exploration became focused on production.

This resulted in economic gold discoveries at the Joe Mann Mine, the Renabie Mine, the Shear Lake Mine at Cullaton Lake, and the S-3 gold-copper deposit in Anorthosite Complex, the first discovery outside the regional structure in the Chibougamau camp.

This was accomplished by applying new geological concepts in the search for economic mineral deposits near known mining camps or prospects which had been passed over by previous explorers because they incorrectly based their interpretation on different geological models of mineralization.

Earlier attempts to bring the Chibougamau Explorers Mine, owned by Meston Lake Resources, into production had failed and the owner went into bankruptcy on three occasions. In 1983, under a management agreement with Meston Lake Resources, Campbell initiated an exploration program at the mine, now renamed the Joe Mann Mine.

The gold mineralization was thought to be a vein type in volcanic rocks. When I examined the underground workings, I recognized the stratigraphic control of gold mineralization was associated with banded massive sulphides and carbonates, modified by shearing. This led to follow-up drilling which outlined 800,000 tons of ore averaging 0.25 ounces per ton close to underground workings.

Bill Zukerkandal, then Chief Geologist, supervised the program. Production commenced in early 1987 when gold was trading at less than $500/oz and continued until 2007. Joe Mann Mine with grades of 0.25 oz/t, was one of the highest-grade gold mines in Canada. It produced 1.2 million ounces of gold, 607,000 ounces of silver, and 28.7 million pounds of copper.

In July 1982, as part of the financing and restructuring, Campbell Resources assumed management of Cullaton Lake Mine producing 40,000 oz. per year. In 1983, Cullaton Lake Mine, a fly-in and fly-out operation in the Eastern Arctic, was in trouble because of dwindling mill feed and falling gold prices. As Vice-President of the Company, I initiated a major summer exploration program with a budget of $3 million, organized by Bill Hamilton and John Thompson. This led to the discovery of a small gold deposit under Shear Lake.

The discovery hole intersected 0.57 ounces gold per ton over a width of 17.5 feet. Four additional holes confirmed a zone with a strike length of 400 feet and to a depth of 150 to 280 feet. Gold assays ranged from 0.26 to 1.4 ounces per ton. This deposit provided a substantial portion of the mill feed in later years. We set a Canadian record by advancing that project from discovery hole to production within a period of ten months.

Gold mineralization was found in a limonite/saprolite altered shear zone in Hurwitz quartzite, a one-of-a-kind oxide gold deposit in a geological setting that was previously unrecognized in the Canadian Artic.

In 1975, my first job as Research Geologist at Campbell Chibougamau Mines was to compile all historic data in the Chibougamau area including logging of the drill core of about 50,000 ft., collected over a 25-year period. I was intrigued by the presence of carbonatite in core from a drill program in the early 1950's carried out to test a magnetic anomaly for magnetite mineralization.

Chemical analysis confirmed the carbonatite with an anomalous concentration of niobium and tantalum. In 1982, Camchib Mines Inc. purchased the property from Shell Canada. Systematic exploration, including bulk sampling, was organized by Peter Potopoff and confirmed a phosphate-niobium deposit with an estimated resource of 145 million tons averaging 20% P_2O_5 and 0.35% niobium oxide. The Martison Phosphate-Niobium deposit was a residual apatite-rich zone, formed through a weathering process from an underlying carbonatite - an uncommon deposit, I believe, previously unrecognized in Canada. After I left Campbell, these claims were allowed to lapse and were then staked by a prospector in Timmins and sold to PhosCan Chemical Corp., a public company listed on the TSE.

In early 1982, Ned Goodman and I met with Peter Munk and his financial partner, Adnan Khashoggi, a person who became a billionaire by selling arms to Contra rebels in Nicaragua.

They had a plan to build a major mining company, now Barrick Gold, in Canada. They asked Ned to find advanced gold projects in Canada. Recognizing that the Renabie Gold Mine, which was owned and privately operated by MacIsaac Mining & Tunnelling Co., a well-known mining contractor, could potentially be a take-over target, Ned asked Gordon Strasser and I to evaluate the project potential.

A few days later, we arrived at the site via train and a dirt road to the mine. They had no geologist on the job. Mining was at the bottom level near the shaft where the grade had dropped from 0.25 to 0.15 oz/t.

But they had an excellent record of all the existing maps and plans. A detailed study of the historic production and level plans led to the identification of a series of white quartz vein sets and their structural controls which were responsible for the gold mineralization. If our interpretations were true, we knew we could expect a repeat of a new vein set below the shaft level.

Subsequent drilling based on this interpretation and managed by Bill Hamilton and Derek McBride, confirmed a high-grade orebody of 1 million tons averaging 0.25 oz/t below the mine workings. Gold production continued until 1991 and totaled over 1 million oz. This was the first gold mine in the old Wawa mining camp in Canada to reach that production level.

In 1983, Campbell acquired the Goldlund Mine and its 200 TPD mill, which was on care maintenance at that time. Chester Kuryliw, who worked on the property for several years, had identified three gold zones. Gold mineralization consisted of narrow high-grade quartz veins in granodiorite intrusion. Detailed underground drilling and sampling did not meet expectations; Campbell decided the mine was not economic and shut it down after 1 1/2 years.

The Nickel Plate claims in southern B.C were acquired in 1983 from the Bronfman Group for few hundred shares of Campbell. A major drilling program was started with a view to establish resources. Chris Jennings later joined Corona Corp and developed that property. The mine development commenced in 1987 under Mascot Gold Mines. That mine operated from 1987 to 1996. Soon after the mine ceased operating, the site was officially designated a Provincial Heritage Site.

At the annual company gathering in 1983, while cruising on Lake Ontario, Ned and Myron came up with the idea of creating one junior exploration company for each mining camp in Canada. To enhance the long-term growth of Campbell, I helped establish independent public exploration companies operating in several different major mining camps. With the financial and technical support of the parent company, these junior companies focused on projects with the potential for near-term production.

I hand-picked the initial projects for these start-up companies. They included Greenstone Resources for the Chibougamau Camp run by Clark, Yorbeau Resources for the Val d'Or Camp managed by Glackmeyer, Glen Auden for the Timmins Camp and the Nickel Plate project for Mascot Mines in Southern B.C.

It was during this period of corporate expansion that Ned negotiated a private deal with Murray Pezim, acquiring an option to purchase Murray's control block whereby he would end up controlling International Corona Resources with a promise to support Corona's legal battle against Lac Minerals for the ownership of the rich Williams gold mine in Hemlo. After an initial court battle, and an appeal, Corona won the legal fight, another first of its kind in Canadian corporate history.

By the late eighties, the total market capitalization of all the companies controlled by Ned exceeded a billion dollars. In terms of gold production, the company became one of top ten mining companies in North America. Ned had achieved what he set out to do in 1980. After winning the Corona versus Lac legal battle in August of 1989, all the companies were consolidated under Corona Corp and Campbell Resources and subsequently sold to Homestake Mining and Patino Mining in 1992 for a total consideration of over $1 billion.

I want to recount a few personal experiences with Ned that show what sort of mining and financing guy he was. Shortly after the Corona win, just a few days after the party at the Hyatt Hotel to celebrate the success, Ned walked into my office.

He wanted to get my opinion on some of the projects he was working on. It was at that time that I told him about my plan to reorganize a junior exploration company that would be focused in the Timmins area. He thought it was a good idea and said " Remember, if you need any financing come back to me".

Sure enough, he fulfilled his promise years later, when I approached him on two different occasions. In 1991, I met Ned in his office with a one-page memo requesting a US$18 million financing to fund the first heap leach gold mine at La Libertad, Nicaragua. He gave me the backing.

Later, in 2014, my second request was for a US$10 million

financing to develop the first silver mine in Cuba. This request was approved immediately. He even advanced US$1 million the same day, into the account of Holmer Gold Mines Inc., a private company holding a 50% interest in the Cuban project.

He did so without asking me to sign any documents. Unfortunately, this project got held up in the Cuban courts in a fight with the Cuban Government. It was only recently in 2019 that I return this advance of US$1 million, along with interest, to Dundee Corp. I had the privilege of working closely with Ned in his effort to build a billion-dollar mining company. It was the most exciting period of my career. I learned a lot about project evaluation techniques, take-over tactics, corporate reorganization, both simple and complex and innovative project financing.

Above all, I gained the confidence to start a junior mining company. One of things I will never forget is he had told me that, "the purpose of restructuring is to make it complex enough that no two analysts will have the same interpretation".

In my opinion, he is one of the most successful geologists who went on to build many successful mining companies and financial institutions in Canada. He is my friend, my financier, my mentor and ultimately, my mining guru.

The Prospect Club's Judy Baker, *by Dave Rogers*

$\mathbf{B}$ack in about 2012, Judy Baker came up to my cottage near Pembroke to try and settle an option deal on our RRS Syndicate Batchawana Property north of Sault Ste. Marie. Judy was not successful in making a satisfactory deal with Roy Rupert and myself. So, the next morning I talked her into the tractor bucket and told my hired hand to take her over and dump her in the Ottawa River. The final photo is censored. Judy was a good sport about it.

That Woman, *by Ross D. Lawrence*

Mary-Claire Ward was hired by Tom Griffis to join Watts, Griffis and McOuat in 1981. Mary-Claire was a keen volunteer and was a director of the Geological Association of Canada, serving as president in 1995. She also became a member and chair of the geoscience committee of the PDAC, where she worked tirelessly to further the cause of geoscience.

Before the mid-1990s Canada's mines ministers knew little about mining and even less about geoscience. Every year since 1997 Mary-Claire attended the mines ministers' annual gabfest. And every year Mary-Claire made her presentation on behalf of PDAC to prod the ministers to increase their support for geological mapping.

Her dedication to geology was matched by her enthusiasm and the dash of wicked humour that she brought to her efforts. Her crusade eventually paid off when the ministers agreed to a new program called the Cooperative Geological Mapping Strategy. The story goes that the host mines minister told his deputy that he had agreed to support the program "to get that woman off my back." The story was leaked -- to the particular delight of "that woman."

Mary-Claire was born in Dublin and earned her BSc from University College. Her first job was working for Mogul Mines – but not in the field – that was off limits for women. After emigrating to Canada, she had jobs at Kennco and Esso Minerals before joining WGM. She had an outstanding career at WGM for 24 years and was the firm's chairman at the time of her death in 2004.

Yes – chairman! Mary-Claire was not a member of the politically correct gang who want to re-invent the English language and she was not shy in telling everyone of her views.

Every year the Northern Miner designates someone as their Mining Man of the Year. In 1991 the recipient of the honour was Peggy Witte and some considerable comment followed. The 20 January 1992 issue of the Miner contained a letter to the editor entitled Brave Decision. It read:

At the risk of being forever condemned to the ranks of the "unpolitically correct" may I offer my heartiest congratulations to the editors for their brave decision to retain the title "Mining Man of the Year" while recognizing that "the best man for the job is a woman". I am heartily sick of the current plethora of attempts to legislate our vocabulary by people whose knowledge of the English language is clearly limited. To have changed the traditional title at this stage would have detracted from Margaret Witte's very real achievements. Keep up the good work and stick to your guns. Sincerely, Mary-Claire Ward, Senior Geologist, WGM.

After her passing, there was an amazing collective desire to mark her time with us in a meaningful way. An endowment was created to provide a $5,000 grant to a graduate student whose thesis is based on an important contribution to increasing the understanding of the Canadian geoscience knowledge base through mapping.

Michelle DeWolfe was the first recipient and her PhD thesis at Laurentian University was to study the world class, gold-rich, VMS ore system well-exposed in the Flin Flon camp. The results of this work have aided in exploration in the Flin Flon camp, and our understanding of VMS deposit formation and the factors that control the localization of VMS deposits during the evolution of submarine complexes.

She described the award as the one of several of which she was most proud. She noted that it came with a better than average financial grant, a fully-funded trip to the PDAC convention in Toronto and unexpected prestige and publicity in the industry. She describes an encounter with an industry geologist to whom she was introduced, who then asked, "Aren't you the person who won the Mary-Claire Award?"

And all because of "that woman".

Gord Fancy, *by Richard Hogarth*

I knew Gord from the 1960's, when we both worked for T.A. Richardson & Co. Subsequent to our both leaving the Company to join other firms, we often met for lunch at Hy's Restaurant, in the Arts & Letters building on Richmond Street.

On one occasion in the mid-1990s, he asked me to meet Catherine McLeod of Arequipa Resources in Chile, to discuss the possibilities of her Pierina gold project. After lunch, he phoned me to ask my opinion of its prospects. He told me that in his opinion it did not measure up to his expectations and would not recommend it to his clients.

On the other hand, I told him I liked the story, and would do so. The stock at that time was selling for about $1.50. Gord missed out on this one as Barrick's first offer was $27/share and final offer was $30/share. That was a massive 20 banger!

We had many lunches where we discussed mining stocks and projects. We even talked about joining forces, when we wanted to work less and travel more   This all came to a tragic end, when Gord lost his life in a private plane accident on his way to Florida, for a long weekend.

More on Gord Fancy, *by Dave Rogers*

Gord Fancy was an early member in the Prospect Club, and he was our broker working for T.A. Richardson & Co for buying and selling shares.

Gord won the Brass Ball award in 1987. We had a good party and then went to the Richardson office. Gord did not have a private office at the time so against his wishes I mounted it on the wall behind his desk facing out for all to see in the Bull Pen. The manager was not pleased and made Gord take it down first thing the next morning. That was the same guy who had the first computer in their office. He of course had no clue what to do with it. Just had it mounted on a credenza behind his desk to look important. NO! He would not let some of the more computer savvy types in the office use it. Life in the fast lane of brokerage offices and computers in 1987.

Gord and I had lunch at Hy's about a month before his fateful flight. He mentioned that his Dr. Friend who owned and flew the plane was lackadaisical about his aircraft maintenance and that he felt he should not fly with him anymore. When I heard of some of the instances, I bluntly told Gord that if I was in his shoes I would absolutely refuse to fly with this guy. Gord agreed but then one month later he decided to give it one more flight. Very sad. Ironically the only item that survived the crash was a bottle of good scotch which Gord had wrapped tightly in a towel and tucked inside his golf club bag.

Some Interesting People I've Met, *by Chris Jennings*

Three generations of Oppenheimers of De Beers fame. One in a nasty dispute over ownership of the Marsfontein mine. Nicky Oppenheimer saying I had stolen 32 of his top people for the Klipspringer mine and me saying he had illegally stolen my Marsfontein mine discovery. Actually 30 of the 32 came to me asking for jobs and the other two responded to advertisements.

Having lunch with Seretse and Ruth Khama under the same acacia giraffe tree at our camp. Seretse soon after went on to become the first Premier of Africa newest and best democracy - Botswana.

Meeting Kwett Masire, Khama's successor as Botswana's second Premier and having a long conversation with him in both English and Setswana. Many years before this, he and I had spent three days camping together on his newly acquired cattle ranch in southern Botswana where I found underground water for him, using a variety of geophysical instruments.

Flying to South Africa with Marsh Cooper and Howard Keck (Superior Oil) in his Gulfstream G2 jet. It was largely through Keck that I was transferred to Toronto in 1981 to become Vice-President of Exploration for Falconbridge.

Receiving two phone calls. "Hello this is Mrs. Mandela (Winnie). I hear you are in a Supreme Court dispute with De Beers over Marsfontein. I can help you win your case." On both occasions I thanked her and turned down her offer. Not long after the second call, one of Winnie's assistants, who had once worked for me as a field assistant, came to me and mentioned the cost of Winnie using her influence on the judge would have seen me (SouthernEra) paying off the million Rand mortgage on her house! (that is about $1 million Canadian at the time)

Meeting wonderful Graca Machel, who was Chancellor of Cape Town University and second wife of Nelson Mandela. We had arrived early for a small dinner party, and so had Graca, who was hosting the dinner.

During a long conversation with her, I found out that she was very familiar with the work of the Portuguese poet Fernado Pessoa. My father had spent the latter part of his life studying Pessoa's poetry, writing about him, and translating many of his poems into English. Graca was wife of Samora Machel, premier of Mozambique, before he died in a suspicious plane crash, so was the first lady of two different countries!

Two very sad memories. A dead gorilla shot by locals in East Congo and a magnificent maned lion shot by locals in central Botswana. Another memory never to be forgotten was being chased by an angry lioness in a remote area in Northern Botswana. Each bound she took, as she drew rapidly closer, despite me making Usain Bolt look like an old lady on crutches, was accompanied by a terrifying grunt.

Fortunately, she stopped a few meters from the person behind me who had turned and grabbed the trunk of a small tree. She stopped about five metres from him and 10 metres from me for a few terrifying seconds twitching her tail from side to side and then turned and went back to mind her small cubs.

Our game scout who was supposed to guard, us threw his rifle away and led the field of fleeing geologists. One of our party sprained his ankle badly when tripping over a small log in the grass but continued to run at high speed.

Seeing grizzlies from the air and on the ground. Having a grizzly flatten a steel door with one blow and steal a whole leg of beef. Watching salmon in Northern British Columbia leap up waterfalls, seeing herds of migrating caribou near Lac de Gras. Having a grizzly bear, in my humble opinion far more dangerous than lions, rip the scalp of one of our geologists which required about 40 stitches.

Mike Bates and Grey Owl in Bisco, *by Ian Thompson*

Geology has allowed me to travel the world and meet all manner of oddballs, crackpots, and rugged individualists, to say nothing of all the non-geos I have met, like Mike Bates. Bates was the Canadian Pacific Railroad telegraph operator in Metagama, Ontario, for many years, the operator of a number of tourist cabins in the area along the Spanish River and other waterways.

He was also the inventor of the very useful Bates Humane Snowshoe Harness and the friend and confident of the famed conservationist and con artist Grey Owl, aka, Archibald Belaney from Sussex, England.

I met Mike in 1959 while mapping the CPR rail line from Metagama to Biscotasing. Dave Rogers, who was responsible for mapping the Biscotasing area for the then Ontario Department of Mines, hired me as a senior assistant. For me, the opportunity represented the chance for some real field work with my newly-minted geology degree after spending the previous two summers doing exercises in hot, cramped, and noisy Sherman Tanks as part of the Army Reserves.

Mike's cabins were too expensive for our meagre exploration budget from the Ontario government. But Mike had good stories about Grey Owl, who he met years earlier in the 1920s, and I greatly valued the snowshoe harnesses he made.

The patented Bates harness was revolutionary because it allowed the wearer to turn their foot out of the harness without using hands or trying to undo the webbing. The logo on the bag said "no more blistered toes" because the toe was so flexible and you walked pigeon-toed to give you balance, the whole foot moved, not just a rigid toe.

The harnesses provided great comfort when traversing lake ice alone in storms and late in the season, carrying a long pole. Luckily, I never dumped. Over muskeg the harness also worked well but was a bit awkward for climbing and descending hills as it provided little lateral and heel support. Bates designed the harness for Moosehide boots and leggings, but we got our damn Gum boots to work as well anyway.

As for Grey Owl, Bates recalled the budding celebrity would make visits from his homestead on Lake Temagami, 150 miles away by canoe. Grey Owl tended to visit when he was on the outs with his young wife Anahareo, aka Gertrude Bernard, a strong-minded Mohawk-Algonquin woman from Mattawa who changed him from a fur trapper to a conservationist.

The union only lasted a few more years, and Grey Owl didn't last much longer, dying in 1938. Grey Owl's cabin on Ajawaan Lake in Prince Albert National Park remains a popular tourist destination, Mike Bates' tourist cabins, if still standing, perhaps not so much. But those snowshoe harnesses, they were the best.

Mining's Baritone, *by Kerry Knoll*

The first time I met Bill James was when he worked for me as a bartender. It was the annual picnic for a group called Women's Association of Mining In Canada. Today you would expect that title to apply to an organization of women engineers and geologists who worked in mining, but back then it was a group of mainly housewives of mining men. At the various mining conventions, these women organized talks on subjects like the pros and cons of plastic surgery, fashion trends and the latest diets. The picnic was their large annual fundraising event that, oddly, was managed almost entirely by their husbands.

As a rookie reporter for The Northern Miner, Leon La Prairie somehow saw big things for me in the mining industry, even if I didn't see them myself. He talked me into running the bar for the event, and furthermore suggested that I write a letter to the presidents of all the big mining companies and ask them to do an hour shift as bartenders. For me, Leon explained, it will give me a chance to socialize with and get to know these guys. Who knew what that may lead to in my career, he added. I followed up and got a great response, with the first "yes" coming from Bill.

When the big day came, it turned out to be one of the hottest September days on record, in the mid-30s and humid as hell. To top it off, the picnic had a record crowd. And miners are a thirsty lot. I bought the same amount of booze as they had in the previous year, but the heat made the beer from the kegs flow like foam and we couldn't keep the bottled beer cold. Leon kept doing beer runs in his station wagon, but we still couldn't keep up and there was a mob around the beer tent all afternoon. The other bartenders hightailed it out of there the minute their hour was over. But not Bill. He rolled up his sleeves and worked the whole four hours. At one point he got the bright idea of gathering a couple of the garbage cans, spraying them out with a garden hose, and filling them with beer foam and waiting for it to settle. It worked. As he dipped the cups into the garbage cans and handed the beer across the table, he'd say with his infectious grin, "don't worry, I certify it's sanitary."

It was around that time that Bill had become the new CEO

of Falconbridge, a once-successful company that had become bloated and in dire need of a fixing. Bill had earned a PhD in geology at McGill and eventually joined his father's company, which were engineering consultants to the mining industry. He eventually joined Noranda under that company's iconic leader, Alf Powis, where he quickly rose to the head of the mining portfolio. He left that job for Falconbridge, and when he took the reins that company was bleeding $2 million a week, which was a boatload of money in 1982.

I went to interview him about the changes he made at Falconbridge, and he gave me an office tour. "It'll be short," he said in his always booming voice. "We had three floors and now we have half a floor. We had 23 vice-presidents, of God knows what, now we have six." He took me to the kitchen and showed me the schedule for making the daily coffee in this giant pot, which previously had been the job of secretaries. Now, he and the other vice-presidents were all on the list. Bill got rid of the special washrooms for the executives, the two private jets, the fleet of Jaguars. He faced down the union and laid off 40% of the staff in Sudbury, where Falconbridge's main operations were.

Within 18 months he had the company back in the black with its first quarterly profit in ages. A few years later, he bested his former boss at Noranda by purchasing the Kidd Creek mine and smelter for $1.3 billion. He was known for going to drink beer with the union guys in Sudbury.

Anyone who knew Bill could well visualize his run-in with Robert Mugabe in Zimbabwe, not long after the strong-man took power from the white Rhodesians in the early 1980s. Rebels opposing Mugabe were attacking Falconbridge's Blanket gold mine. The miners had no weapons and were running out of food. Bill flew 24-hours straight to Harare and went straight into the dictator's office. As detailed in the Globe and Mail, Bill's demands, delivered in his signature loud, gravelly baritone, were simple. He wanted food for his employees and assault rifles for protection. The next morning five truckloads of maize showed up at the mine, along with a dozen AK-47s.

One of the most frightening occurrences in the mining business is an underground rock-fall. In 1984, when a rock burst trapped four miners underground in a mine near Falconbridge, Ont., he raced to the scene. Against the advice of safety personnel, he went underground himself and through a small opening held the hand of a lone survivor, 22-year-old apprentice mine mechanic Wayne St. Michel, who was trapped under a giant rock. For more than a day, Bill stayed with the man.

"It's going great, Wayne, it's going great," he told him over and over. "We're coming for you." After 27 hours, St. Michel was freed, but, cruelly, he died shortly after in the hospital.

"The only time when I was a kid that I ever saw him cry," said son John James of his father.

I remember covering one of Falconbridge's annual meetings, which were normally very staid affairs. There was the dour-looking board of directors in their stuffed suits. I heard Bill had to be talked into putting on a tie. His head of investor relations dutifully handed out his carefully written speech to the press beforehand. Bill didn't even look at it, he just talked, told stories in that voice of his, and generally put on the most entertaining annual meetings in Toronto. In fact, they got so popular the organizers had to rent larger and larger rooms every year.

During question period, someone asked for more information about a discovery Falconbridge had mentioned in a press release a few months before.

"Well," said Bill. "I can't say much about it." He paused for effect, a born comedian. "But I can tell you this. Do you remember what Adam said the first time he saw Eve naked?" He paused again. The room was silent, apparently nobody recalled what Adam had said. "Well," he continued, "Adam said, 'honey, you'd better stand back, because I've got no idea how big this thing is going to get'." The audience howled. The board of directors looked on in horror. Bill asked for the next question.

In the late 1990s, when Bill was running Inmet Mining at the age of 70, John Zigarlick and I were trying to buy the big Izok Lake zinc project from them and put it together with our Back River gold project. Izok Lake was discovered by Texasgulf Sulphur in the 1950s and had resisted several attempts to turn it into a mine. It was only accessible by air, and in the summer the planes landed on the lake while in the winter, ski planes landed on the ice. It took its name from the habit of the exploration crews to spray paint a big IZ OK on the snow if the ice were suitable for landing. Izok was a rich zinc deposit not far from Back River, but it was stranded due to the difficulty of getting its concentrates to market. Somebody would need to build a road and some kind of port. Inmet's feasibility study said it would cost $400 million to build. John wanted to extend his ice road up to Bathurst Inlet, giving himself another customer and making our Back River deposits more feasible.

I remember Bill telling us about his summer trip in his 9-metre Zodiac boat, with not one but two 400-horsepower engines, exploring the coast of Labrador as if it was an afternoon paddle down a lazy river. He and John made vague plans to take the boat on a thousand mile ride up the MacKenzie River the next summer, but I don't think it ever came to fruition.

Bill was a delight to negotiate with, razor sharp as he picked up on every nuance, all the while writing everything down in his notebook which looked like those scribblers a junior high student would be using. We secured an option to buy Izok for $40 million but were unable to raise the money as metal prices had slipped into one of their frequent canyons. A few years later, as metal prices began to spike, a company named Wolfden bought the project for $50 million in shares and sold itself to a Chinese conglomerate a year later for $263 million.

Timing is everything.

Small Time Promoters & Characters I Knew *by Mackenzie I. Watson*

Ken Wheeler: Kenny, I believe was American, bragged that he had slept with Barbara Walters, and was always impeccably dressed and groomed. Once, while visiting Chibougamau to buy claims from prospector Adrian Tremblay, Kenny asked Adrien where he could get a manicure. Adrien replied, "I give you de manicure wit de axe."

Buying claims from Jacques Duval in the Mattagami rush, Jacques remembers Kenny counting out $40,000 in one-hundred-dollar bills. "Now," asked Kenny, "What are you going to do with all that bread?"

I once recalled seeing Kenny in the old King Eddy at the bank of pay phones, likely talking to a broker. In his hands he had a coloured geophysical map. I overheard him say, "I got a 'Rembrandt' in my hands."

Lyle "The Knife" Smith: Lyle came from Killaloe, Ontario, and probably started in the business as a prospector and eventually into promoting. I first met him in 1974 during the Hebecourt Township staking rush. He somehow managed to control the helicopters flying down during the staking. He got paid but stiffed the helicopter company. He also owed money to George at Cyranos Restaurant, but instead of paying, he'd bring in a dozen roses for George's wife in lieu of settling another tab.

Scotty Stevenson: Scotty was an entrepreneur, hotel owner and fur trader. I first met him when I worked with Icon Syndicate in the early 60s. Scotty competed with the Hudson Bay Company, trading with the Crees. He flew his own plane, a Cessna 180, so was able to fly into the remote camps and buy directly from them. Emmit McCleod, Jimmy's father, was a partner in this enterprise. I only flew with Scotty once—he usually had a bottle of beer in hand when he flew.

Scotty owned the Waconichi Hotel, which was home mainly to the lumberjacks and prospectors. Saturdays were special, starting in the morning when the lumberjacks would get out their guitars, accordions and whatever else they had, and play

French western music. Wish I could have filmed them. On the weekends, the Waconichi would have a band in the basement bar. You always sat with your back to the wall because with guys outnumbering gals by 4-1, fights always broke out over the girls.

The stairs down to the basement bar from the main floor were steep. I was there when a drunk fell down them and lay motionless at the bottom. The hotel called for an ambulance; they came in with a stretcher but did not load the unconscious man onto it. Nothing seemed to be happening. Scotty appeared and began arguing with the ambulance owner.

"What's going on here?" I asked. As it turned out, the ambulance owner had not been paid the last time he'd hauled someone out of the bar and wasn't about to move the man until Scotty paid up front. No Medicare in those days.

Twelve-Foot Davis, *by Kerry Knoll*

When I was about eight years old, my Dad had a job selling auto parts to gas stations. His territory covered Edmonton and all of northern Alberta, so he was on the road a fair amount. One summer, he decided to take three of his boys with him. I'm guessing that with six kids and summer holidays in full swing, my mother had something to do with this decision.

Anyways, one stop along the way has stuck with me for more than half a century. It was to see a statue of the legendary prospector, Twelve Foot Davis. My little brain thought it must be some giant who was 12 feet tall. But this is the story my father told us (with a little help from the Canadian Encyclopedia):

Henry Davis tried his to make his fortune in the California Gold Rush as one of the original 49ers and like most, he didn't get lucky. But he didn't lose the bug and in 1860 heard about the Barkerville discovery in British Columbia, and so headed north. He arrived to a thriving gold rush town, even though road access wasn't to happen for another five years. Hurdy Gurdy dancing girls charged the miners a dollar a dance. Gambling and drinking were accepted, and horse races and prize fights were common. There were also church services, the Cariboo Literary society and the Theatre Royal.

But he soon discovered that everything was already staked. Undeterred, he started going around measuring everyone's claims, which were supposed to be no more than 100 feet of riverbank. He discovered two claims side by side that totaled 212 feet, and so staked the 12 feet right in the middle of them, and the mining recorder accepted it after a survey. He started digging and pulled out nearly 800 ounces of gold from his little claim, worth about $15,000 back then (and worth more than $2 million Canadian today). There is no word on how the claim owners on either side fared. The area eventually yielded more than five million ounces of placer gold. Osisko Royalties now controls the area and has another five million ounces drilled off.

From then on Henry was known as Twelve-Foot Davis. He took his fortune and began trading along the Peace River in northwestern Alberta, forty years before Alberta became a province, where he successfully competed against the Hudson Bay

Company for the rest of his long life. To this day Peace River Country is sometimes referred to as The Land of Twelve-Foot Davis.

I'm thinking that this just might have been when I got the gold bug.

How I met Robert Friedland, *by JJ Elkin*

Robert Friedland had just come off his Voisey Bay triumph in 1995. He had turned to the Far East and Indonesia for his next exploration project. I was convinced about Indonesia's potential and wanted to meet and team up with Robert in some way.

I found out from his assistant he could not meet me, as the following week, on a day she specified, he was going from Los Angeles to Jakarta. I figured he would go on that marvelous airline, Singapore Airlines, on the non-stop to Singapore and then switching to Jakarta. I was successful in persuading a Singapore reservation agent to put me in the First-Class seat next to Robert. And thus, I had a fabulous private "tete a tete" for 11 hours.

We became friends and I spent a number of weeks with him in Jakarta as his shadow, and to all, as his "advisor". We obtained the concessions we desired.

RAISING MONEY AND DOING DEALS

You Never Know, *by Dave Rogers*

Gord Fancy had a connection in the United States who knew of a retired U.S. Admiral who was a lawyer and was involved in private financing of junior exploration companies and individuals with the right story.

I was introduced and invited down to give a show-and-tell to a group of private investors. The meeting was for 3 p.m. The Admiral told me to be in his office at 2:00. We shook hands and I gave him my prepared spiel. He spent the next half hour asking questions then proceeded to really dump on my project and harangue on me to see if he could shake me loose, I suppose. I held my tongue and gave him straight answers.

Finally, he smiled and shook my hand and said let's go in and meet some potential investors. We did. I could hardly believe the flowery and positive introduction he gave the investors about me. I gave my spiel and answered their questions. Turned out to be a great day and I walked out with agreements totaling $500,000. You just never know.

"My Name is Santa Claus", *by Kerry Knoll*

Wheaton River was listed on the Toronto Stock Exchange in the summer of 1991, the only mining company that was listed that entire year and it took a Herculean effort for Ian McDonald and myself to raise the $1.5 million to get there. Two years later the company was still struggling, out of money, trying to find partners for our various projects. We had bought two closed gold mines in the Yukon: the old Ketza River mine from the dregs of Canamax, and Total Energold's Mount Skukum mine and the adjoining Omni deposit, located on the banks of the Wheaton River. The idea to buy the Skukum stuff came from a broker named Gord Fancy, who'd lost a bundle of money in Omni and wanted to get some of it back.

We believed that old chestnut that the best place to look for a mine is in the shadow of a headframe, and thought that having a permitted mill and tailings facility would make even a small discovery more likely to get into production. But it wasn't working, and our shares were trading at a dime, down from the 50 cents of our IPO. Ian and I weren't getting paid, so we leased a big office and rented single offices to a bunch of junior mining companies. It covered the bills, barely.

One day the geologist Laurie Curtis walks in to talk to one of our tenants, Peter Tredger. Laurie was on the board of North American Metals, which owned the Golden Bear mine near Telegraph Creek in British Columbia. I'd first heard about the Golden Bear in the Yorkton office in London, where I'd gone to visit Don Moore, one of the original directors of Corona, when Bob Dickenson gave a presentation on it.

The Golden Bear was the Hunter-Dickenson group's first operating mine. It had originally been a joint venture with Chevron. The two were joint operators, which was a recipe for disaster. It went way over budget, costing $120 million. The original cost estimate was $36 million . The Chevron employees would work a two-week shift, then head home while the NAM crew came in for their two weeks. The two sides were always blaming each other for all the problems. At some point, for reasons I'll never understand, Homestake made a takeover bid for NAM, but only got 89% of the shares. Finally, Homestake bought out Chevron, but the problems at the mine persisted. One issue was that in order to avoid the place getting unionized, they'd hired a general manager who was a big union guy. Bad idea. It was a great place to work, but not a great place to own.

"Homestake is closing the Golden Bear," Laurie told Peter. I heard him from the next office and went and knocked on the door. I'd met Laurie a few years earlier when he was on the drill at Nuinsco's Cameron Lake discovery in Ontario. I'd flown in as a reporter with David Bell who was keeping an eye on it for Nuinsco's partner, a Hughs-Lang company.

"Do you think they'd want to sell it," I asked Laurie, thinking that at the very worst we could add another mill to our collection. His cautious answer was, "maybe. But this hasn't been announced yet, the employees don't even know."

We had hired a South African mining engineer named Vic Jutronich as the COO of Wheaton River. Small world that it was, he had played rugby in university with fellow South African Peter Steen, who was by that time president of Homestake. Vic called his old drinking buddy, never letting on that we knew it was closing. They chatted for a while and Peter said he'd have one of his colleagues contact us.

Several weeks later we got a call from Homestake's Corporate Development guy, Lee Graber. He was coming to Toronto and wanted to meet with us. Ahead of the meeting we signed the confidentiality agreement and they sent us a bunch of information.

The meeting finally happened and most of it was taken up showing how they had looked for more ore but come up empty handed. There was less than a year of reserves left. However, they were in the process of permitting Eskay Creek, and didn't want to be shutting this mine down before they had their permits. Eskay would have some messy tailings. It was all optics. They had decided to get rid of it instead, and at this point we were the only ones interested. After what seemed like an eternity, Vic asked Lee, "So you haven't told us, how much do you want for it."

"Well," said Lee, "I was getting to that. Let me put it this way. Imagine that today is Christmas and my name is Santa Claus."

We were dumbfounded. Not only did Homestake offer us an operating mine essentially for free, but they were also going to put up a bond with the government to cover the entire eventual cleanup, and pay all of the employees whatever severance they would have been due. It had cost about $100 million to build the mine. All we had do was replace the $500,000 working capital NAM had in the bank at the time, and we would own a producing mine, with the reclamation money already in place. Okay the reserves were a little skinny, but you can always find more of those, can't you? The problem was, we didn't have that 500 grand. We had less than $100,000 in the bank.

Ian and I had been supplementing our income working for a new royalty company called Repadre, funded by Ned Goodman and run by his son Jonathan and a banker named Gerry McCarvill. The only royalty they had was on one of the diamond exploration properties in the Northwest Territories, but no discovery had been made there as yet. They were finding royalties hard to buy, and we were working to find them some.

We went over to see them and offered them a royalty on the Golden Bear production. For $500,000 they would get a 6% royalty until payback, and then 2% after that. You can't run a mining company with no cash on hand, so we asked, and by the way, do you guys want to do a private placement for another half million? The answer to the second question was no, we are strictly a royalty company. A few days later Jonathan called us said he'd talked to his dad, maybe his family trust would be interested in the shares if we could agree on a price, which we did at 33 cents. We had the money lined up and an extra half million for walking around money.

The problem was we still didn't have a signed deal and there was a bunch more paperwork to get cleared up and loads details to look after so we flew down to San Francisco with our lawyer, Paul Stein, to finalize things. We had to tell Paul that we couldn't afford to bring him in business class, and he was gracious about that (I think he paid for his own upgrade). We'd had several very lean years and my clothes were looking like it, but I put on my best suit and hoped for the best. Part way through the meeting, I crossed my legs under the table and the sole of my shoe fell off. Looking very serious, Paul handed me a note saying: "Put that in your briefcase!"

At the closing, the Homestake lawyers had required us to bring our original copy of our articles of incorporation. So naturally, our lawyer requested that they do the same.

Ian McDonald and Kerry Knoll at the Golden Bear with their first gold pour still hot out of the smelter, July 1993

They dug the old document out of the vault and brought it to Vancouver. There it was, in beautiful calligraphy, signed in 1877 by none other than the company founder, the legendary George Hearst, who started as a dirt prospector during the California gold rush and founded several mining companies in addition to Homestake including Anaconda, owned the San Francisco Examiner, and became a U.S. Senator. I still have a copy of those articles somewhere.

The next thing we knew we were the proud owners of the Golden Bear gold mine, cranking out 5,000 ounces of gold a month.

Stan Hawkins, Mac Watson and Flow-Through, *by Dave Rogers*

Near the start of "Flow-Through Financing" becoming popular on Bay Street. I had a joint venture involving one of The "Hawk's," Stan Hawkins companies. We both needed exploration funds. Mac Watson introduced me to a lawyer in Montreal who was very good at raising flow-through funds. We got an invite to make our presentation in Montreal.

At the last minute something came up and I could not go. The Hawk reluctantly agreed to go. When he came back, he called me up laughing and said he had a successful trip raising one million dollars for his company and six hundred for my company. He had been very impressed. First, he briefed the lawyer on our projects. The lawyer led him into a large boardroom where 10 potential investors sat with their cheque books handy. The Hawk gave them our show and tell. After questions, the lawyer said those of you who wish to invest bring me your cheques. Two guys got up a left—not interested.

The lawyer pressed a bell on the table and two guys with their cheque books in their hands walked into the boardroom through another door and completed the financing. The lawyer had his first-choice clients in the main boardroom. In an adjoining room he had the presentation and screen shots relayed to a second smaller group of interested investors ready to step up to the plate. The Hawk and I were very impressed with the lawyer's technique.

Hey Kid, You Wanna Run a Mining Company? *by John Paterson*

Geomaque Explorations Ltd. had been delisted for being inactive when I took over as president in 1992. Dan Hellens, who was in his mid-80's, was the principal shareholder and was looking for someone to do something with the company. His son Leith had been running it but had left the business and moved to North Carolina. The stock was traded on the old Over-The-Counter. Bid 5 cents, asked 10 cents. No trades for about a year. The company was about $50,000 in debt, no cash, but had been recently consolidated so had only 4 million shares outstanding. It held patented claims in Elliot Lake, Cobalt, and Val d'Or.

Although I was from Toronto, I had spent my first ten years out of school, working in the coal mines of British Columbia and Alberta. So, I didn't know a lot of the mining and financial people. I was now consulting on my own and with Roscoe Postle Associates who were a new consulting firm at the time. I worked mainly with John Postle doing economic modelling of exploration stage mineral deposits but also visited numerous projects around North America and Mexico.

I recently returned from the Ivory Coast where I helped build a small heap leach operation for Marshal Minerals and Eden Roc, which were run by Harry Quint. Joe Hinzer, now president of Watts Griffis and McQuat, was the chief geologist on the project. I worked closely with Mike Cassiday of Kappes Cassiday Associates and learned a lot about heap leaching gold.

I told Dan Hellens I wanted to option a gold property in Mexico. He knew it was going to be difficult but wanted to see the company succeed so he exercised 50,000 stock options at 10 cents to put some cash in the till for travel expenses. Then he kindly gave me the 50,000 shares. I went to Mexico, checked out the property and made the option deal with David Giles at Peñoles.

Lac Minerals had 300,000 Geomaque shares from a previous deal. I was trying to buy them but negotiations through their landman Bill Cavalluzzo, but we weren't getting anywhere. I knew Chris Pegg, who was Lac's V.P. Exploration at the time from university and he talked to Peter Allen for me. He convinced

Peter to sell me the block for 3 cents a share.

It was around that time that I met Don Empey who had been working many years as a mining analyst but had recently gone out on his own. Don knew all the Toronto mining analysts and most of the mining fund managers. I told Don I wanted to develop a gold project, but he told me that brokers weren't interested in gold stories because the price was so low, around $350/oz.

But you will remember that 1992 was when the great diamond rush broke out in the NWT. With Don's connections on the Street and my technical background, we made a great team. Over a few lunches at Ed's Warehouse, one of Don's favorite restaurants, we developed a plan.

John Paterson at the San Francisco Mine
in Mexico, 1995

The idea was to raise some money, stake some diamond

properties in a private company and merge it with Geomaque thereby taking the new investment public, financing Geomaque and getting it re-listed on the TSE.

But staking was all by helicopter and expensive. So, we took the government airborne magnetic data and used a complex algorithm developed by Paterson, Grant and Watson. It's also handy to have a father who's a geophysicist to pick bullseye targets in the Lac du Gras area. Then we went looking for money to do the staking. We needed $35,000 to put postage stamp sized claim blocks over 20 targets.

Our first stop was Southern Era which was run by the famous diamond expert Chris Jennings. Chris liked the idea and Southern Era invested $10,000. I remember leaving the meeting and Don and I were "high fiving" in the elevator. We knew that having Chris as an investor would certainly act as a vote of confidence for other investors and it turned out to be true. The Southern Era stock was flying high and Don had just bought a limited-edition minivan with profits from his investment. The van sported plates with the company's trading symbol, "SUF." We had no trouble putting together the rest of the money. Ten more came from a company called Stall Lake Mines, which was run by a second cousin from Winnipeg, Don Paterson. Don was the first cousin of Richard Hogarth. Another ten came from John Carroll, a New York mining investor with whom I was to have many future dealings. I think Don Empey put in the last five.

The next step was till sampling, but we had to wait until summer. In the meantime, we hired Wayne Beach, of Beach Hepburn to do the legal work. You'll recall how hot the diamond rush was, and the market couldn't get enough of it.

So, we went out to raise some more money in the private company prior to the merger. That's when the fun began.

Don got on the phone to all his analyst contacts and pretty well everyone wanted in. Egizio Bianchini from BMO, John Lydall from National Bank, probably a dozen of the analysts in total. In those days, the analysts could own shares in the juniors as long as they declared it.

We took our roll of maps around and told the story to anyone who would listen. Chris Jennings name was dropped in each meeting. Pierre Lassonde came in big and brought along some of his friends, and so did John Embry from RBC. Then the Toronto

Stock Exchange told us we needed a bigger float, so Wayne Beach issued certificates to dozens of his clients and contacts.

He wrote each a letter saying they could pay him for the shares any time in the next six months and he would send them the certificate. If they didn't want it, he would buy it back. The next thing we knew, we had raised a half a million dollars at ten cents. And we valued the diamond properties at $100,000. So, we did an RTO by the private company with Geomaque issuing another 6 million shares. The company now had 20 "highly prospective" diamond properties, $500,000 cash and 10 million shares outstanding.

Geomaque's stock had been halted pending the merger and the analysts talked up the company leading to the resumption of trading on the TSE. When it finally opened, there were no sellers. The Hellens family held on to their stock. Most of the old shareholders had forgotten about the company and didn't realize it was trading again until they got their monthly statements in the mail. The new investors who got in at 10 cents and Southern Era and the other "first round" investors who effectively got in at 3.5 cents were eager to see where it would open.

Lassonde and some others put in bids in the market and we were all ecstatic to see it start trading at $0.60! Chris Jennings told me it was the best investment he ever made. His $10,000 outlay a couple of months earlier was now worth $170,000 and went up a lot more down the road. Although extremely pleased with the outcome, both Don Paterson and John Carroll told me I'd caused them tax problems and ended up giving most of their gains to charity.

Summer came around and we did our till sampling of the 20 targets. Unfortunately, like many of the other companies that picked up ground during the staking rush, we didn't turn up a single indicator mineral. But the gold price had started going up and we were flexible. We changed our focus to gold in Mexico and used the rest of the proceeds to acquire and do a feasibility study on the San Francisco mine property.

It wasn't our biggest financing, but it was certainly one of the most fun.

"Good Morning, Dave" *by Dave Rogers*

I was looking for a clean, listed shell company. When talking with George Kent he said he had Duration Mines listed on the Vancouver Stock Exchange. It was clean and he would be interested in making a deal for me to take it over. We chatted about it over a two-month period while I did my due diligence on the company. Finally, George and I came to terms and George said ok Dave get the lawyer to write it up and we will sign off on it. I phoned George on a Friday and said drop into the office I have the agreements as we had agreed to all printed out for signing. George dropped in and read the agreement and agreed it was as we had discussed.

Then he began complaining that he should be getting a better deal. He went on and on. I was getting hot under the collar. I stood up, took his second copy and put it in his hands. I said George you can take Duration and stick it up where the sun don't shine. Now get the fuck out of my office.

He looked at me somewhat startled but got up and walked out of my office with his unsigned copies of the agreement. Monday morning there was a light tap on my office door and George stuck his head in and said good morning Dave. Have you got time to get these agreements signed? I smiled and said good morning George and yes come on in a we will get everything signed and witnessed. We did it.

Duration Mines – A Follow-up, *by Dave Rogers*

I had Duration up and running. Good properties with a lot of promise. Interest in the company on the Street. I met with the TSE and went through the procedure to get transferred from VSE to the TSE. All went well. The Engineer's club started letting companies use the "Discussion Room" downstairs for "Show & Tell" sessions. I had a sell-out crowd in the room. About 5 minutes into my spiel, I looked down and noted that all four of my directors sitting in the front row were sound asleep. Ed Thompson, Bill Hill, Bill Allen and Ted Wade. Talk about in-house support when you are trying to persuade the street that your company is going places. No further comment.

The Blue Pearl, *by Kerry Knoll*

$\mathbf{I}$an McDonald and I started a public company in the 1990s called Patent Enforcement and Royalties Ltd (PEARL), which financed inventors who had their patents stolen. We won a number of cases, the biggest one being $48 million by a jury in a New York City court against Conair over a hair-dryer safety mechanism. Another big one for us never even went to court, it was a fellow who had actually patented technology that was required for the internet to function, and the announcement of that lawsuit put our share price over two bucks in the late 1990s. But winning in the United States and collecting the money are two very different things, as the fellow who invented the windshield wiper delay mechanism found out during 30 years of litigation. After a while we couldn't raise any more money and we found ourselves with a shell company and went looking for a mining deal.

In 2004, John Kalmet, the former Noranda executive who had been our president at Wheaton River, called us and said he owned a small interest in a large molybdenum project near Smithers B.C. called Yorke-Hardy, that had been drilled off by Amax.

"Molybdenum," I said to Ian, "I know about molybdenum from my Northern Miner days. Its price goes through the roof for a cup of coffee about once a decade and then heads for the sewer as metal from the Climax mine floods the market."

But Climax was closed, moly prices were rising, and the numbers looked pretty compelling. We cut a deal, halted the stock, and organized a special shareholders meeting for approval. Ian and I each put in $200,000 at a dime to reseed the company, giving me by this time about three million shares and Ian a bunch more than that. Quotes on moly prices were hard to find in those early internet days, but we learned it was trading at $7 a pound, up from $4 only a year before. Our office was closed between Christmas and New Year's, but I took time off from building the Bellavista mine in Costa Rica and went in and created a Power-Point to help raise money for the new venture. The phone rang one afternoon, and it was John Willett, a corporate finance guy now at Raymond James.

"I'm looking at your deal," he said. "Do you know the moly

price has doubled this week? It's trading at $14 a pound." He had found some obscure metals website in India that provided a quote. The name was changed to Blue Pearl and the shares started trading at 30 cents and went to 50 cents when we started doing some infill drilling. The market can be stupid sometimes and they treated our drill intercepts like a new discovery, despite full disclosure. We kept drilling and the share price went to 80 cents at which time a German group financed us for a couple of million dollars. Moly prices were inching up to $20.

The people of Smithers got into the stock in a big way and we were the talk of the town. Drillers handling the core without gloves had their hands turn blue from the mineralization (which is why we called it Blue Pearl Mining). These guys were easy to identify walking down the street and were often accosted by people looking for the latest drill information.

John Kalmet pitched in again, introducing us to Steve Mooney, the former COO of Amax and now the owner of the private company Thompson Creek Metals, which owned the Endako mine down the road. We made a deal to custom mill our ore there, making permitting much easier, capex much lower, and production much sooner. An old Placer Dome holding, Endako had been on life support for years but was now raking in the cash and talking about expanding. Our shares went to $2.50, with Eric Sprott now leading the charge as our largest shareholder with 14%.

Anyone in the mining business knows, or should know, when your shares become over-priced, it's time to make a deal or raise some money. We went to Mooney in early 2006 offered him $200 million for Endako, with Gene McBurney at GMP Partners agreeing to raise us the money. Steve Mooney was 72 years old, his kids wanted nothing to do with mining, and we reasoned that he also had the bigger Thompson Creek mine in Idaho and the profitable custom roaster in Pennsylvania.

He said he didn't trust investment bankers as far as he could kick them, having been burned several times in the past. However, he was friends with John Kalmet, who told him to trust us, and a handshake deal was done.

Thompson Creek had been formed by Mooney, a Colorado School of Mines alum, out of the merger between Amax and Cyprus Mining in 1993. The merged company would have owned all of the primary producing moly mines in the U.S. and that was a no-no. So, they put the money-losing Thompson Creek mine up for sale and got three offers. Door One was, pay us $10 million and we'll take it off your hands. Door Two was, "give it to us for free". Standing behind Door Three was Mooney, who was going to lose his Amax job in the merger, and who said he would pay them $10 million for it, provided they loaned him the $10 million.

It was their best option and Mooney picked up a $500 million complex for next to nothing. The next year he bought Endako, on similar terms. In 1995 the moly price shot up for a couple of months and he paid off all the loans.

We were getting ready to go to the market for the $200 million, and we got a bizarre call from an investment banker in New York, at UBS. He said he'd been engaged by Thompson Creek to evaluate the deal on their behalf. And then he said, "If you guys can raise $200 million to buy Endako, do you think you could raise $300 million to buy the whole company? We value Thompson Creek at $700 million, and we'd lend you $400 million."

Not thinking this could possibly be real, Ian and our lawyer Paul Stein flew to New York and had a meeting with about 30 UBS bankers in their giant boardroom. It was real, and they thought they could pull it off in 60 days, no less. The folks at GMP were ecstatic.

Around that time, Ian and I were celebrating the 25th year of our business partnership with a big party. Eric Burden and the Animals were playing, and McBurney pulled me aside and said we'd better hurry, Stan Bharti was making a proposal to Thompson Creek.

Our brilliant CFO, Derek Price, worked like 20-man team 18 hours a day to model the company to the banker's satisfaction and by August we made the announcement. Moly was trading at $24 a pound by then, and Thompson Creek was making $1 million a day profit, weekends included. The bank had valued moly long term at $12, and that was what the $700 million purchase price was based on.

As sometimes happens, the market lost its collective mind. When we made the announcement, all hell broke loose. Usually when a junior company announces a large financing, the share price goes lower. Not this time. On the conference call before the market opened, Eric Sprott asked our lawyer if there was any way Thompson Creek could get out of the deal if a better offer came along. The answer was no. "Then I'm subscribing for $50 million of the issue as your lead order," Eric said, for everybody on the call to hear.

Our shares opened at $7, up $4.50, and we wound up doing the financing at $5.50. Ian gave 90 presentations on three continents in three weeks and sold the deal. The money was in the lawyer's trust accounts, the closing documents being drawn up, when another bizarre call came in, this time from the Ontario Securities Commission.

The guy said that there was a new rule that the seller of a private company had to continue to have some skin in the game. He faxed over the new policy, but it clearly applied only to private family trusts going public, which this one clearly wasn't. It didn't matter, the OSC was sticking to its guns. I had learned early on that the OSC staff hate to see people make easy money, and with their $60,000 salaries some of them would do anything they could to prevent it. The bottom line was, the seller had to keep a meaningful portion of the company or they were going to block the deal. We brought in a lawyer that had previously been chairman of the OSC, arguing in our favor, to no avail.

We went to Mooney and asked him if he would take 10% of the purchase price in stock. Having realized by this time he had sold way too low, his answer was a quick no. Then Paul Stein came up with an idea. We had not disclosed in our news releases that Mooney was entitled to the first $50 million in working capital on closing, and we would get the rest.

A quick review of the working capital showed that it was closer to $100 million. We would change Mooney's portion to $70 million and have him subscribe for $20 million worth of shares on his behalf. By this time, threatened with a lawsuit from us, the OSC just wanted it to go away and they quickly agreed to the solution.

The deal finally closed, Mooney taking an extra $20 million from shareholders' pockets thanks to the OSC, which pretends to be protecting shareholders.

The market loved the story. While the analysts were pricing moly long term at $12 a pound, the market was thinking $35, and our shares were priced accordingly. We got listed on the New

York Stock Exchange when the shares were trading at $15, Ian and I went down to ring the bell with some of the management.

At the bell ceremony, Mooney pulled us aside and said, "Well, I didn't know if you guys were going to be able to pull this one off. Congratulations. You know, I had had another offer on the same terms waiting in the wings, just in case. Are you curious about who it was from?" It was from a group backed by Warren Buffett. With the bonus shares and warrants that the OSC had forced us to give him, Mooney eventually made an extra $100 million on the transaction. History doesn't record whether he sent the OSC a thank-you card.

Jim Cramer, with his Mad Money program one of the most popular investing shows in the United States, made us his top pick and the shares surged to $24. There was a column in the National Post called "If You Had Invested $1000 A Year Ago" and listed the top and bottom 10 stocks on the Toronto Stock Exchange. We were on top of the list for the full year they ran the table, and I'm sure we were the reason they quietly dropped it. We paid $135 million in income taxes that year. In early 2008 we raised $200 million at $22 per share, and with that and mine profits, paid off the $400 million loan 18 months after the purchase and we owned the mines free and clear. The market cap got close to $3 billion.

Sprott, who was by now a billionaire, told us that Blue Pearl was his biggest score ever. But even the best parties have to end at some point and this one did with the 2008 crash with moly sinking from $25 to $7 in a month, and our share price crashing to $3, before recovering to $15 or so in 2010.

As an aside, in July of 2008 and just before the crash, Ian and I were having a beer with Eric at a patio off Bay Street. My personal wealth was at its highest point in my life. I asked Eric, what should I do. It's simple, he said. Sell everything and buy gold. Of course he would say that. The gold price was around 800 bucks and our stock was at $24. Had I listened, I'd be worth five or six times what I have now. Smart guy.

THE CENTRE OF THE UNIVERSE (ONTARIO)

Timmins, *by Dave Rogers*

In September of 1957 I was assigned to the Timmins Resident Geologists office of the Ontario Department of Mines. In December 1957, Dr. Stuart Ferguson, resident geologist was transferred to Toronto and I was given the title of "Acting Resident Geologist".

In January 1958, the Local CIM held a mining reception where the Minister of Mines, Mr. Spooner, was the head speaker and full of himself. I was invited and the resident geologist from Kirkland Lake, Dr. W.S. Savage, took me under his wing. We had a few drinks.

Spooner came over and was introduced. He smoked like a chimney. He threw an empty package in the waste basket, looked at me and said, "Hey boy, run down to the corner store and buy me a couple of packs of cigarettes". I replied, "Mr. Spooner, I am not your boy. I am a graduate geologist. Find yourself a political flunky," and I turned and walked away.

There were some shocked faces and Spooner was sputtering out loud. Dr. Savage steered me across the room to the bar where we replenished. "Well David", he said, "you sure put him in his place. Well done. Be interesting if you still have a job by month-end."

He then took me over to a group of three very tall, older men in their 40's and 50's. I was 23 and he introduced me as the new resident geologist. All three were the mine managers of the Hollinger, McIntyre and the Dome mines.

I told them I had been toured underground and given an explanation of each mine by the respective chief geologists and that I was very impressed and pleased with their reception. "Well then", said the manager of the Hollinger mine. "Tell us, from what you observed and learned do you have any suggestions from a geological perspective?"

This was the era when the concept of open pits, apart from iron, coal and a few copper mines was being introduced into base metals and gold etc.

"Well gentlemen, I actually do," I replied. "I was fascinated at the tight mining control you have on the gold bearing gold veins and structures. And I think I understand from the operating viewpoint that this is necessary in order to mine basically the higher-grade zones and make a profit. However, as I perused the detailed underground and surface maps I was taken by the large number of isolated high grade, medium grade and low-grade intersections were recorded outside and within the veins systems. I was told that not a lot of extra assaying of "interesting looking" mineralized zones etc. was carried out because of budget restraints.

Your geologists of course recognized the same as I did that there was an excellent potential for much larger tonnages of lower grade material, which if mined as an open pit concept might be worth investigating for the not-too-distant future. I respectfully recommend that you add some funding to the geology budget to allow your geologists to build up a better knowledge of the rocks, structure and gold mineralization grades between the veins you are currently mining."

"Well Rogers", they basically said in unison. "There is no budget money for that kind of day-dreaming with the price of gold as it is today." And with that they turned and walked over to another group of their cronies. "Well," Savage said, "you sure know how to stir the pot. Let's go get another drink."

And no, I was not fired.

Fast Forward to 1994, and Dome opened their Super Pit and closed it in 2004. It was 286 million tonnes of rock, 340m deep and 800m to 900m across.

The Windfall Affair, *by Ed Thompson*

The Windfall affair had a severe impact on the Prospectors and Developers Association and on the exploration and development industry. Viola MacMillan was president of the association and, as such, really represented the junior exploration industry. People nod knowingly whenever they hear mention of the Windfall "scandal," but most don't really know a damn thing about it except what they've heard second- or third-hand.

I was very much involved in the exploration business at the time. In fact, I was competing against Viola and others for the Windfall claims near Timmins, Ontario and was a shareholder in Windfall Oils & Mines. So, my understanding of the events is better than that of the popular press.

In a nutshell, I believe Viola and the junior mining industry were unjustly crucified. That is my interpretation of events "from the trenches."

To set the stage, 1960-63 was a depressed period and little exploration work was being carried out. Canada was heavily oriented toward gold, yet the gold price of US$35 per oz. combined with rising costs made most projects uneconomic. Only a few broker-dealer companies were doing financings and the regulations made the raising of capital difficult and expensive.

And with no exploration success, everyone lost money. Some complaints were made to the Ontario Securities Commission and both it and the Toronto Stock Exchange were threatening to abolish junior financings.

In late 1963 and early 1964, rumours emanated from Timmins of a significant base metal discovery by an unknown U.S. company with the funny name of Texas Gulf Sulphur, ("TGS"). They had been exploring across Canada for almost a decade, flying helicopter electromagnetic surveys and drilling anomalies. We had encountered them in Amos in 1960 and were envious of their use of helicopters.

Finally, on April 16, 1964, TGS announced a major find of zinc, copper and silver massive sulphides and, as the saying goes, "all hell broke loose."

The next day on the Toronto Stock Exchange, more than 30 million shares changed hands, a record at the time, as speculators clamored to buy stocks of companies they had never heard of before, so long as they held properties somewhere near Timmins.

All of us in the exploration business went ballistic as well, including Viola, who had been semi-retired since 1960, when she suffered a heart attack. She had sold off her principal companies to Art White and was devoting her time and energy to promoting the PDA and fighting the industry's various battles.

But like an old warhorse that hears the last bugle call she rose to the occasion, partly because the find was in the Timmins camp where she had got her start and partly because she was a good friend of John Larche, a knowledgeable prospector who had some attractive parcels of land.

The prize was four claims in Prosser Township which had been left out of the TGS staking by mistake. These had a great airborne anomaly and good geology. Everyone agreed that this was the best property available and was a sure mine. I should explain that even before the announcement, companies had started flying the area and at least six now had airborne surveys. At Teck we had flown a large area and considered this anomaly a great target. We were busy buying and optioning properties and selling portions of our survey. Base metal deposits usually occur in camps so the expectation was that other deposits would be discovered.

Viola flew up to Timmins to talk with John who was negotiating with about six companies, with Noranda having the most money. He was trying to do a million-dollar deal: $100,000 down and $900,000 in one year. This was a lot of money in 1964 and no one was immediately prepared to pay it.

Viola bugged John to get a quick answer from Noranda, so John called the field man, but the company couldn't decide. Viola then cornered John in a hotel room and worked out a deal: $100,000 cash and 250,000 shares of a shell company. After signing him up, she flew back to Toronto and offered the deal to Windfall Oils and Mines for what she had paid plus an option on 200,000 shares for five years and a royalty. A fair deal and subsequently approved by the TSE.

Most of us thought she had a mine and had out hustled the industry again. I called her husband George to congratulate him and sold him our airborne coverage of the property for $5,000.

Again, some vital background information is required. Viola was in the underwriting business through her company Mac-Millan Securities and had been financing companies for more than 20 years. She was financing Windfall and had options on blocks of stock at progressively higher prices, which was a perfectly normal business practice, but as you will learn, it caused problems.

It wasn't long before a drill was turning on the property. We all thought a hit was a foregone conclusion and so we started buying a little stock. A day or so later, on July 6, some buying started in Timmins and everyone said, "This is it." And by closing time, the stock was over $2.

As I mentioned earlier, Viola had been financing Windfall through two other companies she controlled and had options on 900,000 shares at three-month intervals at prices ranging from $0.40 to $0.70.

The TSE at that time had a crazy rule that if the price of a stock rose to double the option price, they were due and payable into the company's treasury immediately. Therefore, on July 6, she got a call from the TSE ordering her to pay all the money for the options into the Windfall treasury within the hour. The amount came to $400,000 which, in 1964, was a lot of money. She had to dash over to her bank and negotiate a personal loan of $200,000 and sell enough shares to meet the TSE requirements.

Viola later stated that these shares that she had to sell to meet the TSE's regulations were the only shares she ever sold and that none of the other directors sold. She wanted to sell other shares to maintain an orderly market but her solicitor, fussy old Tom Cole, whom I would later inherit, said the exchange's regulations did not permit it.

The next day, prices kept going up and the company issued a brief statement saying the drill had entered a "mineralized graphitic shear" at a depth of 416 ft. This did not mean a valuable discovery had been made, but, because of the euphoria at the time and because there was a lot of graphite at TGS, the share price continued to increase. The rise was also probably helped by the fact that Viola had been forced to exercise all her options. Speculation was intense. People were flying over the drill in helicopters and sneaking in on the ground to try to see the core and take sludge samples for assaying. On the same day, July 7, George

MacMillan ordered that a core shack and a bunkhouse be built, and drilling was halted for a few days. Bradley Bros., the drillers, reported that they were having trouble keeping snoopers away from the drill. George took the core and locked it in the trunk of his car.

On July 10, the TSE sent a telegram demanding an explanation and the company reported that a core shack was being built. On the July 14, the OSC called a big meeting, including the president and vice-president of the TSE, and everyone apparently agreed that the proper procedure was not to assay the core until the hole had been completed and there were to be no visual or partial assays. George was ordered to keep the core under guard, which only deepened the mystery. There were fake assays being circulated by at least one group.

The shares hit a high of $5.60.

However, in short order, the hole was completed, the core assayed, and the results released on July 30.

Everybody involved will remember where they were.

While some copper mineralization had been encountered, less than 0.5%, it was not what was expected, and the stock dropped from above $3 to $1. It was over in three weeks, though a number of other holes were drilled. The mob wanted blood. Viola was the Queen, and they went after her head.

No one seemed to appreciate that it was mostly the TSE and OSC regulations - and regulators - that had been a big part of the problem and that the speculators had themselves to blame.

I had never seen a government move so fast.

Within a couple of weeks, Justice Kelly was appointed to allocate the blame. The actual hearings did not get started until the spring of 1965 and when he handed down his report in the fall, Kelly suggested that George and Viola were guilty of fraud and strongly criticized both the OSC, whose commissioners had done some trading, and the TSE.

It was a perfect excuse to kill junior exploration financings, which the TSE and the OSC did immediately. Soon afterwards, in the late fall of 1965, George and Viola were charged with two counts of fraud whereupon she resigned from the PDA and withdrew to her farm. Viola was the PDA, so the association collapsed and the industry, for reasons I never understood, did not rally around. In Canada we often take a perverse delight in destroying our heroes and we certainly abandoned Viola.

The fraud case was weak and didn't come to trial until three years later and Viola and George were acquitted in February 1969. The judge ruled they had acted quite correctly. However, Viola had also been charged with "wash trading," a common practice, then and now, of creating the impression of activity in a stock by buying and selling into related accounts. A broker at the time compared it with spitting on the sidewalk or practicing birth control, both of which were technically illegal at the time.

The authorities could not find anything wrong with Viola's Windfall activities, so they widened the search to other companies and found that Viola had sold 200,000 shares of Consolidated Golden Arrow to George.

She said George had been after her for some time for some shares in this company. The sale was done through a broker and because it was a large block, speculators thought something was going on and jumped on board. She also sold a few shares to nine friends and neighbours. Her lawyer later wrote that Viola had no idea that she might be breaking a law by selling some shares to her husband.

In my mind, it was an unjust decision, and her appeal was denied. Viola spent nine weeks in jail, her 40 years of achievements negated and most of her friends gone. She was later given a complete pardon, but the damage had been done.

The fall-out was immense:

- The Royal Commission uncovered serious weaknesses in the regulatory practices of the TSE. Branded a "private gaming club," it was criticized in particular for approving the press release and failing to suspend trading.
- The OSC also came under criticism. Commission director John Campbell was suspended for his involvement and a new Securities Act was brought in.
- The junior mining industry was decimated in Toronto and eventually resurrected in Vancouver.
- The PDA went down with Viola, and we were all unfairly branded crooks. The big companies abandoned the association and some actually forbade their employees from going to the convention. The junior mining industry has been unjustly tarnished ever since.
- Viola's and George's careers and reputations were

destroyed. Although they continued exploring, it was half-hearted, and they had no success.

The dollars involved were miniscule. The Commission estimated that the public had lost $2 million, part of which went into various public companies. As far as I know, Viola and George never made a dime from their efforts.

Finally, a warning to all. No matter who you are or how careful you might be, if you get caught in the headlights and the mob wants blood, you're done for.

Windfall – The Aftermath, *by Dick Hogarth*

$\mathbf{A}$s an addendum to Ed's story on Windfall, the following dissertation is offered.

At the time of this scene, I was employed as a salesman with the firm of T.A. Richardson & Co. Ltd. This firm, whose head office was located in Toronto and had a number of branches in mining communities including Timmins.

A few years prior to the Windfall event, Viola MacMillan, had perpetrated a serious trading infraction and was never to have an account with the firm in the future. This was personally told to me by their Chief of Trading.

After the first hole was drilled by TGS, with its exceptional results, people lined up around the block in Timmins to buy stocks. Shortly after the find, Windfall became a focus. I recall keeping a "Swing Chart", on the movements, and as a result only had one client, on his own volition, buy the stock.

Our President, Marshall Stearns, son-in-law of Sandy Richardson and President of the TSE, on a Saturday morning, when the announcement was disclosed, that there were no values of significance. I recall my total surprise and shock with this news. Two people, that became aware of the results from the assay office, I believe located in Kirkland Lake, had access to these results. They both made a handsome profit on their investment.

Market Opportunity Due To the Texas Gulf Mystique, *by* *Dave Rogers*

Joining Texas Gulf in the fall of 1966, I soon realized that there were a couple of promoters who employed claim stakers to follow our geologists and as soon as we began to stake small claim blocks in any greenstone belts in Ontario targeting Airborne EM anomalies. They would then move in and tie on to our claims.

They did not interfere with our staking. They just stood back and when our stakers were finished they moved in immediately and tied on. These claims were then recorded in one of their many shell companies.

They would wait until we started follow up with ground geophysics and drilling. Then they would get the rumour mill going and move the share prices from say the $0.10 level up to $0.15 and pile on the promotion about Texas Gulf drilling on our claim borders.

I got to know who some of these guys were. At that point, say $0.15, I would buy a small block of shares. They nearly always ran the share prices up to $0.25 to $0.50 per share and I sold immediately into that market.

Almost guaranteed to make 25% to 75% capital gains. And this was before the Federal Government imposed the Capital Gains Tax on December 31, 1971.

The Boulder Syndicate, *by Dave Rogers*

I phoned Wally Bruce, exploration manager for Dome Mines Ltd. for an appointment. I re-introduced myself to him as the young student with Jim Proudfoot who showed up on his doorstep back in November of 1956. The Geological Survey of Canada had presented a talk at the Engineers Club on the 1971 Reverse Circulation Drift Prospecting program they sponsored in the winter of 1971 across Northern Ontario and Quebec. The analytical results were to be released later that summer. I had been retained by the GSC to run the program but was not privy to the analytical results.

Wally Bruce, and a number of exploration managers had attended. So, I then proceeded to explain to Wally that I would like to form the Boulder Syndicate. Say three companies at $400,000 each to be front and centre in the follow up when the results were released. Wally liked the idea and took me directly into Mr. Jim Repath, President of Dome Mines Ltd. Mr. Redpath Sr listened to my brief pitch and said he liked the idea and would participate. What other partners do you have in mind?

I carefully responded that I was not sure but that perhaps they might suggest two partners who they would like to partner with. He immediately said how about Imperial Oil (Fenton Scott) and Jorex (Joe Rankin). I agreed that they would make good partners. He said I will phone Fenton and get him on board. Meanwhile he picked up the phone and got Joe Rankin on the line. Joe, he said I am sending over a young geologist with a good syndicate proposal. We are in and I am sure Fenton will join. Listen to his proposal and if you like it tell him so and we can make up an agreement.

I skedaddle over to Joe Rankin's office. Joe was a huge man 6'6'. He welcomed me into his office and said, tell be about the syndicate I just became part of. I did just that and he said ok I am in. How much money are you looking for?

I said I thought $400,000 from each partner would do the job. He looked at me and said did Jim Redpath agree to that amount? I said no because he did not ask. Things moved so fast that the dollar amount was not discussed. Joe said I can come up with $350,000 for the first year. So, times 3 can you manage to operate on $1,050,000 for the year? I replied I guess I will have to.

If we make a significant find, then I will be back for more money. That, he said, I can handle. He phoned Repath to say he was in and what each contribution would be. Redpath said fine Fenton and Imperial Oil are in. I will get an agreement drafted up. Now, if I do say so myself, that was a very speedy and successful business deal.

We had some technical successes using the basal till sampling technique and we had one miss.

I proposed to do several reconnaissance drill profiles along the down-ice side of the Gabbro Complex in Montcalm Twp. as indicated by the Ontario Government airborne magnetic survey. At a meeting in my office in Ottawa for some reason Fenton Scott turned me down. He persuaded his buddy Don Kemp, Jorex geologist, to vote with him against the proposal. Wally Bruce was in favour with me. I got a bit upset and told Fenton that he joined the Boulder Syndicate with only a $350,000 investment out of his $6,000,000 annual budget to see what I could come up with using the basal till sampling system. I was pissed and said when I was with TGS I was running $1,000,000 programs without the bosses second guessing me all the time. Fenton would not back down, and Wally got me cooled down.

Getting to the quick of the matter, some company, I can't remember who, flew an EM survey over the complex in the next year or so and came up with a one-line anomaly which they drilled. Ended up with a 3.9 million tonne ore body grading 1.25% Ni, 0.51% Cu and 0.051% Co. It would have been a nice technical advance for basal till sampling and a feather in my cap at the time. But thanks to Fenton it was not to be.

Moosonee, *by Howard Stockford*

A new niobium-rich, pyrochlore-bearing carbonatite was discovered by a team led by Wally Boyko in 1966, 40 miles south of Moosonee, Ontario. Consolidated Morrison Explorations/ Argor Explorations (Art Stollery companies, financed by Imperial Oil) controlled the concessions at that time. Canadian Bechtel was asked to supply support staff on the project and I was assigned to look after a definition drilling program, starting in January 1967.

I took our family from Montreal to live in Moosonee.....again, a bit of a culture shock for them! Getting there was interesting....Included a 3 hour train ride on Ontario Northland's "Polar Bear Express" from Cochrane to Moosonee, there being no road access. We were kept sane there by having an associate membership to the local CFB radar site's officers' mess which also allowed access to all the base facilities, including Curling Club and swimming pool/gym etc. I was transferred from Bechtel to Argor Explorations in the spring of 1967. During the change from Bechtel, which coincided with the first week of Expo 67 our Montreal apartment was well-used by friends and we attended this wonderful event for four days before returning to Moosonee.

I reported to Robert M Smith, Arthur Stollery and James Walker, who was the Project Manager. At the Argor site we had a 3000ft airstrip made by packing the snow on the muskeg. We used Austin Airways' DC 3's and Beaver/Otter fixed wing aircraft and a 47-G4 Bell or Hiller 12E helicopter operated by Niagara Helicopters for servicing the site and for exploration projects. Most of the helicopter pilots were "green", coming straight from learning to fly in Niagara Falls so we had to train them in navigation skills in the flat James Bay Lowlands. There were some hairy moments, including two engine failures!

Subsequently Bechtel was commissioned to complete a feasibility study on the Niobium (Columbium) project, including metallurgical studies at Lakefield. A test shaft and small drift was driven on one level to generate a bulk sample for developing the flow sheet. The deposit has not yet been developed and is now owned by others. This deposit could have supplied the whole world's market at that time

We moved to Cochrane to continue exploration in the area from there, in 1969, and then to Toronto in 1970, where I set up a new exploration office in the old schoolhouse at the corner of Kennedy Road and Major Mackenzie Drive, on the Angus Glen Farm property owned by Arthur Stollery, a great Boss! He sent me to look at properties all over Ontario and included a review of several properties in Guatemala and evaluation of the Yukon with a view to opening an office in Whitehorse. I liked the potential for gold in Yukon but Cons. Morrison only had about 400,000 dollars annual income from its shareholding in Noranda from it's potash mine in Saskatchewan, not enough to carry the cost of a helicopter alone in the Yukon. Art also had me do a review of the future of the lithium market in 1969....always thinking of commodities that would be in demand in the future! This market, of course was dominated by the solution miners, particularly Foote Minerals in the U.S.

We found another large, Noobium-bearing carbonatite in Valentine Township, close to the Otter Rapids hydro dam. Two holes were drilled, one containing very light, honey-coloured pyrochlore. This carbonatite is overlain by 400 feet of Paleozoic sediments and exploitation would be limited to underground mining. To my knowledge this has never been followed up.

While in Moosonee there was some difficulty getting the local workers to adhere to the times for the helicopter departures and my wife, Jeannie was a big help in getting this done. We finally fixed this problem by giving one of the locals a contract to do the bush work. Somehow their new boss got them under control with some innovative methods!

Due to Morrison's close association with Siscoe Mines (George Smith, CEO and brother of Bob Smith) we had access to Siscoe's Turbo Beaver. It was flown by Grant Davidson, a former Air Canada pilot and de Havilland test pilot. There were stories that although he was an excellent pilot he took a lot of chances, landing the new Turbo Beaver on remote bush trails and he once demonstrated the STOL performance of that aircraft by landing across a dock 300ft wide in New York Harbour. He and I once went into Nakina where the strip was soft and muddy in the spring. I was there to look at the Prairie Lake Carbonatite. The aircraft was on amphibious floats (with only small wheels in the front that dug into the mud). He had me stand on the back of the floats to get the front wheels free and I had to jump in halfway down the runway....hairy stuff! I don't think Grant is around any more!

Texas Gulf Sulphur, *by Dave Rogers*

Before joining Texas Gulf Sulphur, I had put together several exploration projects which I was in the process of dealing off to exploration people and a company. The most important one was the Lyon Lake Proposal which I had discussed with C.C. Huston, but he told me they had flown the area that summer with their ABEM Swedish Two Plane E.M. system and found no anomalies in the area.

He had the ABEM system under contract for Canada. I told him I had seen it in action in Bolivia and talked with the geophysicists who pointed out several serious flaws with the system. I then showed the project to Dr. Duncan Derry who was looking for projects for clients. He liked it but before we had a deal signed, I had joined Texas Gulf.

Immediately upon joining them I had given a letter to both Dave Lowrie, Manager and Dr. Holyk, V.P. Exploration, requesting if they would be interested in my idea. If so, I wanted to retain a 5% net profits interest. They had their hands full with the famous lawsuit by Leitch Gold Mines v Texas Gulf Sulphur re the Kidd Creek VMS discovery near Timmins, Ontario.

I was annoyed that they would not at least give me a letter saying they were not interested and that even while I was an employee of Texas Gulf, they recognized that this was a business arrangement of mine before I joined them and that I was free to deal it off to whomever was interested.

I had written up the exploration proposal well before talking with any of the above people and had it under lock and key in my lawyer's office. Stupidly, I would not proceed with Dr. Derry until I had TGS signed off. Nothing happened that fall. In the New Year I went after Lowrie again to give me a letter of sign off. Nothing and I was still being stupid and not just going ahead with a deal on the project.

Cut to the Quick. That fall I was the only geologist in the office and Holyk walked in, sat down and said Dave buy Mattagami shares. They have made a big VMS discovery near Lyon Lake south of Sturgeon Lake in northwestern Ontario. I looked at him, trying to bring myself under control to no avail.

I stood up lifting my steel desk up and slamming it down.

I blurted out to Holyk that is exactly the location of my project that you would not sign off on and I was too stupid not to just go ahead and make a deal. Holyk was shocked at my reaction. He got up and as he was leaving said Rogers don't be stupid. Buy as much Mattagami stock as you can afford this afternoon. It is trading in the $10 to $11 range. Word will be out tonight, and the market will soar tomorrow. I knew that Holyk and his Bay St. cronies were connected and heavy market players on Bay St.

I stormed out of the office and home to make immediate financial arrangements to buy 5,000 shares at $10.75 which I sold a few months later in the mid $20's. This more than doubled my Texas Gulf salary. Before capital gains tax. But was a long way from what a 5% net profits interest would have paid me if I had taken the bull by the horns and signed a deal off with Dr. Derry.

The next day a guy showed up at the office and wanted to speak with the boss. I was the only one in so Holyk's secretary showed him into my office. He took out a rolled map and spread it out on my desk. It was a copy of the InPut EM survey of the discovery area and he had claims for sale on two anomalies located not far from the discovery anomaly.

I said we are interested. Can you leave the map with me and come back after 2.00 pm and I will speak with the boss? He said fine and walked out the door. I immediately put the Xerox machine to work to make a copy for me. When Holyk showed up I showed him the map and asked if he was interested in talking with the prospector about his claims. He took a quick look at the data and said no. I turned and walked out. When the prospector came back, I gave him his map and said that the powers to be were not interested in his claims.

Ironically, I was so pissed at the whole affair I went into the confidential exploration files and searched for anything on the Sturgeon Lake area. An amazing find. Dr. Leo Millar a very smart Texas Gulf geologist who Holyk did not really get along with, had recommended flying the area for VMS about two years before. Holyk had turned his proposal down.

As background: I had mapped the Sturgeon-Metionga Lakes area for the Ontario Dept. of Mines in 1961 (see the Moose stories). My preliminary report and maps were published when I was still in South America. I had recommended that the acid volcanic centres in the area be subjected to close examination with a view to potential VMS deposits. Leo had read this. He flew up and examined some of the available outcrops and came back with his recommendation which Holyk had nixed. So, Leo was ahead of me and missed out on having another significant VMS discovery for TGS. TGS and I missed out because of my reluctance to proceed without a letter of consent. I vowed never again.

West Timmins Mine - Discovery to Production in Only 100 Years, *by Sethu Raman*

On February 8, 2016, Tahoe Resources Inc. and Lake Shore Gold Corp. announced a friendly business combination deal valued at $945 million. As a major shareholder of Lake Shore and discoverer of the West Timmins Mine trend, I was in an enviable position of being able to contemplate my possible retirement in Florida. This chapter of my life, which took place over a period of 25 years, includes my role in purchasing control of Holmer Gold Mines Ltd. and the subsequent discovery and development of multiple gold mines on the west side of Timmins leading to the aforementioned business combination.

The Timmins Gold Camp currently is enjoying a second life. High grade gold in drill results from Lake Shore Gold along with a $1,900 per ounce gold price has started an area play, with many junior companies staking and exploring properties all along the Destor Porcupine Fault. The Timmins West Mine, which has been in production since 2011, is a perfect example of the tenacity that is sometimes needed in the mining business.

This is a story about a gold discovery that unfolded over a period of 100 years.

Gold was first discovered at the Timmins West site in 1911, by prospectors McAuley and Bridge, who staked 3 claims to cover the location of the original gold showing. Between 1911 and 1925, these prospectors sank two shallow shafts on the McAuley Bridge showing.

Between 1925 and 1937, various companies including Hollinger Mines and McIntyre Mines, carried out trenching on a large quartz vein and drilled two holes in the vicinity of these two shafts. In 1938, the property was acquired by Orpit Gold Mines. Over several years, 87 holes, totaling 13,800 m, were drilled by Orpit or its successor companies. The gold mineralization was associated with carbonatized volcanic rocks that had siliceous sections and quartz, or quartz-tourmaline stringers which tended to parallel bedding.

In 1959, Paul Meredith purchased the property from Stanwell Oil and Gas Ltd., which was the ultimate successor to Orpit Mines. In 1964, the property was transferred to Holmer Gold

Mines Limited, a company Meredith incorporated in Ontario. The company name of Holmer was derived from Hollinger and Meredith. Under an option agreement, United Buffadison Mines Ltd. drilled 10 holes across what was called the Fockler zone totaling 2,116 m. From this work, it was concluded that the gold mineralization occurred in stacked quartz veins that dipped about 50 degrees to the north.

Holmer Gold Mines then became the operator of the property in 1968 and over the next 13 years drilled 45 holes which was combined with stripping, channel sampling and bulk sampling. Based on this work, it was determined that two mineralized zones occurred, the western or Main zone, which had a northwest strike and was dipping steeply to the south, the opposite of all the earlier interpretations, and the eastern or Shaft zone which had a northeasterly strike and unknown dip.

At this point, an estimate of 720,000 tons of probable reserves grading 0.124 oz/ton (653,000 tonnes grading 4.25 gm/tonne gold) was generated for the Main zone.

In 1984, Douglas G. Sirola, then a director of the company, convinced Noranda to option the property and that company carried out a program of airborne EM-Mag surveys, a ground magnetic survey and limited geological surveys. Four holes were drilled to test the gold mineralization west of the major diabase dyke. The previous resource calculations for the Main zone were considered invalid by Jarvi in 1984, who then revised the estimate down to 427,000 tons grading 0.099 oz/ton. Noranda's drilling failed to confirm the gold mineralization west of the dyke and the average grade was lower, so the option was terminated in 1985.

Paul Meredith, Founder and President, was looking for a way to reactivate the Company, which was now trading on the OTC market in Toronto. At that time, as Vice-President of Royex Gold Mining Corp and its related companies, I worked closely with a Dr. Stephen Ogryzlo, a Canadian Mining Hall of Fame Inductee, and a consultant to their mining operations across Canada.

In 1986, Steve Ogryzlo introduced me to Paul Meredith. After looking at the Holmer data and some negotiation, Stephen and I, as equal partners, privately purchased control of Holmer from Meredith. I became the President and CEO and soon after that, Holmer shares were then listed on the Alberta Stock

Exchange.

In February of 1987, I negotiated an option agreement with Chevron Canada. Under the option, Chevron carried out an extensive exploration program including compilation, major stripping, geological mapping, systematic channel sampling, geochemical and geophysical surveys. Eighteen holes were drilled along three fences spaced 100 m apart along the strike of the Main showing. Based on this work, Dr. Stewart Fumerton identified three main zones of alteration.... the Fockler zone, the Hanging Wall zone and the South Holmer zone. All were close together, auriferous and hosted in strongly silicified and tourmalinized volcanics and sediments.

Of all the zones, only the Fockler zone was known in any detail and it consisted of three ellipsoidal pods. Two of these were larger than average. One pod occurs between 150m to 200m below surface near the diabase dyke and had been the main drill target in the early years. As was common in those days, it was this pod that saw numerous drilling programs that were used for stock promotions to raise funds to keep the Company going, with Holmer shares trading as high as $18 in one gold cycle.

The other pod extended from surface to 175 m below surface. The best intersections were 7.02 g/ton over 11.65m and 10.99 g/ton over 7.24 m. The Hanging Wall alteration zone intersections mostly returned low gold values over narrow widths. In 1989, Chevron decided to discontinue its entire exploration program in Eastern Canada, although it did decide to maintain its 20% earned interest in the property, which at this time had grown to a total of 23 patented and leased claims for 920 acres. During the years between 1990 and 1994, I was deeply involved in negotiations with a Chevron official in San Jose, California and eventually, Holmer was able to purchase back the 20% earned interest from Chevron.

It was also during this time that I was able to complete a detailed compilation and reinterpretation of all available drill logs and assay data in level plans and sections. I found that these results were inconclusive and the conclusions sometimes erroneous. The geological interpretations were significantly distorted by the lack of pre-1984 drill core, inadequate rock description and assaying coupled with un-surveyed drill holes. I made the decision to primarily use the Chevron data as the basis for further follow-up work.

Fortunately, one result of the Chevron drilling was that it clearly identified two pods of gold mineralization in the Fockler or Main zone. The main gold mineralization was associated with a 100m wide zone of strong alteration and specifically with intense tourmaline/ red carbonate alteration and in the opinion of Dean Rogers, a retired Dome Mines geologist who looked at the data, was similar to that found in ore deposits at Dome Mines east of the Mattagami River Fault. The alteration on the Main zone appeared to pinch out at a depth of about 200m. However, the last drill hole, H88-24Ext, on this zone intersected a second parallel alteration zone, the HW zone, with quartz veins assaying 84 g/t over 1.6 m at a vertical depth of 250 m.

Based on my interpretation of this HW zone as an en-echelon vein structure with significant depth potential, I proposed a $200,000 program, equally funded by the partners. Although the drill results confirmed the interpretation, for the next several years, the property remained unattractive for further financing efforts because of the poor results from the extensive drilling that had been conducted on the Main zone, the discontinuous narrow veins with low to moderate gold values and the perceived limited tonnage potential. In addition, this Main zone appeared to be cut-off by a thick diabase dyke at depth.

It was at this time that Holmer Gold got diverted slightly by looking at exploration possibilities in Cuba. I had gone to Cuba when it first opened up to foreign exploration in 1991 and acquired numerous mineral exploration concessions for Holmer. So, in early 1992, Holmer Gold went to Cuba and over the course of the next year made two significant mineral discoveries - the Loma Hierro high-grade silver deposit and the San Fernando/Los Mangos massive sulphide deposit. These discoveries gave Holmer the promotable news with which it was able to raise funds for both the Cuban exploration programs and for further work at the Timmins Gold property.

In early 1995, I became a significant shareholder of Holmer with my participation in a private placement financing and in also purchasing Steve Ogryzlo's interest in Holmer, which was now being financed by myself, Ed Svoboda and our associates.

Holmer began exploration drilling on the Timmins West

Gold property in May of 1996, to test the depth potential of the Hanging Wall HW zone. This drilling program, supervised by Babu Gajaria, who had discovered the Detour gold deposit, and Dave Beilhartz, who discovered the Cote gold deposit, confirmed not only the depth extension of the HW zone, but also discovered a new Footwall, FW, zone, which had a width of about 25m and showed consistent gold values.

Sethu Raman holding the first gold bar from Timmins West Mine- August 2011.

The FW zone contained fine disseminated gold that is associated with pyrite with distinct albite-silica alteration that was like the ore zones at the Harker-Holloway Mine east of Kirkland Lake.

Continued drilling in 1997 resulted in the discovery, with

drill hole DDH97-56, of a new parallel "Ultramafic Gold Zone", the UM zone, in ultramafic rocks below the Footwall zone at a vertical depth of 800 m. Multiple intersections included 0.27 oz/ton over 12.2 ft., 0.23 oz/ton over 11.3 ft. and 0.18 oz/ton over 63.5 ft. The Ultramafic zone contained visible gold associated with quartz tourmaline veins and coarse pyrite in altered ultramafic and alkalic intrusive rocks. At that time, this was one of the best deep drill holes ever drilled in the Timmins Gold Camp. Most of the previous drill holes on the property had been terminated as soon as they entered the ultramafic rocks. When drill hole DDH 97-56 intersected alteration at the mafic/ultramafic contact, I made the decision to extend the drill hole into the ultramafic unit. This resulted in the discovery of the high-grade gold mineralization. The geological setting of gold mineralization in the UM zone was the same as that of the Red Lake gold camp. It is my belief that "chasing the alteration" was the key to developing this deposit.

On May 6, 1997, Holmer shares were listed on the TSX, accompanied by a $4.2 million financing, and on that very same day, BRE-X was delisted.

The 1998 program was designed to test the continuity of the gold zones. All the zones remained open down plunge while the UM zone was only partially tested between the 200 m to 800 m levels. In 1999, Holmer entered into an option agreement with St Andrew Goldfields. However, St. Andrews was unable to meet the first-year expenditure commitment and the option agreement expired in November of 2000. As the entire mineral industry hit bottom during this time, Holmer was not immune.

In early 2001, the TSX notified Holmer that it was being reviewed for eligibility for continued listing. At this critical point in Holmer's history, I personally advanced $400,000 in a private placement for working capital and the Company was able to maintain its listing. Due to this financing, Holmer was able to drill an additional 22 holes to complete definition drilling at 25 m intervals in contemplation of an open pit.

In November of 2002, an independent mineral resource study was completed by Watts, Griffis and McOuat Limited, leading WGM to estimate a total indicated resource of 232,000 ozs contained in 422,000 tonnes with an uncut grade of 17.78 gm/tonne gold and an inferred resource of 890,000 tonnes averaging 6.4 gm/tonne (183,000 ozs). If all the known mineralized zones could be traced to a depth of 2000 m, then the deposit had the potential to host 7 million tonnes with an estimated grade of 7.8 g/t, equivalent to 1.6 million ounces of gold in known zones.

Dan Innes, who was then President of Lake Shore Gold Corp., became aware of the potential for a high-grade gold deposit on the Holmer ground and after reviewing the quality of the field work and geologic interpretations by Holmer geologists, was confident in that assessment. This led to Holmer entering an option agreement on May 27, 2003 whereby Lake Shore Gold Corp. could earn a 50% interest in the property by increasing the indicated resource to 500,000 ozs. This would roughly entail moving what was then the inferred tonnage into the indicated category. Gold closed at $360/oz on that day.

Drilling by Lake Shore Gold Corp. focused on exploring the partially tested down plunge extension of the zones between the 400m and 800m levels. In September of 2004, Lake Shore completed their vesting requirement by confirming an indicated resource of 1,369,000 million tonnes at an uncut grade of 16.45 gm/tonne or 724,000 ozs of gold, a 200% increase over the 2002 estimates.

On December 31, 2004, Holmer and Lake Shore completed a plan of arrangement that resulted in Lake Shore Gold Corp. Between 2005 and 2007, Lake Shore completed a resource expansion drill program that would become the basis for a pre-feasibility study. In 2007, Lake Shore purchased Bell Creek mine and mill in Timmins, for a total consideration of $10 million.

In January of 2008, when Anthony Makuch became President, Lake Shore had been very aggressive in conducting advanced exploration involving further drilling, shaft sinking to the 700 metre level and a surface ramp to test shallow veins with all the development ore being produced currently being processed in the company's Bell Creek Mill. In addition, Tony Makuch negotiated a business combination with West Timmins Mining Inc., giving Lake Shore control over a 130 sq. km area covering most of the western extension of the Timmins Mine trend.

In February of 2008, Lake Shore entered into a strategic alliance agreement with Hochschild Mining. Through a series of private transactions and two private placements for total proceeds of $ 144.3 million, Hochschild's interest increased to approximately 40% on a fully diluted basis.

Under the terms of that strategic agreement, Hochschild entered into standstill agreement which limited its shareholding to 40% until November of 2010 and no voting control at the BOD level, with only two members as directors. A few years later, Hochschild, as the result of internal problems, decided to sell their entire equity position into the market.

Lake Shore continued as an independent mining company, something rare in the Canadian context, and developed the mine into production with reserves and resources totaling over three million ounces.

After 100 years of perseverance, the Timmins West gold deposit had finally gone into production in 2011. Continued exploration along the 5-km Timmins West trend established three more deposits and therefore production is expected to continue for several decades.

Another Missed Discovery Opportunity, *by Dave Rogers*

$\mathbf{I}$ had done a bit of research into the mafic and ultramafic intrusives in Northwestern Ontario with a view to perhaps drilling a few holes through them to test the base levels of the intrusions for Ni-Cu-PGM deposits. I ran the idea past Dave Lowrie and Walt Holyk, and they did not feel that this was something they wanted to spend money on.

I resigned from Texas Gulf in December 1971, but I kept in mind the above file with the idea of staking two or three of the potential exploration targets. My first choice was Lac des Iles.

However, I got tied up on other things and left it to spring. When I checked to see if the ground was open, much to my surprise and saw that Lac des Iles and all the surrounding intrusives were staked. Guess who.

All in the name of the infamous Patrick J. Sheridan, P. Eng. My procrastination did me in again.

The Lac des Iles exploration, discovery and mining is well known. Ironically a couple of years later Pat made a hell of an option deal with Texas Gulf. A cash payment up front of $1,000,000. Texas Gulf drilled a slew of holes but dropped the option a year later. The mine is still in production.

I hope if Holyk is reading this in his grave that he realizes that perhaps he should have followed more of my recommendations. Actually, he did take up other recommendations of mine, but unfortunately, they did not pan out as economic discoveries. C'est la vie in mineral exploration.

Wunnumin Lake 1959, *by Ed Thompson*

In the summer of 1959, as the newly minted chief of Pickle Patricia Explorations, I found myself in August of that year with prospector Ed O'Donnell prospecting the Wunnumin Lake greenstone belt which is located about 100 miles north of Pickle Crow. I had started the summer with a fairly large crew and two bush planes but by August there was only Ed and I and dependent for air service on Hooker Brothers out of Pickle Lake.

Ed somehow had fashioned our accommodation into a large teepee that some of the local Cree found interesting. They would often visit us at night and sit around inside the teepee, drinking tea with copious amounts of sugar. Ed seemed to take great delight in trying to have some limited conversation. I say limited as we both only had a few words of Cree and they of English.

One day we decided to freshen up a small showing we had found on the shore of the lake. We had a plugger and some powder, so we drilled and loaded a half dozen short holes. I was about halfway through lighting the fuses when Ed pointed out our Cree friends in two canoes paddling down the lake toward us.

Ed shouted, "Fire, Fire", and tried to wave them away but they just waved back and kept coming. We barely got under some cover when the holes started popping and rocks flying. After the last shot we emerged, fearing the worst and then nearly falling over with laughter, partly from relief.

Up the lake the canoes were flying away, hell bent for leather, the paddles flashing.

They never visited us again. The showing was mainly pyrrhotite and no one in the next 60 years ever discovered anything of interest in the Wunnumin Lake greenstone belt.

The Head Forester and his Introduction to "Irish Mist,"
by Dave Rogers

In Biscotasing, northwest of Sudbury, Ontario, at the end of our mapping season, I purchased a large bottle of Irish Mist and gave it to the head forester at Bisco who had been most helpful in everything we needed that summer. He said he had not experienced this drink before. I suggested that he just take one shot glass and no more, each night as he relaxed after his supper.

The next morning my crew and all our gear are at the train station ready to disembark. My forester had said he would be down to see us off. The train was pulling into the station when he came down. He apologized for being late and said he was feeling a bit down. Actually, he had a massive hangover.

I took one look at him and said, "My friend, you did not listen to me, did you? You drank the whole bottle yourself last night." He sheepishly acknowledged that he had done just that. I shook his hand, and we boarded the train south to Sudbury then Toronto.

A Wild Portage Ride, *by Dave Rogers*

The Biscotasing-Ramsay area had been logged over many years before. The lumbermen built a unique type of log railway over the longer portages.

In 1959 decided to use a facility that was still operational over a 3/4-mile portage. We loaded our canoe on the trolley type flatbed with all our gear in the canoe. Picked up the brake log which seemed strong enough, but I did not make a backup pole. We pushed our way up the first half and then there was a long quarter mile stretch downhill to the lake. Everyone jumped on board for the ride down. I was on the brake log and gravity started to overcome.

My assistant joined me holding the brake log but about 100 yards short of the lake, the brake log broke and we were free running to the water. The carriage stopped up short as it entered the lake. The canoe, our gear and ourselves were launched unceremoniously out into the lake. No broken bones, luckily the canoe was still in one piece and only our collective egos were bruised, and we were somewhat chagrined.

English Ray and the Norseman, *by Dave Rogers*

Ray, an Englishman was the senior assistant and canoe partner, in the summer of 1955 near Nakina, Ontario. Ray, with absolutely zero field experience, had done his Ph.D. at Queens in a record 11 months. Because of my canoe and bush skills, learned growing up in the Ottawa Valley, I was assigned the job of hopefully teaching, but at least keeping Ray alive during our canoeing and bushwhacking while mapping the area geologically.

Our first task was to get him to pay attention on how to operate around a canoe. I showed him how to get in and out, keep his balance and to be one with the centre of gravity of a canoe. The next day we are heading out for our first traverse.

I am in the stern, balanced and as Ray approaches, nose in the air, balancing his map pack, hammer, jacket, I speak up and remind him to pay attention on how to load his stuff in the canoe first and then to step in with both hands on the thwarts for balance and sit in the front seat.

I was holding the canoe as tight and balanced as I could. I

guess he thought he was Lord Nelson and boarding his battleship. Ray, everything dangling, put one foot into the canoe in front of the seat followed by his second foot and with no sense of balance. The canoe of course jiggled a bit.

He lost total control and fell overboard maps and all. He came up sputtering, threatening me as I sat in the stern patiently in my balanced canoe. The party chief and his assistant went paddling off laughing.

About 6 weeks later I had Ray understanding and paddling the canoe reasonably well. In addition, I had shown him how to raise and balance my ground sheet and sailing rig in front of him in the bow. I controlled the vertical position by two ropes from the top of the sail back to the thwart in front of my seat. Hold tight and with a wind you can sail downwind quite fast. If trouble looms, I holler, "Ray throw the mast overboard." I flip the ropes loose and the sail is in the water and the canoe is still upright.

So, one afternoon, having completed our mapping traverse we were paddling back to camp when the wind came up in our favour. We were on a roll and had just entered a narrow 400 ft. wide gap between the shore and an island. I had heard the airplanes landing and taking off on a drill camp move, but not actually focused where the Norseman was landing.

We are on the dead tear down wind in the gap. Suddenly, I spot the Norseman on the dead tear landing up wind in the gap. Whoops! "Pitch the mast Ray!", I holler and turn the canoe sharply into the reeds at the side of the gap. We make it ok.

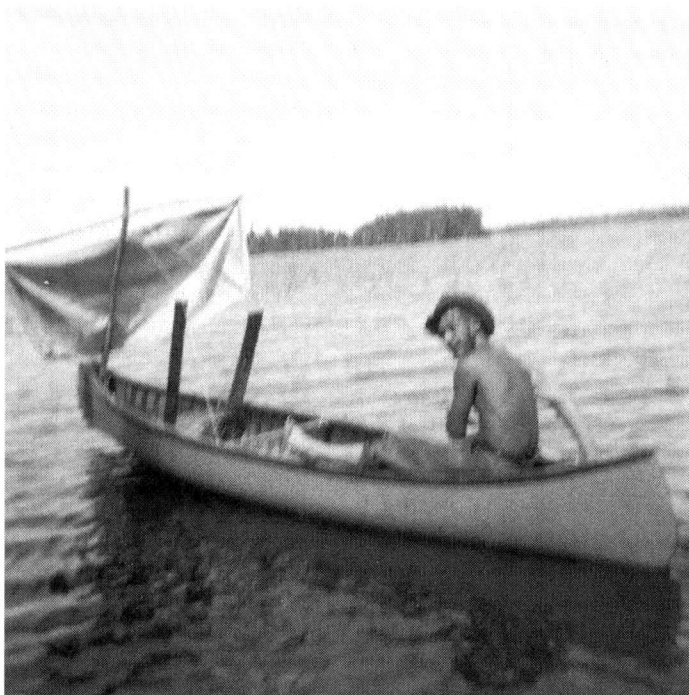

I look over and the Norseman pilot has his window open shaking his fist and swearing at me. I waved, smiling and swearing back at the plane as it climbed and told Ray to remount our mast and sail and we proceeded like hell downwind back to our camp.

Ray was earning his canoeing spurs.

Them Bugs Eat Uranium! *by Peter Bojtos*

Agnew Lake uranium mine was, to this day, one of the most modern and "out of the ordinary" mines I have ever been involved with, and that was back in the late 1970's. Located east of Elliot Lake, Ontario, it had leaching, both on surface piles and underground ores. Massive stainless steel pumps to circulate 100 million gallons of acid, post-stressed concrete floors to prevent cracks forming so acid leaks wouldn't seep into the ground, ion-exchange columns uniquely designed for the mine, a Pulldozer, invented and designed at the mine, which was a backwards operating bulldozer used to clear out drawpoints, massive underground bulkheads to hold back up to 150 foot heads of acid and we had to teach the mine inspectors how to come up with an authorization for them. Also, very large ventilation and mine air heating systems and of course, bacteria to make the process work.

Bud Roswell was Kerr Addison's Vice President in charge of the mine, and he gave a detailed presentation in Espanola during a public meeting for approval of the mine explaining how the bacteria would work and all the safety precautions that went along with it until someone asked him where the mine got the bacteria from.

He explained that the required thiobacillus ferrooxidans strain of bacteria was created and cultured in a special research laboratory in British Columbia where the scientists incubated and then put the bacteria into special cylinders to preserve them and keep them safe.

These cylinders were wrapped and boxed in Styrofoam packaging and then sent from Vancouver on a Greyhound bus. The bus driver then dropped off the bacteria at the Texaco station in Nairn Centre for pick-up by the mine.

The stunned, incredulous silence from the audience was deafening.

Uranium recovery didn't come up to plan and Bud Roswell lost his job and at the mine we were told that the President of Kerr Addison was coming up from Toronto to talk to us. I was in my office when I heard a loud, booming, hoarse voice at the other end of the building. The next moment Bill James came marching into my office, introduced himself, sat down in my chair and got on the phone for the next hour.

What a gruff, lovable, happy-go-lucky task master he proved to be, and I always enjoyed working for him over the next few years both at Agnew and in Toronto. Many, many years later, even at quite recent Prospect Club meetings before he passed away, he could still quote me some of the numbers I had generated for him, especially on a 1981 evaluation and bid for the acquisition of the Patino mines in Chibougamau that I had done.

He never forgot that one, the one that got away. Northgate got it. Amusingly enough, about 10 years later, I was a Director of MSV Resources, and we acquired the Copper Rand and Portage mines from Northgate.

Agnew Lake closed down in the early 1980's and I was in charge of the reclamation of the property. The buildings, headframe and hoist were sold to Noranda who needed it for their new mine at Hemlo.

I had provided them with all the Kilborn Engineering drawings. The riggers disassembled the headframe and labelled each beam and girder with chalk marks to help with the re-erection before loading them onto trucks for transport to Hemlo.

But on the way they stopped in Sault Ste Marie and all the ironwork was sand-blasted clean. So much for the chalk marks! It must have been fun putting that jigsaw puzzle together at Hemlo. But the headframe stood until recently, so someone did it correctly.

Meanwhile back at Agnew the tailings had been stabilized. These were not a conventional type of tailings because the operation utilized leaching of run-of-mine ore, so the tailings pond was really an effluent discharge pond containing very low uranium grades, thorium (we did not recover that) and some rare earths all wrapped up in a mixture of gypsum, formed from the neutralization of the leach acid with lime, and colloidal iron that resulted from the bacteria oxidizing the pyrite in the ores. This slimy mixture was contained in a valley with a well-constructed dam at its west end, the dam having a deep key trench below it filled with bentonite. The surface leach pile had been transported to this tailing area and the rock mixed in with the slime in order to stabilize and solidify it.

Due to the high gypsum content the whole area set solid like a low-grade concrete. For the next few years, I carried out regular sampling at several pre-set sampling points across this area. Finally, in the later years of the 1980's, we arrived at the close-out determinations. The reclamation program fell under the auspices of the Atomic Energy Control Board, but their aim was to have the land revert to the Province of Ontario when the reclamation was complete.

This involved a series of quasi-judicial hearings where the Company and AECB presented the reclamation results so that Ontario, represented chiefly by the Ministry of Environment in Sudbury, could accept a hand-over of the land. One of the main points of debate was whether the tailings area would remain intact for the next 10,000 years and survive an ice-age glaciation. The Ontario Ministry of Environment was dubious on this point.

The containment dam at the west end of the tailings had been designed by Prof. Eli Robinsky from University of Toronto Engineering so I had him present his work at the meeting in Sudbury.

He gave an extensive and detailed presentation of his design and calculations for the dam. When he was finished the judge in charge of the proceedings asked for any questions. Sure enough, a particularly vocal young member from the Sudbury Ministry of the Environment sprang into action and asked Eli what made him so sure that his dam design would withstand 10,000 years and an ice-age. Eli stood back up and humbly explained, "I have shown you my calculations and tried to demonstrate why this dam is a safe structure, but like everything in life nothing is an absolute certainty". And then he puffed himself up in his most professorial manner, looked directly at the Ministry guy and said, "But if it makes you feel any better, I designed the foundations of the CN Tower." Game, set and match.

Geochemistry, *by Ed Thompson*

The big story in 1964 was the Texas Gulf Sulphur (TGS) copper-zinc-silver discovery in Kidd Township, near Timmins. This was a major find and the first in some time. It created a staking boom around Timmins and sparked a tremendous amount of speculative interest in junior mining companies. Base metal deposits usually occur in camps and we all expected that there would be other discoveries.

The TGS discovery was made by drilling airborne geophysical anomalies located by flying over prospective areas with a helicopter or fixed-wing aircraft. The aircraft had an electromagnetic system which detected anomalies that were caused by massive sulphides, graphite, water-laden shear zones, conductive overburden, and so on. TGS and other companies had been doing this type of work for the previous decade but with only limited success.

Suddenly half a dozen companies, including mine, were flying the Timmins area. There were actually hundreds of anomalies and the challenge was how to test them effectively and cheaply. The ground was a hodgepodge of Crown lands, timber company lands, and "vet lots" (privately held lots mostly owned by logging contractors, which were originally land grants from the time of the Boer War in South Africa). Frank Wank, our land man, had a huge challenge which he handled admirably. We ended up with 65 or so properties to test and set up a separate ground geophysical group headed up by Doug McLeod to locate the anomaly on the ground and decide whether it merited drilling.

I thought that by using geochemistry, we might be able to determine whether drilling, or even optioning, the property was advisable. Mercury was now being touted as a possible trace element that could seep through the soil and result in an anomaly. Problem was, overburden in the Canadian Shield can be up to 200 ft. thick, which effectively masks any geochemical signature. The overburden varied greatly throughout the Timmins area. Besides, there were no case histories for mercury anomalies. I therefore decided we needed to do some sampling across the TGS discovery, and it would have to be done on the q.t. as there was still competition for properties.

And so, it was that one summer day I made my way out to the TGS property in Kidd Township, leaving my vehicle on an old road and walking a couple of miles through the bush while dodging TGS crews. They had several drills working and a fair amount of activity. I scouted the area and estimated where the orebody should be and where I would sample, then settled in for darkness. There was a moon that night as I paced off along my lines and started digging samples about every 100 ft. The sounds and lights from two TGS drills working nearby assured me that I was close to the orebody. I sampled most of the night, which wasn't easy, and made my way back through the swamps and bush to my car, which I found at first light. I was bushed.

Back at my hotel room, I tidied up my samples and tried to correct my night's writings, then flew back to Toronto. I submitted my samples to the lab for all the base metal elements plus mercury and anxiously awaited the results. Nada. No anomalies. Many years later, when case histories were published, there were some high values several miles to the south, pushed down by the glaciers. So, we had to option the properties, do ground geophysics and drill, which we did for a couple of years without success. To date there has not been any other base metal mines discovered in the Timmins mining camp.

"Dey Save da Ball" *by Dave Rogers*

I came up with the proposal to duplicate the Elliot Lake Uranium stratigraphy under the north shore of Lake Huron. Fringes of the basal Huronian rocks were mapped along the shore and nearby islands. We had taken out Licenses of Occupation from the Ontario Government to cover the 20+ miles of strike length. I had spotted a hole about four miles offshore.

It was mid-January and -40 degrees below zero. The drillers were on 12-hour shifts and had a Batch Camp set up on the ice near the drill. About 2 a.m. the young French-Canadian drill helper was up top during the rod change. He had been warned to stay clear of the swivel.

Somehow, he got caught up and spun senseless and thrown to the drill shack floor, buck naked, with only his boots and the top of his turtleneck sweater around his neck. No broken bones but his scrotum had been torn open and his testicles were hanging loose.

The driller got him in the Batch Shack and warmed up but only had a few aspirin to give him. He was in pain and shock. They tried radioing out to their base camp near Blind River. Their radio call was picked up by an American shortwave operator and forwarded to Blind River. They in turn called me in Thessalon where we had a Bell 47 chopper.

Our pilot and engineer said they could not legally fly under -30 degrees below zero. They put the Herman Nelson on to heat up the chopper anyhow and by 7 a.m. the outside temperature was approaching -30 degrees and the pilot took off for the drill rig.

The drillers bundled up the injured lad and forcibly strapped him into the passenger seat. He was screaming with pain from his exposed injuries. The trip then was fast to the Blind River Hospital where he was put in good care. About 11:30 a.m. the drill boss came in to see how his man was doing.

The lad had just wakened up from the anesthetic, checked himself out and had spoken to the doctor who assured him that his package, although painful for a while, would be soon be back in perfect working order.

The young driller, thrilled to hear the good news, bound

up and shouted out to all, "Tabernack et Caline de binne, Dey save da Ball....Dey save da Ball!"

Within a few hours this story was the talk of Blind River and it spread from there.

Culture Shock, *by Kerry Knoll*

J im Ashcroft, a mining engineer who used to run the Sudbury operations for Inco, was on my board at Glencairn Gold. He told me this story. When Vale took over Inco, it was an unfriendly bid and so the South American brass had never visited Sudbury before the takeover was successful. When the deal was done, a group of Vale people came up from Brazil to check out what they had just paid $13 billion cash for.

They met in the boardroom, which had a huge picture window overlooking the smelter. In between was a large parking lot, with more than a thousand cars.

The Vale head cheese asked, "What are all those cars doing here."

"Those belong to our employees," somebody replied.

"You pay your workers enough to buy cars?" the shocked Vale boss asked.

Vale decided to try to break the union and reduce wages, resulting in the longest strike in Sudbury history, just short of a year. The union prevailed.

Musselwhite Grubstake and Mine, *by Ed Thompson*

From Google: "Gold was first discovered in the area [north-western Ontario] in 1962 by brothers Harold and Allan Musselwhite of Kenpat Mines Ltd., who found erratic gold mineralization in a quartz vein on the north side of Opapimiskan Lake and several showings in iron formation on the south side of the lake."

Harold and Al Musselwhite, two old prospectors, beat the bushes for more than 40 years starting in 1933. They were a low key, soft spoken pair, with one of them completing the sentence the other one started. In 1973, they showed up in my office looking for a little grubstake money. They were raising about $15,000 for a summer program of prospecting and were taking subscriptions of $500 to $1,000. My companies didn't have much money in the early '70s, but I was used to grubstaking prospectors and, after a short chat, agreed to subscribe $1,000 out of a total of $15,000.

One of the areas they wanted to prospect was around Opapimiskan Lake, 120 km north of Pickle Lake in northwestern Ontario, where they had found a small gold showing some 10 years previously. Gold was priced at $35 per oz. then and so was of little interest. However, by the 1970s, the price had started to rise, and companies were again exploring for it. Harold and Al did a lot of panning of the overburden that summer and found a surprising amount of gold in several locations. Members of "the syndicate," headed up by Wally Bruce of Dome Mines, were encouraged and we continued to explore every year until, by the early 1980s, more than $2 million had been spent, much of it on drilling. Harold said the area looked like a pin cushion. The Syndicate members had shaken down to only four: Dome, Imperial Oil, Inco and Lacana, my company.

The syndicate sank a decline on the West Anticline zone to "shake hands" with the deposit, take bulk samples, and do some underground drilling to try to firm up reserves. A preliminary feasibility study was done, but capital costs were high because of the remote location and lack of power and other facilities. Native groups came out of the woodwork and environmentalists made every swamp a pristine wetland to be protected. We had meetings every month in the 1983-5 period and spent probably $10 million.

I lost contact with the project when I left Lacana in late 1985. Lacana was merged into Corona, and Corona disposed of its interest. Inco Gold was converted to TVX Gold and Dome Mines was merged into Placer Development.

In 1989, two of Placer's senior geologists reviewed the project again and got a budget to follow the iron formation band some 1,200 metres to the north. Using up to six drills, they showed that the deposits contained probably more than 10 million tonnes grading about 9 grams per tonne.

Finally, in February of 1996, the project was given the green light and a 3,500-tonne-per-day project was opened at a cost of $340 million. The Musselwhite project is a good example of the long-time frames and the tremendous amount of work required to develop a mine. Al and Harold were long gone, as were all the original people who explored the deposits in the 1970s and '80s. Only Wally Bruce, the original champion of the project when he was the exploration manager at Dome, made it to the official opening, and that was perhaps only because of a letter I wrote to Placer Dome explaining his early involvement.

Today (2020), the Musselwhite Mine, now owned by Newmont, is one of the largest gold mines in Canada. Since it first commenced production in April 1997, the mine has produced more than four million ounces of gold and has reserves of over two million more.

HEADING OUT WEST

The Oracle of Telegraph Creek, *by Kerry Knoll*

On our first visit to the Golden Bear mine after we "bought" it from Homestake, we were driving up the hill from the mill to the mine site and a beautiful bear with very blond fur wandered into the road, forcing us to stop the truck. A few moments later, three very dark brown cubs followed her. I turned to my business partner, Ian McDonald, and said, "It's a sign! That is the Golden Bear. And the three cubs mean we are going to discover three new deposits."

Ian said that was one of the most idiotic things he'd ever heard. I told a few other people about the oracle of the Golden Bear and got similar reactions. I then approached a couple of the First Nations employees, thinking their spiritual sides would understand. They looked at me, shook their heads, and walked away without a word.

The mine was down to one year of reserves, so we had to get busy looking for more ore. Vic hired Dunham Craig, a brilliant geologist who had just left Cominco. Dunham in turn hired Randy Smallwood, unemployed at the time, and whose wife was expecting their fifth child. Ian remembers the first time we met noticing that Randy's socks didn't match.

We started drilling beneath the current workings, but the core came out looking like shit and we didn't even bother to assay it. The mine site was about half way up a steep mountain. Higher up, Homestake geologists had found a few rocks grading three or four grams, which wasn't of interest to them, the grade was considered too low. The mine operated at 400 tonnes per day, typically processing ore grading about 10 grams per tonne, and had a roaster, as the ore was refractory.

The stuff up top was oxidized, and so we wouldn't need the roaster, and we made the decision to try to find the source of those rocks. In the meantime, we did a $5 million financing, the largest of our career to that point. It was done by Glen Milne over at Canaccord and another guy we had never met, Eric Sprott at his new firm.

We brought in a geologist with a strong background in geochemistry, who looked over the situation and sat the team down for a lecture to the growing exploration team. First, we were going to lay out a grid, then we were going to sample at certain intervals, he droned on for several hours. Randy Smallwood recently reminded me of what happened next:

"Dunham ducked out the back door, grabbed the bulldozer, and headed up the hill, and started cutting a channel through the area where the gold-bearing rocks were found. Not an hour later he came back down, went back into the meeting, and said, "Don't worry about the geochem, guys, I found the deposit.""

We mobilized the drills and the first hole pulled good looking material from surface down to about 60 metres. While the drilling was going on, the lab wasn't busy and finally got around to assaying the core from the earlier hole, beneath the mine workings. I'll never forget the life-changing date Ian and I got the call: October 15, 1993. It was Vic on the phone. "Are you boys sitting down?" he asked.

That shitty-looking hole graded 15 grams over 15 metres. We were expecting assays from the hole up top later that afternoon. We called Jonathan Goodman and Gerry McCarvill over to the office to tell them the news. Jonathan was especially happy because his family trust owned a couple of million shares. He still likes to tell the story of that day:

"Ian said, "My lawyers have instructed me not to say anything, so I'm only going to tell you this once.""

While they were there, we got the call on the second hole. Forty-eight metres grading 5.24 grams per tonne gold almost from surface. Holy fuck! Two new deposits in one day! And yes, we eventually found that third deposit, so my bear cub theory wasn't so absurd after all. We had proven the "within the shadow of the headframe" myth to boot. We put out the press release Monday morning and the shares, which had been trading around a buck, soared to more than $5 and we quickly raised another $5 million, this time in a couple of hours.

To celebrate we had a big party and invited everybody we knew from Bay Street. We had the honour of introducing Ned Goodman to Eric Sprott – two future mining billionaires whose paths I'm sure crossed many times afterwards.

But operating problems persisted at the Bear, and eventually we shut down the mine and transformed it from an underground, refractory deposit to an open pit heap leach. We let Vic go. When we were looking for the new operator, we got down to a shortlist of four people. Oddly, all of them had used Graham Farquharson of Strathcona Mineral Services as a reference. So, Ian and I went to see him.

"Brave bunch of guys," Graham remarked when we told him why we were there. He was known for his bluntness, amongst other things. He recommended John Kalmet and it turned out to be the best move we could possibly make. John had been manager of the Pamour mine in Timmins before moving west and heading up   Noranda's western Canadian mining division for many years, with five operating mines under his direction.

Under John's capable management, Wheaton River turned the upper deposit into Canada's first successful heap leach mine. Nobody on Bay Street would finance us. They actually didn't think heap leaching worked in Canada because it's too cold, or so they told us, though we explained until we were blue in the face that there are plenty of heap leach mines in Idaho and Montana. We managed to borrow $10 million from Barclay's Bank in the U.K. for the restart. Five grams per tonne open pit, and we were getting 92% recovery after a couple of weeks of leaching. Our mine manager Dennis Bergen once told me, "we could leach this stuff with hot tea." Soon we began producing close to 100,000 ounces per year starting in 1997. The Barclay's loan was paid back part way through the first year.

We bought the Red Mountain deposit from whomever had it the time, the Bellavista project in Costa Rica from Rayrock, and eventually took over Kit Resources, acquiring the Back River properties with their two million ounces. We had a mine! We had a project pipeline! We had cash! The Golden Bear was making gold for $125 per ounce and, unfortunately, selling it for $275.

Red Mountain had an interesting backstory. It had been owned by Lac Minerals before Barrick took that company over, and was located smack dab on the top of a windy, snowy mountain near Stewart, B.C., with only helicopter access. Lac acquired it when it bought out Bond Gold, the Australian miner founded by the high-flying, art-collecting, yacht-racing billionaire Alan Bond. A while after we bought it, I spoke with a guy who had been Bond's project geologist. He told me that when the company was negotiating with Lac's Peter Allen, he got a call from Bond himself and was told to drill the best possible hole he could on the project. Which he did, straight down dip. It was a whopper and apparently swayed Allen to pursue Bond. A couple of years later Alan Bond declared bankruptcy was sentenced to seven years in prison for fraud on another mining deal.

Wheaton River was now in full blown development mode, but the market cap hovered around the amount of cash we had in the bank. It was 2001 and the gold price still had a two in front of it, for the third year in a row. Then one day Frank Giustra called us to a meeting with Pierre Lassonde and Ian Telfer, and said they wanted to buy control of us. Fund Manager Frank Holmes was there as well as a couple of others. Holy shit, I thought, if you think gold as a religion, we had six of the 12 apostles wanting our company! We were lousy promoters and were trading at less than the $25 million cash we had in the bank, all profit from the Golden Bear, and so we said yes. Our lawyer, Paul Stein, commented that we were the only client he'd ever had that would give up on such a quality company, but that it was the right move given the individuals who wanted it.

When we were trying to put a pin in the deal, our share price started moving up. It was thirty cents, then 35, then the next day it was trading at 42 cents, on volume. Frank was sure we were leaking something, but we weren't, Ian and I were the only people in the company who knew about the negotiation. On the Friday before the PDAC and the shares closed at 52 cents. Ian and I were setting up our booth at the show when his phone rang. It was Frank. He wanted a deal and he wanted it now, before the market opened on Monday, between the lines suggesting that we were telling all of our friends. So, we got everything we asked for in terms of severance.

A few weeks later the phone rang, and it was this guy calling from the Jersey Islands. He said he was a commodities trader and that he had bought three million shares out of the market in late February. "Are you curious why?" he asked. When he was doing some research on the Saskatchewan Wheat Pool, he stumbled across Wheaton River's website and saw that it was trading for less than cash with all of these assets and decided to load up.

Ian Telfer took over as president, and with help from Lassonde and Giustra, raised a barrel full of money and started buying gold mines all over the Americas, just as the big bull market in gold was getting under way. Wheaton River was the top volume trader on the Toronto Stock Exchange in 2002, with the shares eventually going to $11.

Randy Smallwood, by the way, stuck with the company and eventually landed a job running its subsidiary, which is now called Wheaton Precious Metals. It had a $24 billion market cap last time I looked, with Randy still at the helm. Wheaton River hooked up with Goldcorp in a merger of equals and was eventually sold to Newmont for $12 billion. What's that expression about acorns and mighty oaks?

The One That Got Away, *by Ed Thompson*

In early 1962 I flew to Vancouver to check out the exploration scene and the possibility of opening an office for the Keevil Mining Group. We were interested in finding large open-pit copper deposits. Geochemistry was in vogue and that summer I assembled a team to geochem the west coast of Vancouver Island by boat and from logging roads for copper using the portable Holman test. We did not locate any deposits of interest.

The following summer, I and my partner, John Poloni, followed up airborne magnetic anomalies and prospected in central B.C. We worked mainly out of McLeese Lake and optioned a copper property (Gibraltar).

At Gibraltar, there was a short adit into the hillside that ran about 1% copper in a shear zone and we hoped to discover a major tonnage of about 0.6% copper. We tried to locate higher grade zones by geochemistry but the whole mountain gave high copper results.

At Keevil's, we tried all types of geophysics. There was a new process called IP. We did an IP survey but couldn't find background (later discovered that the whole mountain was mineralized).

In the winter of 1963, I was back exploring the Gibraltar copper property, this time with prospector Gus Macdonnell. Our previous small program of a few drill holes and an IP survey (probably the first such survey in B.C.) was encouraging, but copper was only 30¢ per lb. at the time. There were abundant amounts of 0.3% copper but not much in the range of 0.6% to 1%, which is what we were looking for. Gus and I stayed at a small motel at McLeese Lake for six weeks, collecting geochemical samples and trenching and blasting various locations for rock samples. Gus would carry the "plugger" around the bush with ease, though it must've weighed at least 70 lbs. I don't remember where we bought the dynamite and fuses or if we even had a permit. It would take forever now to do this kind of work. Luckily there was little snow that winter (whereas in the following winter there were several feet of the stuff).

I worked on it for two years, and in early 1964, Ken Rose supervised our drilling project. We were always short of funds in the '60s, so when an option payment came due, the project was dropped. A few years later, a junior company picked it up and carried out a large drilling program of 60-70 holes and outlined a resource of 0.4% copper. In 1972 Placer Development optioned it and, after a feasibility study, put it into production at around 40,000 tons per day. The mine had continuous production until the end of 1993, then intermittent output until October 2004 when high copper prices allowed it to operate fully once again. Today it operates under the name "Taseko mine."

Today, after spending some $700 million on expansion and renovation, the operation is the second largest open-pit mine in Canada with a milling rate of 85,000 tpd and a reserve life of 21 years (667 million tons of reserves at 0.26% copper and 0.008% Mo).

I think of it as the big one that got away, but it was probably only a mine for Placer.

The Falconbridge Years, *by Howard Stockford*

I was offered a job as Senior Geologist in Manitoba/Saskatchewan in November 1970. I reported to Colin Coats, Falconbridge's Exploration Manager in it's Winnipeg office, and to Stan Charteris who was Exploration Manager for Falco in Toronto. We moved the family to The Pas, where Joe Brummer had a company house built before the road was opened to Thompson. Colin and Doreen Coats occupied the same house from 1965 to 1970.

I spent most of my time during the following four years in the company's field offices in Wabowden in the Nickel Belt or in Snow Lake/Flin Flon VMS belt. We typically had a budget of $1 million/year and ran an average of ten drills split between the southern Thompson Nickel Belt and Snow Lake, with large land packages in each area. Most of the drilling was done in the winter to take advantage of the good ice conditions in those days. Falconbridge had one nickel operation, the Manibridge Mine, a small deposit of about 1 million tons @ 2% Ni. The exploration of this property was conducted by our exploration team operating out of Wabowden. Incidentally the settlement was named after W A Bowden, who was the section foreman at the end of the CN line before it was extended to Churchill and later, Thompson. A significant underground exploration program came under the direction of our team in Wabowden at Bucko Lake It was a j/v with Cons Marbenor, Stephen Kay's and Joe Hirshhorn's group.

I was Falconbridge's representative on the Boards of Dickstone Copper Mines, Maskwa Nickel Chrome Mines and Stall Lake Mines, where I first met Richard Hogarth and James Richardson Sr. Falconbridge's team discovered the Rod deposit in about 1968 on the Stall Lake mines' property in Snow Lake.

This deposit was high grade (about three quarters of a million tons @7%Cu, had a shallow plunge to the NE and was shaped like a ruler, deformed along with the enclosing felsic volcanic rocks. One of my first tasks was to supervise the drilling of a shaft pilot hole to about 2000ft, in an area where there was a lot of hole deviation. We had to install 11 wedges in the hole to minimize deviation from vertical. I had never set a wedge before and Colin Coats went through the procedure with me over the phone, an interesting experience indeed! This deposit was subsequently mined under the terms of an agreement with HBMS (the Rod Mine).

Falconbridge controlled the Linda Claims, up plunge from the Rod Zone. Talking of scoundrels, there was prospective ground further up plunge from Linda owned by Bill McKayseff, a retired RCMP officer. I offered to option the McKayseff property for $10,000 cash and a minimum $100,000 work commitment over several years. He said that if I doubled the cash payment he would split the cash with me, personally!! I said "we don't do business that way in Falconbridge" and stuck with my original offer. He replied "it's done every day"! I said, "not here". This definitely tainted my view of the RCMP!

These claims ultimately went to Falconbridge Copper and then Thundermin. A large, NE plunging, pyritic VMS deposit (about 12 Mt grading 3% Zn and 0.050pt gold) was discovered on the Linda property, based on a program devised by Barry Simmons. The massive sulphides are connected to a broad chlorite alteration zone which also plunges NE onto the Rod property. The deepest holes to date have the best copper grades at around 2000 ft depth. I still believe there is a big copper deposit further down plunge close to the Rod boundary.

We moved to Winnipeg from The Pas in 1974 and I became Exploration Manager, Winnipeg Office for Falconbridge. Subsequently I was promoted to Chief Geologist, Canada in 1981 (by Dr Chris Jennings) but by 1982 the company was being prepared for sale by it's parent, Superior Oil and one of my first tasks was to close several of the regional offices in St John's, Timmins and Thunder Bay, leaving Quebec City, Winnipeg, and Vancouver on a reduced staff size basis. Fortunately, we were able to place staff that were laid off at other companies.

One of the highlights of our time in Winnipeg was running the CIM Convention in 1979. Jeannie shared the responsibility for the spouses' program and was able to arrange for a special performance of the Royal Winnipeg Ballet, with Evelyn Hart....a big success for the finale! It was difficult to persuade CIM to do this.....an opportunity for the Mining Industry to experience one of the world class cultural benefits of Winnipeg!

QUEBEC & POINTS EAST

Quebec Cook and his Sutures, *by Dave Rogers*

It was 1956 and we were out from La Sarre, Quebec. One day the cook asked me if he could come out and help on the line cutting and placing of survey pickets. He was about 55, eyeglasses about ¼ inch thick and used binoculars to look 100 feet ahead in the bush.

About 10 a.m. he hollered at me for some help. I went back and he said he cut himself and the back of his wrist was a deep cut about 2 inches long and it wasn't bleeding. His skin was as thick as horse hide. He was wearing bib overalls and he reached in a little pencil pocket and pulled out a good size needle with a thread all wound up on it.

"Ok", he says, "you hold the skin tight together and I will sew it up." I am trying hard not to faint.

Holy smokes he just stitched himself up and he didn't flinch! Then he took a bandana from around his neck and he wrapped around the suture and said, "OK now we finish the line."

I said, "No. You go back to camp have a rest then get supper ready." I carried on with cutting the survey grid. In those days a good man cut and chained one mile 1.6km in one day with a sharp axe. I was a good man.

Boiling Tea in the Crotch, *by Dave Rogers*

We were in northwestern Quebec in 1956. My junior assistant and I had backpacked six miles back in the bush for a one-week mapping and prospecting job. On the second day the junior boiled up the teabilly. I'm sitting on a log and hold up my cup for him to fill it.

He fumbled and poured the whole Billy Can of boiling tea right on my crotch. I had severe second and third-degree burns. Luckily I had a tube of trusty 'Ozonol Cream' the ointment to cure all in the 1940's and '50's.

I covered the burn area completely and then we had the six-mile walk out. Me, bare assed and holding my broiled scrotum up away from my inner thighs. We get to the truck and my assistant drove me to the hospital in La Sarre where they attended me for a week. It was 3 weeks before the scars had settled down and I could get around readily again.

Early Years in Quebec and New Brunswick, *by Howard Stockford*

As Mine Geologist at Coniagas, I was responsible for daily grade control, guiding development headings, exploration drilling and exploration around the mine to try and keep the mine operating (1963). Grades in the mine were up to 14% Zn but prices were were only 14c/lb. When we hit good grade we drifted out to it right away several times....it was hand to mouth, without defined reserves ahead of it! Sturgeon River Mines (also part of the Boylen organization) had a gold property about a mile from the Coniagas shaft and there I had one of my scariest experiences....mapping the shaft down to 700 feet on night shift working from the rim of the sinking bucket, with heavy rain in the shaft. This was later to become a gold operation operated by Bachelor Lake Gold Mines.

The late Dennis Sheehan came to work for us in 1964 and was a great addition to the team, having come from the Willroy operation in Manitowadge. We became lifelong friends and he and Heather stayed with us in our trailer when she visited Dennis before they were married. Both of our children were born whilst we lived at Coniagas, Roger in Val d'Or and Sally in Chapais.

Mike Knuckey had become Mine Manager by 1964. He managed to keep the mine going until 1967 although I left to work for Bechtel in 1965, initially at Mt Pleasant in New Brunswick and then in their Montreal office.

So, we basically moved from one trailer to another, on the top of Mt Pleasant, New Brunswick where Mt Pleasant Mines were exploring and trying to develop a tin/tungsten deposit. After mapping the tin zones on surface and in exploratory underground adits and a couple of raises I found that the whole deposit had been misinterpreted by Mt Pleasant Mines. Although isolated, Mount Pleasant was a beautiful place, near St Stephen and St Andrews on the Bay of Fundy. We showered in a waterfall under a small, quintessentially Canadian, wooden covered bridge on the way to the project near Mt Pleasant.....a beautiful place!

Bechtel was essentially hired to develop a process for extracting the tin (cassiterite) and to mine enough material to run metallurgical tests. As soon as the client received our report the stock fell and Bechtel was kicked off the job! I suspect that Bechtel was not paid for their work! The project had obviously been over-promoted but subsequently some tungsten was produced from the property (the Fire Tower Zone) but it was not a success story.

In Dec 1965 we loaded all of our belongings and two babies into the car and drove via Maine and Vermont to find accommodation in Montreal. At the US border the customs people opened the trunk of the car and closed it quickly, saying "lady, you could have 200 lbs of heroin in their but I wouldn't touch it with a barge pole"! (It was half full of diapers).

Bechtel put me to work in the Paré St office on the Iron Ore Company of Canada's major mill expansion project at Carol Lake. I learned a lot about heating and ventilation as well as pump design and procurement at that time.

Nova Scotia in the Early 1970s, *by Dave Rogers*

$\mathbf{A}$t the PDAC I got talking with my old classmate Avard Hudgins, Mr. Nova Scotia Geology. I went to Nova Scotia in May.

Avard showed me the Gay's River property and explained the setting and potentials to me. After a week of going from showing to showing around the province, all the while drinking and arguing a bit, we settled on forming a syndicate to stake, sell and explore the Zn-Pb deposits in the Windsor Formation in Nova Scotia and Cape Breton.

The Gay's River area discoveries had been previously staked and drilled by Cominco and Texas Gulf. They both walked away saying the ore horizons were too thin and grades were way too low. Avard's prospector, Merton Stewart, later a recipient of the Prospector of the Year Award, had located 15' to 30' thick glacial float assaying 6% to 30% Zn + Pb. This float had not been moved far by the glacial scouring.

Randy Mills the famous Chibougamau Camp promoter, his partner Dr. Harry Morgan & Avard Hudgins comprised the Millmor Syndicate. The Rogers part consisted of DPR's new Grubstake. We formed the Millmor-Rogers (50/50) Syndicate.

I gave Avard a cheque for $5,000 to map stake all of the favourable Windsor age sediments in Nova Scotia....for our syndicate.....which he did the next day. We had the Province tied up.

We then parceled up the areas based on the known geology into 5 land packages. Randy Mills who knew everyone on Bay Street phoned selected promoters with good market shells. The following week Avard and I made the rounds in Toronto and made deals with the ones we thought would actually move a drill in and explore plus perform best in the marketplace.

I had visions of the Rogers Grubstake making a ton of money from our portion of the shares in these companies and putting the money to work in the Grubstake. I fortunately phoned Bob Fasken, Camflo and syndicate member. He quickly explained that was not the way to do it... David it will be nothing but grief and second guessing by the members at what you could have/should have done....after the fact. He said David send each member his prorate number of shares in each company and let them be the author of their respective actions and results. I clearly got the message. Some made good money. Some did not. DPR made good money.

Randy Mills controlled a junior called "Cuvier Mines Ltd." The MillMor Syndicate had vended the Gays River deposit claims into that shell. Then when we formed the MillMor/Rogers Syndicate for the province the Rogers syndicate was earned into the Gays River/Cuvier package. Our agreement was one half page long signed by all of us plus a handshake. No lawyers.

The Cuvier Mines shares were trading in the $0.05 to $0.10 range. I personally bought an extra 300,000 free trading shares. Our other earned shares had various levels of escrow attached at the time. Cut to the quick. A broker in Montreal by the name of Bert Applegath began placing shares in a number of client accounts, authorized and un-authorized. They moved the price up steadily over the next few months. Imperial Oil was drilling and getting good results. Soon the shares were trading in the $1.00 range....Then up through $3.00. The final high hit $5.45/share and I happened to hit the bid for 45,000 shares. $245,250 in my account thank you very much. I had 15,000 shares still in escrow but supposedly coming free in one week. In hindsight I should have just sold them then and told the broker he had to get delivery of the shares.....Not to be....But I did sell them a few weeks later in the $2.75 range.

Applegath left Canada for the States and did not come back. His history is the subject for a complete book written by the right author and at the right time. Shades of New Cinch. Everything. Sex, theft, lies, murders, fortunes made and lost and professional standings destroyed through a series of 3 to 5 publicly trading companies over the next 20 years or so. He was front and centre in the Diamond Rush in the N.W.T. with two or three companies. Gord Fancy and I bought shares in the $0.20 to $0.35 range in three of them and made three to seven times on our money.

To earn our 50% interest in the Gays River Play I was assigned to try and sell the Gays River/Cuvier project to Fenton Scott, Manager of Imperial Oil Mineral Exploration. Fenton was known as hard and tough, but fair, to deal with. I flew back to Ottawa on a Friday. I cold called Fenton Scott. He gave me an appointment for 10 a.m. Monday morning in Toronto.

I had been forewarned about Fenton's penchant for using

long pauses and staring at the person across the table. I was familiar with the technique from my father's dealing with English timber buyers from London. Quite the art of encouragement and finesse to reach a settlement.

I arrived on time and was shown into Fenton's large office. We introduced ourselves and then Fenton called in Stan McEacheran, his business manager. I made my presentation in about seven minutes flat they asked a few questions and I sat back. Fenton began his act. Stan was doing the same. I sat, without a twitch and glanced back and forth from one to the other with no facial expression. Finally, Fenton said, "Stan what do you think of Rogers proposal?"

Another long silence and stares. Then Stan said, in his precise manner, Fenton, Rogers tells this story a lot better and with more geological persuasion than Avard or anyone else ever has. Fenton agreed...... Silence....... Fenton said to Stan do you think we should take on this project? Another long pause. Stan finally says yes! I sat trying not to twitch, sneeze, or blink. After another long pause Fenton stood up put his hand across the table and said we will take the deal as offered. Your terms are reasonable. The cheque for $35,000 and a draft agreement will be in the mail to Hudgins tomorrow. I shook both their hands, expressed my thanks, gathered up my notes etc. Turned and walked out the door. I hardly took a breath until I reached the street and was about a block away. Holy crap I could hardly believe what had transpired.

Back on the bus to Ottawa. That evening I phoned Avard and told him I sold the Gay's River Project to Fenton and Imperial Oil and the cheque/agreement will be in the mail in the morning. A long silence. And "Rogers you are so full of shit...how can you be so cavalier over this deal?"

I pulled a Fenton and stayed silent...After a couple of minutes Avard's voice changed and he quietly said, "you really sold our deal to Fenton?" "Yes," I said, and you can inform your partners that the cheque plus the deal as we outlined will be in the mail tomorrow. And note that the Rogers Grubstake has earned its 50% interest in the Gays River Play. So have a good weekend and go fuck yourself and I hung up the phone.

Friends in the Mining Business, *by Dave Rogers*

Casa Berardi days. The street knew I was going to move a drill in on very prospective claims held by Aurogin Resources. My phone rang and a French-Canadian voice said Dave Rogers please. Yes, I said how can I help you. A chuckle on the other end of the phone. He gave me his name which I no longer recall. He said Mac Watson suggested I give you a call. So now he has my full attention.

You plan to move a drill in on the XYZ claim block next week. Yes, I said that is public knowledge. The voice said, "Unfortunately Mr. Rogers the claim block you paid to have staked was never staked."

My body ran a flush. I have a crew ready to stake it now. I called Mac Watson to see if he was interested in the claims. He said they belong to Aurogin. I told him they were never staked. Mac said give Dave Rogers a call and give him a chance to have them staked. He is a friend of mine. I said I paid a reliable contractor to have those claims staked. Yes, said the voice but the guy he paid to do the staking took the money and went on a toot. He is shacked up and partying and did not stake the ground.

I immediately asked the voice on the phone will you stake the block properly for me. Yes, he said, and he gave me a fair price and proceeded to stake the block and record them in Aurogin's name.

He phoned me a couple of days later to say the job was complete. He said we checked out the party boy and the claim tags, a roll of money and the claim staking sketches were all in his packsack on the floor of his new girlfriend's house. I had already sent the new cheque to the voice on the phone.

The Human Skull Mystery, *by Dave Rogers*

Out of Senneterre, Quebec in 1956 on a prospecting trip with four assistants. We had set up camp in a bay near an old trapper's cabin. One junior was nosing around behind it. He found a human skull covered in moss and just laying on top of the ground. We looked at it and I said, well why don't you polish it up and let's see what it looks like.

There was a hole on the top of it which you could just put the tip of your little finger in. Yes, it could've been a bullet hole, but it also just looks like chipmunks or something had been chewing on it. The skull was by itself no other bones around just sitting in the moss.

Then we used it as a toothbrush holder at the end of our small dock. Three weeks go by and we are ready to move on to the next job. The pilot when he landed said the policeman in town wants to talk to you guys about the skull. So, I went with the junior to meet with the police officer at the end of the day. I gave him a sketch of the lake and cabin location.

He looked blankly at me so I told him how he could check out the location and the history by going through the mining recorder's office and see which claims were owned by which owners over the years.

And also, the trapper's license list and what trapper was registered in there. Check and see if he had family in the area. Then the phone rang, and he had to go off on an emergency call. He said be here tomorrow morning at 9 A.M. to finish this up and off he went.

I picked up the skull, put it in a bag and we went back to the hotel. The next morning of course we left on the seven o'clock train and the junior was able to take his skull home where he put it on his fireplace mantle. No, I do not recall his name.

Reclamation in the Old Days, *by Peter Bojtos*

Back in the mid 1970's, Bill Row, the Chairman of both Noranda and Kerr Addison, had written a memo to his Boards basically stating that if something weren't done, the regulatory agencies and public opinion would make Noranda and its subsidiaries eat all the tailings that they had created. Bill was definitely forward thinking, and Noranda took his directive to heart. A position of "Manager of Environment" was created and Bill Marshall, retired General Manager of Pamour, was given the position.

As 1980 rolled around, whilst I was busy being Chief Engineer at Agnew Lake, Phil Cross, Executive VP for Kerr Addison and Bill Row told me to start taking an interest in several closed down mines that needed rehabilitating. These were Normetal, Quemont and Kerr-American in Bluehill, Maine, and to get ready for the eventual closedown of Agnew Lake, Mogul of Ireland and, of course, the Kerr mine in Virginiatown. With the invaluable help and teaching of Bill Marshall this non-environmentalist got to work.

I tackled Normetal first. The mine had closed in 1975 and all infrastructure had been removed but there was a large tailings area immediately on the north side of the town, the Slam, Quebecois French for slimes.

And I mean immediately. If you stepped off the sidewalk of rue Principale you were already standing on The Slam. Meanwhile acid drainage was seeping into the aptly named Calamity River. Oh, and one more thing, the town had created a large garbage dump in the middle of the tailings area between ponds One and Two.

With the help of the retired Mine Manager, Bob Allen, I uncovered the operating skeletons. These included things that were wrong with the original tailings design, areas where the dam walls had collapsed and released a lot of tailings into the river, an unfortunate regular happening in the old days that tended to be viewed as an operational hiccup, and other hidden quirks.

At the same time a series of vegetation growth studies, using treated Normetal tailings as the growth medium, were underway at Waterloo College, now a University, under the direction of Dr. Ed Watkins. Ed was also doing growth studies for Karl

Winterhalter at Inco and Bob Michelutti at Falconbridge who were pioneering the revegetation of Sudbury and doing a great job and I learnt a lot from these three guys.

In order to reslope and grade the tailings the garbage dump first had to be buried into the tailings, so I got a local contractor with a D8 bulldozer to do the work. He drove his dozer onto the tailings and then trundled towards the garbage dump while Bob Allen and I stood watching from a distance on the site of the old headframe.

The dozer operator lowered his blade and dug into the dump, stopped, jumped off the dozer and ran hell-for-leather back to town. What the ....? We found the very distraught operator in a bar in town who told us that as soon as he cut into the garbage, thousands of rats came swarming up over the hood of the dozer towards him. We got him a clean pair of trousers so he could go home.

The Quemont tailings were a bit different in that they were in a poorly drained area right up alongside the Horne Smelter complex and had sat there, festering, for 10 years since the mine closed in 1971. The liquids emanating from the area were every shade of orange, purple and blue as acid generation was in full swing.

The solution arrived at was to cover the entire area with inert smelter slag from the Horne. This was done and the place ended up reasonably well rehabilitated. Sometime later in mid 1980's the CBC sent a film crew to do a documentary on the environmental work being done by Noranda and they included some film segments on the Quemont tailings.

For their final scenes they wanted a distant view of the entire smelter complex, so they set up in the Notre Dame cemetery on the northwest side of town. The smelter, and Quemont tailings, didn't look that bad in that final scene on the TV but then the camera went from a distant focus to a close–up and as the lens zoom was retracted one of the gravestone crosses in the cemetery, with the smelter in the background, came into focus. End of documentary. I have never quite forgiven the CBC for that miserable ending.

Rehabilitating a mine site in Maine was quite a different matter as everything had to be done with the Maine Dept. of Environmental Protection in a very legalistic fashion. Most things were done with the DEP imposing a Consent Decree on Kerr-American, a Joint Venture between Kerr Addison and Black Hawk Mining (a Denison subsidiary). The mine had closed down in 1977 and the buildings and tailings area had been under care-and-maintenance ever since. The most serious environmental concerns here were due to the fact that the metals in the ores leached out very readily and the local lobsters and other sea-life were showing elevated levels of cadmium. I received a lot of help from Noranda's new VP Environment, Dr. Frank Frantisak, and the Noranda Research Centre headed by Dr. Jacques Nantel.

These two men elevated the Noranda Group's environmental function from an earlier chiefly physical endeavour to a modern highly scientific discipline. However, demolition and disposal of the mine buildings and equipment was the first order of business. Luckily, demand for used equipment was quite good and I soon had various contractors on site removing equipment that had been purchased until one day when someone removing the main transformers broke a drain plug and the PCB oil inside it flowed out. Fortunately, all the oil was contained in the concrete enclosure surrounding the transformers. The Maine DEP jumped into action with their hazmat experts as soon as we reported the incident and they told us what to do. All the oil had to be collected in sealable drums and arrangements made for a licensed hazmat contractor to transport the drums to a PCB disposal/incineration site in Kentucky with tons of paperwork and manifests having to be completed at every step of the way.

But first they told us to immediately go to Sears or Montgomery Ward in Ellsworth and rent a large wet/dry vacuum so we could collect the oil into drums. So off we went to Monkey Ward, got the machine and sucked up all the PCB oil under the watchful eye of the hazmat experts who were placing their seals on the oil drums and recording every step taken. Other drums were filled with rags, brooms gloves and any of our clothing that had come in contact with the PCB. When we were finished, we asked them what we should do with the PCB contaminated vacuum that we had rented. "Oh, just wash it out and return it" was the response from the DEP's hazmat expert.

Two Geology Students & Mr. Wally Bruce – 1956, *by Dave Rogers*

About 10:30 p.m. on a cold and blustery evening, we have our thumbs up outside of Shediac, New Brunswick and a large 1955 Cadillac pulls up. "Where you headed boys," the driver asks. "Bathurst," we say.

"You won't make it tonight, hop in and you can start over in the morning after a good sleep and some food in your stomach," the driver responds. The guy turned out to be the General Manager of the start-up Mutual Funds, a rage of the '50's and '60's which were sweeping the country.

He phones his wife with a heads up for beds and food for a couple of cold wet college boys. For the next hour we were lectured on how to make a fortune in the expanding Mutual Fund Craze. I was quickly being persuaded that it would beat breaking rock in the bush.

The next day we get to Bathurst and inquire as to where the Rio Algom office and camp was located. As we walk over Jim says, "there he is," and makes a bee line walking right up to Wally Bruce who is deep in conversation with Dr. Sandy Seeber, V.P. Exploration for Rio Algom.

Jim approaches Wally and says remember me? Jim Proudfoot. "We met in Newfoundland four years ago and I am here to make a deal on a good gold-copper prospect". Wally quietly suggests that Jim and I go sit on the veranda and he will be over shortly.

Fifteen minutes later Wally comes over. I am introduced and he says slow down Jim and tell me your story. He did. Wally mused it over, said he would think about it overnight. Meanwhile we had just walked into the Rio Algom, Eastern Canada Fall Round Up and they were very busy.

He then asked where you are staying. I stepped in at that point and said, "Mr. Bruce, we are cold, wet and hungry and have only $2.00 between us." He looked at me with his traditional smile-grin and replied, "I like a man to lay it on the line. Come with me." At his office he instructed his secretary to book us a room with two beds, two dinner tickets, one beer each and two breakfasts at the hotel.

Then he asked, "how are you going to get back to Acadia for classes Monday morning?" I shrugged and said, "hopefully some lucky hitch hiking." Wally then had the secretary book two coach class tickets from Bathurst to Halifax on the morning train. And two bus fares from Halifax to Wolfville.

"Ok boys, meet me here at 7:30 a.m. and tell me your story. I am a busy man this week." I spoke up then and said, "Mr. Bruce, I grew up in the Ottawa Valley where my father was the general manager of a large lumber and sawmill complex in Pembroke. I want you to know on behalf of Jim and myself how much we appreciate the direct and kind way you have taken us under your wing. Thank you very much. We will be here at 7:30 sharp."

No, we did not make a deal, but I learned a lot about the exploration business and met Wally Bruce, one of Canada's finest gentleman geologists and successful mine finders.

Gone off to Fight in the War, *by Dave Rogers*

In 1955, paddling into a pleasant bay with a small sandy beach I spied the remains of a prospector's log-walled tent nestled into the hillside. A bush scrounger's delight. It was well-constructed of six 6-inch diameter spruce log walls. A spruce log floor and a spruce pole tent frame. The tent had deteriorated and fallen in. I stood in the doorway checking everything out. The pots and pans on the table. A rusting .44/40 carbine standing against the wall by the door and their prospecting gear piled in the corner. Then I spotted the note pinned to an old pillow.

"September 1943. We have gone off to fight in the War". "We will return." It was signed by two Scottish names which I have forgotten. My older brother had been overseas and returned safely. There I stood spellbound 13 years later.

They had not made it back. Everything was as they had left it. It was just weathering into the ground. I felt humbled.

Stories from the Summer of 1961, *by Dave Rogers*

Down on the Labrador with my U of T Professors, Dr. W.W. Moorehouse, my thesis advisor and Dr. Peter Peach an undergraduate petrology professor.

We were working for Amax Exploration (Southwest Potash) on a NALCO property near Makovik on the coast. I worked directly for Dr. Moorehouse, a great learning experience, for the first half. Then he left for business in Europe. At that point I answered to Dr. Peter Peach. Laugh or Cry.

The Eskimo Girl Had A Request, *by Dave Rogers*

This is the way it was back in the 1960's long before Voisey's Bay Ni discovery. We had hired an exceptional Newfoundlander, cook and storyteller. We were busy setting up our field camp just north of the village of Makkovik in northern Labrador. I had noted the cook wandering around the bushes and talking with a group of young kids who were watching us work.

At lunch time, the cook approached Prof. Moorehouse and said that one of the young people would like to speak with us. Certainly, said Moorhouse, and the cook pushed this tiny, thin, shy Eskimo girl in front of us.

She shyly spoke up, looking at the floor.... "Sir's, I has this parcel coming in C.O.D. on the first boat sometime next week. It costs $11.75 and I do not have the money to pay for it."

Then she looked up and smiled and said very clearly, "After dat I just does it for fun". A dead silence in the tent. But within two minutes she had $12.00 on the table for her parcel and Moorehouse bid her adieu.

The cook was beside himself trying not to laugh out loud. A few days later I was in Makkovik and speaking with the Moravian Missionary Kate who ran the mission. I told her the story and she smiled and said David they are just like rabbits.

The Canoe Capers, *by Dave Rogers*

I had rigged up a 20 ft. double ended Dory with an old 9 H.P. outboard in the centre well. In addition, I scrounged up a 16 ft. canoe. The cobble beaches all along the coast in this area were steep 30 degrees and very tricky to board either a boat or a canoe. I trained one assistant how to manage the bow of the canoe and to make the right timely moves when I called them out. We used the Dory fairly often going to nearby areas of interest along the coast. Dear Peter Peach, bullshitter extraordinaire, decided he wanted to have a tour along the coast to take photographs. I took him down to the beach and explained the manoeuvres, timing and difficulties of getting into and out of the canoe in order to get out to the Dory without tipping or just plain floundering.

This Ottawa Valley lad was not about to get dumped in the ocean by the clumsy maneuvers of Peter Peach. I explained carefully how the waves came in ever increasing cycles of 3, sometimes 4 large waves and we had to move appropriately to avoid getting soaked. He of course said he knew all about how the ocean and waves worked. Yes, I said that's fine. But are you agile enough to move promptly in balance with the wave sequence? I asked him to do a dry run with us first. He refused. We managed by luck to get him sitting in the canoe on the floor and lifted the canoe with him as the wave came in and took up the canoe. We jumped in and paddled him out to the Dory. With lady luck on our side, we got him safely seated and dry inside the Dory.

So, a day was consumed while we took him up and down the coast doing his photography. No geological work accomplished, but he could care less. Then it was time to disembark back at camp. The wind had come up and the waves pounding the cobble beach were quite large. Again, I told Peter what he had to do when we hit the beach on top of the last large wave of a sequence. Ya! Ya! Rogers I know what I am doing. Yes sir, says I. We count the waves and picked our ride, and we went surfing in on a large one. At the crest of the cobble beach my bowman jumped out and held the bow. We were on a 30-degree large cobble beach. As the wave receded, I jumped out and held the stern. I yelled at Peter to get out quickly. He fumbled and fell back in the canoe. We held the canoe as solid as we could when the next much smaller wave hit. The canoe filled with water and Peter was a beached whale. Meanwhile I had hollered to the camp for some help and two guys came down and grabbed Peter hoisting him out of the canoe and up the cobbles to the crest. Meanwhile we had to weather another large wave then where able to run the canoe up and over the top of the cobbles.

Of course, Peter was blaming me for purposely getting him and his stuff soaked with sea water. I just looked at him and said you are "fucking pathetic" and walked away to my tent to get some dry clothes. No Peter Peach did not like any part of David P. Rogers...nor I any part of him.

Dr. Moorehouse had left a list of things he wanted done. Especially for us to visit and examine three additional showings further away from camp. Two entailing 12 hr days and one a minimum overnight trip. I asked Peach about them and he said they were not worth checking out. I asked him if I could take an assistant and do the examinations. He exploded at me saying I told you they are not worth looking at. I held my tongue that time. Moorehouse had specifically wanted them examined.

The Amax Boss, Tony Barker, arrived in camp. He walked into the Cook Tent where everyone was gathered. He threw a couple of Northern Miners on the table. Turns to Peter Peach and says they have just announced a significant tin plus other metals discovery on Mount Pleasant in New Brunswick. Tell me Peter, he says, did you ever actually walk over and around that mountain? Peter had been in charge of exploration covering the discovery area for AMAX the summer before and in his report, he recommended dropping the claims as they were of no interest.

I really lost my control at that point and ran laughing out of the tent into the tundra. If Peter did not like me up to that point he sure as hell hated me from then on.

When I returned to Toronto the last week of August, I phoned Tony Barker at AMAX and inquired if I could have a letter of reference as I was making the rounds for employment. Tony chuckled and said I remember you Rogers. Moorehouse gave you a good recommendation but you were on the top of Peach's "do not hire again list". I reviewed your summer work and am pleased to give you a good letter of recommendation. That was the last summer that Peter Peach was employed by

AMAX.

When I dropped into Prof Moorehouse's office to discuss continuing the Ph.D. program he smiled and asked. How did the summer go Dave? I said while you were with us it went extremely well in my opinion. After you left it just fell apart. Yes, I heard said Moorehouse and we will have to find another University for you to continue on your Ph.D. No problems with that as I will help you.

Thank you, sir, I said but I have accepted a very interesting and extremely well paying, tax free contract with C.C. Huston & Assoc. "Prospection Ltd" to work in Bolivia as part of a World Bank Aid Team assignment. We smiled at each other and shook hands.

Honeymoon Blues, *by Kerry Knoll*

During the Casa Berardi rush in the 1980s, somebody organized a mining conference in Amos, Quebec. I attended as a reporter for The Northern Miner. At the bar after dinner one night,
I'm sitting with the vice-president of Teck for Eastern Canada,
Ken Hymas. This guy comes by, pitching his gold project.

"This was a producing mine in the 1930s," the guy told
him. "What happened was, the owner who was running it got
married and went on his honeymoon to Niagara Falls. The mine
started flooding and they called him to come back but he refused.
The mine got totally flooded and everything was lost, and it has
never been pumped out since."

Ken stared at him for a minute, took a puff of his cigar, and
looking deadly serious, said in his proper British accent, "So,
you're telling me this guy fucked himself out of a gold mine?"

The Founding of Aur Resources, *by Howard Stockford*

I left Falconbridge to help Dr Jim Gill to build his new company, Aur Resources Inc. into a new producer, in 1983. I had spent a few days with Jim, who was consulting on a gold property in the Dryden area. We seemed to get along and the potential for building Aur into a significant gold/base metals company sounded very exciting.

Although I had enjoyed my time at Falco and my relationship with Stan Charteris, Colin Coats and Dr Chris Jennings, the company was being prepared for sale under the direction of Dr Bill James and the company was being reduced to half the size. Superior Oil then sold control of the company to Mobil. Falconbridge was then sold to Dome Mines and then, Noranda Mines, Mobil being an oil company. One of the main assets of interest to Bill James was the Kidd Creek complex in Timmins.

Aur had negotiated the option to purchase a controlling interest in a large land package in the Val d'Or Mining Camp in Quebec controlled by Brominco. Leo Brossard, CEO of Brominco had become disillusioned with the declining gold price in the early 80's and by 1985 Aur was able to merge the two companies, with Aur being the surviving entity. Brominco had about $3 million in the treasury, which we figured would give us about half a million to spend on exploration for about 5 or 6 years. Our first project was to carry out an underground exploration program at Orenada, a gold project and then we carried out similar underground programs at the previously- producing Norlartic Mine property. We connected to the next gold property to the west (the First Canadian property of associated company, Thunderwood, run by John Heslop). With encouraging results at Norlartic and First Canadian, we were able to take advantage of several flow-through financings. One program led to another but we needed a mill to process any gold ore produced. Production of our first gold was achieved in the late 80's at Norlartic and First Canadian but we didn't have a mill to process the ore.

Aur Resources had inherited a $5/ton royalty interest in Soquem's past-producing Louvem Mine through the Brominco transaction. Jim was able to persuade Soquem to trade this interest for an option to spend $500,000 on exploration on the property to acquire a half interest with Louvem Mines having the other half, controlled at that time by St Genevieve.

Louvem/St Genevieve controlled the Chimo gold operation, east of our Val D'Or holdings. Aur offered to buy the Chimo mine through Louvem in early 1989, after drilling had achieved some success on the Louvicourt base metal property; still lacking a mill when the Chimo offer was unsuccessful Aur took control of Belmoral Mines Ltd providing us with a mill and source of marginal gold ore from its underground mine, and the Aurbel Mill, which was then used to treat gold ore from Norlartic and First Canadian deposits.

A number of targets had been tested by the Aur/Louvem joint venture by the end of the flow through year (Feb 1989) on the Louvicourt property. Hole number 30 was released to the public, having intersected approximately 300 feet of 1% copper in a large alteration zone. The previously-producing Louvem Mine stratigraphy had been tested to a depth of 1000 feet. Aur proposed to test the mine horizon to a depth of 2000 feet, below the former mine and then to proceed testing it with deep drilling to the east on 1000 ft intervals across the property, supported by down-hole (DeepEM) geophysics, with the objective of not missing an "elephant". High grade massive sulphides were intersected in June of that year and the results were released. We knew that we were onto something significant. Even the drillers were excited when they called in to Aur's Val d'Or office.... Benoit Drilling's French- Canadian foreman said "we hit the pure rock" (massive chalcopyrite!).

This discovery was the highlight of my career, along with our Val D'Or team (Don Bubar, George Mannard Jr.), led by our CEO, Jim Gill. George said he put a rabbits' foot beside the picket that marked the "discovery hole, #42" to bring luck! Well, it did!

Teck and Cominco came in to Aur with a significant financing following the announcement of the discovery and Noranda supported Louvem. Several lawsuits followed, resulting in a subsequent settlement which increased Aur and Teck/Cominco's interest in the Louvicourt property to 55% and reducing Louvem/Noranda's interest to 45% (subsequently Novicourt). Aur retained the operatorship in the new mine and this established Aur as a new Canadian mine operator. It produced approximately 16 million tonnes grading 4%Cu, 3.5%Zn,with an ounce/tonne of

Ag and 1 gram/tonne Au. The mill averaged 3500 tpd.

Louvicourt started producing in 1994 and achieved payback of the capital (Aur's share of $294m) after one year for Aur and two years for Teck. The mine operated for 11 years and provided jobs for some 300 people (up to 600 during construction) and provided high quality copper concentrates to the Noranda smelter and zinc concentrates to Valleyfield.

Louvicourt was the stepping-stone for Aur, leading to it acquiring two significant copper deposits in Chile, (Andacollo and Quebrada Blanca). Both mines produce high quality (LME grade) cathode copper, which progressed from heap-leach oxide-copper to primary sulphide/milling operations. I went to Chile six times a year to attend the sub-company's Board meetings. Aur had a very good production team in Chile, led by David Brace and VP Operations, David Libby.

Aur offered to take over Inmet, which was subsequently withdrawn and another offer to take over Cambior failed. An offer to purchase Outokumpu's half interest in the Zaldivar copper Mine also failed. The purchase of the Quebrada deposit from Cominco, however, was successful and was a game changer for Aur. We also made an unsuccessful offer for HBMS. All of these required considerable due diligence and occupied a lot of our Toronto and Chile teams during my last few years at Aur.

We looked at the former producing Jerome Mine area in Arizona, hoping to find a Louvicourt analog. A significant zinc deposit was known to exist under the town of Jerome and I don't believe it has ever been developed.

One property nearby, the Bluebell Mine, owned by David Rogers' company was examined by me, guided by Dave himself during the nineties. We walked into the old mine adit and realized that we had walked over some old boards and track materials, under which some rattlers were sleeping, standing up after we passed by! I picked up a piece of old steel track to help defend ourselves on the way out. We were safe but it was a scary experience!

Aur dabbled in diamond exploration for several years, mainly in the Great Bear Lake area of the NWT, under the guidance of Roy Saukko (former manager of Falconbridge's Thunder Bay office). One diamond project that attracted our attention in 1988 was an alluvial project in Bahia, Brazil, operated by Kerry

Knoll and Ian Macdonald's company. Jim and I visited the property at the time of the 1988 Olympics. Inflation in Brazil was rampant at that time and I remember watching Ben Johnson win (and then lose, the 100metres) for Canada. As we watched the TV in the village the price of the beer we were drinking declined by half!

Aur was acquired by Teck in 2007, at which time the company was dissolved. I stayed on the Board until it was sold. When sold the company was generating almost a million US dollars a day in earnings. I retired at the end of 2004 and was retained to consult for Aur for two years to help develop the Duck Pond Mine in Newfoundland. Unfortunately, I had a TIA in June 2006 and then had a brain tumour removed later in that year, cutting short my consulting practice.

INTO AFRICA

Diamonds in the Soles of My Shoes, *by Chris Jennings*

There are a lot of misconceptions about those involved in those early days in the finding of the diamonds in Canada, and perhaps this would be a good idea to clear some of this up.

In January 1957, newly graduated from the University of Natal, with an undergraduate degree in Geology and Physics and a B.Sc Honours in Geology, I joined the British Colonial Service and was posted to Bechuanaland / Botswana Geological Survey (BGS) in Lobatse, of which I later became the Deputy Director.

I was closely involved with people and companies from outside the country such as Consolidated African Selection Trust (CAST), who were exploring for diamonds in the country and I became very friendly with Gavin Lamont, who headed up the small initial diamond exploration team working for De Beers in Bechuanaland.

Gavin himself had only left the BGS two years before I arrived. He lived just a short way up the road from both my house and the Survey office and frequently popped into my office to discuss what they were doing and so, of course, I became familiar with their exploration methods. If Gavin heard that I was making a trip to a remote part of the country, he often asked me to collect samples for him and he would supply me with sample bags and a scoop and give me very precise instructions about exactly how I should collect samples in the wind deflation concentration layer at surface. I did this for him on a number of occasions and soon developed a serious interest in diamond exploration.

Soon after Gavin had repeated the CAST findings in 1958 of both diamonds and kimberlitic minerals in the headwaters of the ephemeral Motloutse River about 250km southeast of Orapa, Gavin came into my office, wondering where the source could be.

While talking to Gavin, I remembered a paper by Alex du Toit, one of South Africa's most famous geologists, published in the S.A. Geographical Journal (1933), where he postulated a N.E./S.W. upwarp running from Rhodesia to along the escarpment forming the headwater termination of the Motloutse.

I showed Gavin a copy of this paper in our library and suggested to him that the river source of the diamonds may have been cut off by this recent upwarp and that, therefore, it might be a good idea for them to look northwest. After a trip to this area by Gavin, Manfred Marx did a traverse along the sandy road to Lake Dow and found a large concentration of kimberlitic minerals.

Gavin again came to my office and explained roughly where these had been found and, as De Beers had no aerial photos of the area, I pulled out the BGS 1945 RAF photography of the area and there we found a huge anomalous increase in vegetation, exactly the shape of the Orapa pipe, as it turned out later.

The Orapa pipe with a surface area of 111 hectares, or 274 acres, turned out to be one of the world's biggest and most lucrative pipes ever discovered. Today 53 years after its discovery by Gavin it is still producing well over US $1 billion worth of diamonds per annum. In 2013 Orapa produced US$1,6 billion dollars of diamonds $300 million more than Jwaneng, long regarded as the world's biggest value producer.

We also found a whole lot of other, smaller vegetation anomalies, all of which turned out to be kimberlites. The irony of all of this is that this may have been a chance discovery as Leon Daniels of Pangolin and I now think that the source of the Motloutse diamonds may be much   closer to where they were originally found by both companies. This is backed up by the unabraded nature of the minerals and different chemistry from that of the Orapa field. I get a lot of teasing from my children about this.

Gavin Lamont was in my opinion the most successful diamond explorationist ever, finding in Botswana the world's richest pipe at Jwaneng, the Orapa mine and the nearby Damtshaa and Letlhlakane pipes all still in production and the main contributors to De Beers still being the world's biggest diamond producer.

After 14 years at the Survey, we decided to move as our two daughters had to go to boarding school as there was no suitable high school in Botswana. I joined Falconbridge Nickel mines in January, 1971 as head of the western division for Africa and eventually became general manager for the whole of Africa including mines in Uganda (Kilembe, Cu,) Namibia (Oamites, Cu, Ag), South Africa (Western Platinum, Pt, Pd, Ni, Cu, Au), Zimbabwe (Blanket and Golden Kopje both Au).

While still at Botswana Geological Survey, I had used geophysical methods for finding groundwater, initially building my own instruments. I still regard the finding of fresh, potable groundwater for literally hundreds of thousands of Batswana one of the most satisfying things I have ever done in my life.

After attending a Mining and Groundwater Geophysics conference in Canada in 1967, I was able to raise funds from the British Government to buy one of almost every kind of Canada's most advanced geophysical instruments for mineral exploration. Canada was a leader in this field at that time. I carried out surveys over virtually every mineral deposit known at that time in Botswana and built a database. Because of this advanced array of Canadian geophysical instruments, we had visits from most of the geophysicists working for South Africa's big mining companies.

I also realized that a major drawback in De Beers exploration methods was their sole reliance on soil sampling for kimberlitic minerals and that geophysics could add a totally new dimension to exploring for diamonds, especially as Gavin had asked me to do many surveys using magnetics, resistivity (EM), and gravity over some De Beers pipes in eastern Botswana, near Mochudi and then, finally, over Orapa.

These surveys showed that geophysics both from the ground or using airborne techniques could be an admirable additional tool in the search for kimberlites when combined with ground sampling for minerals, and especially where pipes were covered with overburden to a greater depth than the depth to which termites could go in their search for water, thus bringing up kimberlitic minerals while excavating their myriads of tunnels in this process. We now know termites can go down to depth of 80 m in search of the water table!

In 1973, I proposed an exploration program, to Falconbridge, for diamond exploration in Botswana. There, like in South Africa, no other companies had the knowledge of the exploration techniques or of the huge potential profits to be made, or had the desire to or dared to compete with De Beers.

In 1978, I proposed a worldwide diamond exploration program and Marsh Cooper, who was head of Falconbridge, became interested in my proposal. At that time, Superior Oil (Supco) was the majority shareholder in Falconbridge and both Marsh Cooper and Howard Keck, chair of Supco, flew in their Gulfstream jets to Johannesburg where I sat with them and explained my ideas of using airborne magnetics and electromagnetics to explore for diamonds. I was also aware of the huge profit margin at Orapa and passed that knowledge on to Cooper and Keck.

Soon after that I was invited to make a presentation to the whole Superior Board of Directors in Bakersfield, California. Keck loved the story and said that Supco wanted to be a 50:50 partner in the worldwide exploration program I had proposed.

I was appointed, by Keck and Cooper, to be in overall charge of the program and had the Falconbridge teamwork in Botswana under John Lee. In addition to working in Botswana we also had a serious look at offshore mining for diamonds in South Africa. In Eastern Canada, the Falconbridge team worked under Roy Saukko and Hugo Dummett was appointed by Supco to join our team.

Hugo was a copper porphyry specialist with no previous experience in diamond exploration. He was delegated to work in western Canada and the United States. I received all the combined reports and controlled and visited all our combined worldwide exploration projects. I imparted all my knowledge on diamond exploration to Hugo who was a quick and smart learner and very ambitious and competitive.

It seems that Hugo may not have told people that the work that he was doing was part of a joint venture between Falconbridge and Superior and that I was in charge of the program. I only I became aware of it later.

This occurred when I called Chuck Fipke, who was employed for the joint venture by Hugo as a contractor. When I called him to congratulate him on the discovery at Point Lake, the conversation went like this. "Hi Chuck, this is Chris Jennings here. I want to congratulate you on your discovery at Point Lake", Chuck, "Hey, I never worked for you", and with that he slammed down the phone. I have had more gracious conversations in my life.

I have always given Chuck, later joined by Stu Blusson, full marks for their persistence and tenacity in trying financial times for finding one of the world's great diamond mines -Ekati in the N.W.T!

When the Falconbridge team started discovering numbers of kimberlites in the late seventies in Botswana, we soon realized how astronomical the cost of making an initial evaluation of them would be. We estimated the cost of this at that time was US$10 million per pipe making the overall cost for 70 pipes US$700 million!

I then started looking for other methods of identifying economic pipes other than through increasing amounts of expensive
bulk sampling and approached John Gurney and felt that he
could assist us, and the rest is history. Forecasting economic kimberlites by probing kimberlitic minerals both from field sampling
or from drill core after a kimberlite had been discovered.

Hugo and I did not share our sponsored Gurney's report
on G.10 garnet analysis and other minerals with Chuck Fipke. In
fact, only three copies were made of which I still have my copy.
This work was valuable, ground-breaking information and highly
confidential and it would not have been appropriate at that time
to share it with contractors, who were running businesses of their
own and could have used it to our disadvantage.

It was only at a later date, after the Falconbridge / Superior joint venture had been canned, that I spoke about this work.
Chuck, by then exploring on his own in Canada, obtained support
from the government of Canada to try to duplicate Gurney's work
for the erstwhile joint venture but was unsuccessful until he hired
someone who had been on Gurney's team.

The Falconbridge/Superior joint venture initially concentrated on two kimberlites, the Sloan Pipe in Colorado and the
GO25, now Ghaghoo, pipe in Botswana. The Falconbridge team
commenced major airborne surveys around the De Beers Holdings at Orapa and, of course, we, flew over their economic
Letlhakane pipes for orientation.

Soon after this, I heard from a friend of mine with top De
Beers connections, that Falconbridge's diamond exploration program in Botswana was discussed at Board level by De Beers and
that they were extremely unhappy at what they regarded as our
temerity at intruding on their exclusive terrain of diamond exploration worldwide, especially as none of the mining majors had
ever dared to explore for diamonds in competition with them.

After completing our surveys around the De Beers areas,
the Falconbridge team carried out pioneering geochemical
ground sampling in the Central Kalahari area of Botswana for
kimberlitic minerals, using helicopters. This resulted in the discovery of several new fields, including that of GO25 all hitherto
unknown to de Beers.

GO25 was found after an initial find of only five

kimberlitic ilmenites from our widely spaced helicopter sampling. Ghaghoo was eventually put into production after passing from our JV to De Beers and finally to Gem Diamonds but is now on standby.

As an aside, some years later, the SouthernEra /Aber/Kennecott joint venture flew over the Point Lake Pipe where Hugo Dummett, now representing BHP, and Chuck Fipke, representing Dia Met, were involved. Hugo rushed out and switched on the generators controlling a ground electric grid to confuse our airborne survey. However, he was too late as we had already gathered the airborne magnetic and EM signatures.

In 1981, I flew to Johannesburg with Marsh Cooper and Howard Keck flew independently in his own jet to meet with Harry Oppenheimer, the Chairman of De Beers, to discuss the GO25 discovery made by the JV.

I was excluded from the meetings, which were held between the heads of the three companies and left in a nearby hotel. Oppenheimer fed Cooper and Keck incorrect information about the economics of diamond mining that I was unable to correct as I was not present, saying that they were generally marginal when I was fully aware of how profitable their Orapa mine was in Botswana. I had also heard from a Canadian mining engineer working for the Botswana Government, that de Beers had misinformed the Botswana Government about the profitability of Orapa.

The result of this was that Botswana initially accepted a lower share of 10% in the mine. In addition, because de Beers understated the profits from the Orapa mine, the Botswana Government lost the revenue from the understated profits. Sometime later, this was discovered by the Botswana Government, who then negotiated a much larger share.

On my transfer to Canada and promotion to Assistant Vice President Exploration in March 1981, I spoke openly about the use of mineral chemistry for the prediction of diamonds in Kimberlites at mining and prospecting conferences in both Canada and the USA. I also tried to educate financial analysts in our industry on methods of exploring for diamonds, the huge profits to be made from diamond mining and the role played by mineral chemistry and microdiamond in this process as I believed that diamonds would be discovered in Canada and that, with an understanding of why this might be so, more people would get involved and be able to raise capital for their projects.

To summarize, the Falconbridge/Superior JV (F/S) was ahead of others in the use of mineral chemistry and microdiamonds as predictive tools. This was confirmed by the De Beers geologists when, on the signing of an agreement between the JV and De Beers over the GO25 pipe, we were forced to hand over the research we had sponsored with John Gurney to the De Beers geologists. The de Beers geologists admitted that we were years ahead of them in this research on kimberlite geochemistry.

After the breakup of the Falconbridge/Superior JV, Chuck Fipke teamed up with Stuart Blusson and, using the knowledge of the presence of kimberlitic minerals found at Blackwater Lake just east of the McKenzie River in western Canada by the FS JV, actually by Hugo and Chuck working for the JV, they continued to search eastwards across Canada. At about the same time, I resigned from Falconbridge in frustration at the cancelling of all our diamond programs and joined BP Minerals as Vice President Exploration and Business Development.

Geologist getting dropped off at Lac de Gras, NWT

At BP I had a team following the mineral train eastwards. Some hundreds of kilometres to the east, we lost the trail. At this time, I was beginning to learn the complexities of glacial transport and I realized that about 10,000 years ago, a very large post glacial lake had interconnected the Great Slave and Great Bear Lakes of today. This lake dried up thousands of years ago and, in the process, deposited a thick layer of glacial clay on the lake bottom.

Once I knew that, I realized that the clay would lie over the east to west glacially transported kimberlitic mineral train and that the source of that kimberlite train with its outstanding chemistry would undoubtedly lie further to the east.

While with BP Minerals, I had a number of phone calls from Chuck Fipke. Chuck stated that he was following the Blackwater Lake kimberlite trail eastwards and was having trouble raising funds for his search. Each time I spoke to Pat McCullough, our President, about funding this, he turned me down. As the BP search moved eastwards, I found that BP Minerals also did not have the staying power to continue this search and once again, I had my budget for diamond exploration cut to nil by Head Office in the UK.

Again, I resigned and joined Corona Corporation as Senior Vice President Exploration and Business Development. While with Corona I soon found that both Ned Goodman, the Chairman and Peter Steen, the President did not want to explore for diamonds, despite the fact that I had told them that I thought that a major Canadian diamond discovery was imminent.

Morning coffee break at Lac de Gras, circa 2000

I "borrowed" funds from other exploration budgets and

sent Leni Keogh to Hudson Bay to sample westwards, looking for kimberlitic minerals, hoping to get ahead of Chuck. Leni reported regularly to me by satellite phone and, on one occasion, excitedly mentioned that she had found an abundant amount of good colour kimberlitic garnets near Exeter Lake, north of Lac de Gras. Not believing that one could find kimberlitic minerals without first concentrating the samples, I flew from Toronto in a chartered plane to Leni's camp. She quickly spread samples, collected from an esker on the edge of the lake, on to the table where they glowed with beautiful red and purple garnets in an abundance I had never seen before. This was about 5 months before the Point Lake discovery by Dia Met and BHP.

By now, I had disclosed, to senior management, that we had found excellent mineral chemistry garnets and even a few small diamonds from that small sample. I immediately asked Corona for $100,000 to stake the area but, once again, was turned down despite the fact that I forecast a major rush of mining companies, including De Beers, to the area.

Ned Goodman and Peter Steyn soon after saw fit to terminate my services with Corona with Peter Steyn offering the opinion to me that I would never succeed as an explorationist and should join a University as an academic. Many years later I had a chance meeting with Ned in a street in Toronto and Ned comment was, "I should have listened to you."

He sure should have. He, Corona, BP, Falconbridge and virtually every other head of all Canada's mining companies that I had spoken personally to about helping fund Canadian diamond exploration all missed a US$25 to $35 billion bonanza from probably the highest value per ton diamond mines ever found.

Fed up with having my diamond exploration budgets turned down by majors, I flew to London, to look for funding for a junior diamond exploration company. While there in early November 1981, I received a phone call from Aber management, Gren Thomas, Bob Gannicott and Lee Barker, asking if I had seen the press release by Dia Met/BHP announcing the discovery of 81 microdiamonds from a small kimberlite drill sample at Point Lake near Lac de Gras.

I immediately flew back and addressed the Aber Board on the potential for the discovery of economic kimberlites in the area. They asked me to outline an area for staking and, rather than take a consulting fee, I asked for a small gross overriding royalty for myself and a net profits royalty for Corona in recognition of the fact that I was in their employ when I sent Leni Keogh up to the N.W.T.

Gren Thomas and I started staking the ground for Aber only a few days later. The initial funds came from an Aber associate, West Viking, hence the name Diavik. And it was on this ground that the four Diavik mines were discovered.

Diavik kimberlite pipes at Lac de Gras, 2005

The people at Aber, Gren Thomas and the rest of the Aber team, helped me to find the SouthernEra shell, which I took over at $0.01c per share. Our high at one stage reached $20!. Some of the ground in the current Diavik ground was optioned to Diavik by SouthernEra. Both SUF and Aber Boards shared a lot of the same directors but after an attempt, by Bob Gannicott to exclude SUF from the Tli Kwi Cho discovery, I asked all the Aber directors on the SUF Board to resign.

Now, going back to John Gurney and De Beers. When De Beers found that he was working on the landmark advanced research project on mineral chemistry with us, they threatened to cut off all support for John's Department at the University of Cape Town and even threatened to stop sending post graduate students to John and funding them. I clearly remember John being extremely concerned about this threat but, to the best of my knowledge, it was never carried out. Perhaps thanks to Barry Hawthorne (De Beers' chief geologist), who was a thorough gentleman.

It was later, with SUF, that we felt the true might and power of De Beers. When we discovered Marsfontein, where De Beers had worked many years before our discovery and found nothing, De Beers first told the world that our press releases on the discovery were fallacious but then, as we set out to mine our discovery, we think they helped the descendants of the original purchasers of the Marsfontein farm in 1918, open up the wills (archived in a government department) over an Easter weekend. We later found that the original purchasers of the farm, with its mineral rights, were dealers (all lawyers) who habitually bought farms and immediately separated and sold off the mineral rights and suspected that this was what would have happened at Marsfontein. When we went to the deeds office in Pretoria, to try to find a record of the sale of the mineral rights, the relevant documents were missing.

We eventually found the business record book in the descendants office (also lawyers and still using the same office) in Lephalale and found that the page recording the transactions for that day had been torn out. We suspect that the record of the sale of the mineral rights is probably lying in some little old lady's scarf drawer and will never be found. There is provision, in the South African mining law, for a situation in which the mineral rights cannot be found. In this case anyone wishing to acquire those rights must lodge a sum of money equal to standard mineral rights payments at that time, with the Department of Mines.

SouthernEra had lodged the required sum of money when we found that De Beers had, over the same Easter weekend, purchased the mineral rights from the "descendants" to whom they had been transferred. I think that it is good to explain, at this point, that many of the big South African mining companies cultivated very good relations with certain of the officials in the various government departments that affected them and their business.

The deal between De Beers and the descendants was that, in exchange for the mineral rights to be delivered by a certain date, the descendants would be paid R80 million in cash, and a 1 carat D Flawless diamond for each woman. SouthernEra disputed this deal, saying that we had followed the letter of the law and that the mineral rights were rightfully ours. De Beers, led by J. Hughs, embarked on a brutal campaign of arrogant, drawn out negotiations. Every law firm of standing was on a retainer from De Beers and, when we finally found a firm willing to take our case, they were curiously inert and accepting of De Beers claims and we discovered, in the Supreme Court in Pretoria, as we were about to go in for a hearing, that they, too were on a retainer from De Beers!

De Beers strategy was to break SouthernEra financially and, as we were a public company and our financial statements were public, they employed the tactic of drawing out the negotiations in order to simply have us run dry. They did this so successfully that, at one point, the manager of the Klipspringer mine informed me that he had no money to pay the salary bill for the Klipspringer mine and I, together with a cousin of Jenny's, rummaged around and raised the necessary funds. At exactly that time, young Howard Bird (whose father was one of my main mentors at Falconbridge) discovered the Sugarbird Blow on a parallel fissure(dyke) to the Klipspringer fissure, we built a road three miles long in mountainous country in a matter of days, started mining diamonds from Sugarbird and sold them in time to save the company.

That Sugarbird Blow produced diamonds worth US$10 million and this had repercussions on our Marsfontein negotiations. The money coming from the fissure, extended SouthernEra's ability to stay in the negotiations regarding the mineral rights at Marsfontein and this pushed De Beers past the date they had set to finalize the purchase of the mineral rights for Marsfontein. The lawyer acting for the heirs, who had contrived the whole scheme and who was also to get a 1 carat D Flawless diamond, became nervous and De Beers knew that she was perfectly capable of turning her back on them and coming to SouthernEra instead if she saw her prize disappearing so they added a little bonus to the reward offered to the heirs. De Beers told the heirs that they could also have the full value of any diamonds found in the overburden at Marsfontein when mining commenced there, and this was written into their agreement.

I'll jump the gun here, for the sake of continuity. What De Beers didn't know, and their geologists didn't discover until it was too late, cost them dearly. On the day that the overburden started running through the processing plant, the plant manager called our Mine Manager in what sounded almost like panic.

"David", he said, "I think you had better get up here as soon as you can. I have never seen anything like this".

Fearing the worst, David Gadd-Claxton, our mine manager, rushed out to his truck and drove up to the plant. He reported to us that he, too, had never seen anything like the quantity of diamonds cascading on to the belt to the sorting room. In all, over R50 million worth of diamonds came out of that overburden as a result of concentration caused by millions of years of weathering during which the diamonds collected in the hollow of the weathering crater. The grade of that overburden turned out to be 8 carats per tonne. The capital of the mine (R29 million) was repaid in three and a half working days. This must be unique in the history of mining. De Beers therefore had to pay the full value of those diamonds to the heirs, in addition to paying SouthernEra the 40% that SouthernEra owned as a result of the terms of the final agreement with SouthernEra.

The very idea of a small company standing up for themselves against De Beers, was ludicrous, when you think about it. We had absolutely no experience whatsoever of litigation, were regarded with some suspicion as Canadian upstarts barging into the South African mining scene, and our very partners, who had undertaken to deliver the mining rights as part of our deal with them, were themselves arrogant and unhelpful in the extreme. We were saved by people who knew me and were willing to step out of the shadows at possible risk of retaliation to themselves.

At a time when the negotiations with De Beers were at a standstill, I got a message from Jack Lunzer, who headed the Industrial Diamond Company, based in London. Jack told me that he had heard that we were in litigation with De Beers and suggested that I contact Charles Wyndham, an ex-De Beers senior employee. Charles flew out to South Africa and we had some detailed discussions on De Beers modus operandi.

Charles had a close relationship with Lev Leviev. Lev was one of the few diamantaires feared by De Beers. Through Charles I flew several times to Israel to meet Lev., Lev not only offered to give us support but also offered to buy all the Marsfontein diamonds from us, should we get the marketing rights for those diamonds. I was fully aware of the huge financial benefit to marketing outside of De Beers, knowing that one got approximately 20% less after various deductions (including for advertising) made by De Beers, than one would if one marketed independently by tender. I was also very wary of the opaque pricing system used by the De Beers selling organization.

We had a weekly negotiation session, scheduled by De Beers, at which we would, with painful difficulty, advance a tiny amount on some point, only to find, the next week, that they had withdrawn that advance or denied it. Soon after Charles arrived, we gathered out team at the meeting room in the hotel in Rosebank and had asked Charles to be a member of our team. We arrived before the De Beers team and were seated at the table when they walked in through the door. As soon as he saw Charles, John Hughes started, blanched visibly and demanded to know who this was. "You know perfectly well who this is", I replied, "What is he doing here?' John demanded, to which I replied that he was a member of our team. "Well then I am leaving", John said. I kept quiet and looked at him. He hesitated for a moment and then turned round and silently took his seat, as did the rest of his team, all looking very upset and flustered.

Charles also introduced me to Robin Sassoonker, one of South Africa's top diamantaires who also had close ties to Lev Leviev and, importantly, had contacts with senior South African ANC politicians with whom De Beers was not at that time very popular.

One morning, when De Beers suddenly changed the venue for that week's negotiations to their head office downtown in Johannesburg, I decided to go in alone, as Jeanne, who had come with me throughout, was exhausted by the long drawn out stress decided to stay at the office. While at the office, she received an extremely distressed call from David Gadd-Claxton at the mine, saying that he needed very urgently to talk with me. Jeanne told him that I was at the De Beers office and when he phoned their office he was told that the meeting room had been changed and they did not know where I was.

David persisted and, having worked at De Beers for ten years, persuaded one of the girls on the switchboard who knew him to help him and she managed to have me called out of the meeting to take David's call. David told me that he had been told that De Beers had sent one of their senior people to see Robin Sassoonker to tell him that SouthernEra had agreed to cede the marketing rights to the diamonds to them and that we had reneged on our handshake agreement with Lev Leviev to give him the marketing rights. The change of venue of that meeting was probably intended to prevent anyone from contacting me in time to prevent me from warning Sassoonker that there was no truth in what De Beers was saying.

The fight between De Beers and a small Canadian public exploration and mining company, had escalated to top diplomatic levels and soon after this, both Nicky Oppenheimer, at that time head of De Beers and myself were summoned, on different days, to see Pennuel Maduna, at that time Minister of Mines, and we were told to reach, as soon as possible, an equitable agreement with which SouthernEra was happy.

We were to present ourselves at the house of one of the most powerful ANC politicians at that time, to present him with the terms of the agreement. What transpired was that I arrived first and was let in. Gareth Penny, who had been the "good cop" throughout the negotiations, was held at the gate and, only after I had stated that we had reached an agreement and that we were happy with the agreement' was the gate opened and Gareth Penny allowed to come in. Gareth later became General Manager of De Beers, after Gary Ralfe retired. I believe that this attack by De Beers on a Canadian junior company operating legally in South Africa, was a factor whereby most   diamonds mined in Canada were not marketed through De Beers.

After six months of really rough negotiations, SouthernEra and De Beers assembled at De Beers headquarters in Johannesburg to sign the agreement. Jeanne and I were wrung out but relieved that the end was finally in sight and that we could at least come back to our shareholders with something. It was agreed that SouthernEra would own 40% of the project, would manage the mine and would market the diamonds. It was only later that we were told, by people in the know, that we had been in a far stronger position that we had ever realized and could have demanded more. However, we were inexperienced, exhausted, and our own Canadian lawyer had given up on us, thinking that there was no way we could win against De Beers.

At the final meeting with De Beers, their lawyer was

brought into the room and tried one more time to change the terms of the deal, including getting the marketing, shaking his head and saying, "No, no, we cannot agree to this", as each major point was read. I stated point blank that I had a handshake agreement with Leviev and that I would rather give up the deal than break my word. Jeanne, in despair, finally snapped and stood up, saying "I have had enough. I am leaving". As she stepped away from her chair, the man sitting next to their lawyer asked her to give him a minute, bent forward and whispered something to the lawyer and they both got up and asked to be excused for a minute, they came back after a short break, the formerly bullying lawyer completely deflated, and stated that they were ready to sign the agreement without changing anything.

News of the fact that I had refused to break my handshake agreement with Leviev spread quickly through the gossipy diamond world earning SouthernEra great good will there.

Marsfontein was, for two- and a-bit years, the world's highest value per tonne diamond mine. When we brought in Black Empowerment partners, De Beers asked me to sit on the De Beers Board (Naka) responsible for managing the mine, I agreed to sit on the Naka Board but refused all fees and any form of recompense or remuneration from De Beers. Johathan Oppenheimer (son of Nicky) was the chairman of this board. For me it was a pleasant experience, working with some extraordinary and talented black entrepreneurs and businessmen and it may have been the first Black Empowerment venture with any of the old mining groups in South Africa.

Now back to Canada.

As a result of the work I had done with Leni Keogh, I chose an area for Gren and I to start staking for West Viking (Aber), we staked East and northeast of the Dia Met claims until we found, in a northeasterly direction, that De Beers was staking there. We then moved southeast of the Dia Met claims with Gren's help. I was confident that the claims we were staking would include kimberlites outside of the Dia Met claims as I had bought aerial photos, while with Corona, of the Lac de Gras / Exeter Lake areas and, I had noticed that eskers, feeding into the one with extraordinarily abundant kimberlitic minerals found by Leni at Exeter Lake, came from both the northeast, east and southeast. De Beers also found some dykes and small pipes on their ground to the northeast, but none has proved to be economic. We were about to mine the huge Camafuca / Camazambo pipe in Angola, we had been successfully mining beautiful alluvial diamonds in Angola, we were active in Canada, Congo, Gabon, South Africa, Namibia, Botswana and elsewhere, when Mantle Diamonds, succeeded in their hostile takeover of SouthernEra.

We have never been able to establish who murdered our mine manager in Angola, who was an ex De Beers mining engineer. The murder was attributed to a UNITA ambush, but we have always wondered about this. He was staying with us in the SouthernEra house in Johannesburg for a few days and approached Jeanne the day before he was to fly back to the project, saying that he had some very important information for me but felt diffident about approaching me. Jeanne assured him that he could speak with me at any time about anything and encouraged him to do so. Sadly, he left without speaking to me and that was the last time we saw him.

Initial staking camp at Lac de Gras which led to the richest per tonne diamond mine in the world

Back in Canada not long after finishing the Aber staking in the Lac de Gras area I was about to take a break and fly to South Africa when I received a phone call from John Collier head of exploration for the giant Rio Tinto company. "Chris, I hear from Bob Gannicott that you know all about a rumoured diamond hunt in the N.W.T." Me: "sorry I have booked a direct flight for my wife and myself from New York to Johannesburg." "Can't you come via London?" "No, I am exhausted from a period camping at -30 degrees in Canada and just before that had spent time in hospital in Canada after coming back from Brazil with a tropical disease of unknown origin."

Anyway, it ended with us flying first class to London at Rio expense. Being picked by a Rio limo on Saturday morning and taken to John's house in Twickenham with me telling him what I knew of the potential for another diamond discovery in Canada, the outstanding mineral chemistry I had had probed and my feeling that there was a good chance of another economic discovery in the area labelled by Chuck as "moose pasture".

Lac de Gras at A154 Pipe, 1992

Not long after that Gren, then chair of Aber, received a call from John Stevenson head of Rio's company in Canada, Kennecott, and as a result Rio farmed in for a 60% interest of what turned out to be Canadas most lucrative diamond mine.

From people involved in the original Falconbridge/Supco JV came the discoveries in Canada of both the Ekati and Diavik mines which catapulted Canada into third place of both production and value of diamonds in the world!

Sierra Leone, by *Hamish McGregor*

It was unusual to be asked to break a trip to Africa with a stop in Sierra Leone, and to expect to receive details of my assignment on arrival. I knew it involved diamonds and I did know there had been mining for diamonds by Seltrust, at the same time (1950's) that it's corporate cousin was my employer in Zambia. But this was 1996 and I was ignorant of what to expect.

Exiting the plane at night on the far side of a sea-inlet from Freetown, and while not comprehending that I was almost alone, I found an ancient "taxi" and we limped into Freetown and to a hotel. In the throes of civil-war, Freetown was guarded by a few soldiers, and, as I quickly learned, there was no money for any-one-else. As I waited several days for my instructions, I passed time on a beautiful beach where a gang of youths were the self-appointed (?) guards. After a little negotiation, I had access and they had food.

I also walked to the local golf course which, to my amazement, was operating (perhaps for diplomats who were in hiding). With several youths to caddy, who produced clubs, balls and tees consisting of short lengths of hose-pipe, we played 18 holes. My instructions finally came - the client was not ready, and I should leave on the next suitable flight. Quickly arranged, I crossed the inlet on a ferry where, chatting with the smartly uniformed captain, I learned that he had not been paid for several months, but just did his job anyway. Life was tough.

Not long after my first trip, I was properly briefed and returned to Freetown where I was met, transported and accompanied by the client's representatives and an armed guard on occasions. Before heading into the field, I visited the local Geological Survey where I obtained useful background information and truly remarkable maps of all the known alluvial diamond occurrences. Knowing that my assignment covered both Seltrust's former diamond concessions and potential alluvial mining, and also knowing of significant reserves and potential, my first question was "what happened to Seltrust?".

Briefly, the answer to my question was that Sierra Leone Selection Trust (Seltrust) was formed in a 1934 agreement, scheduled to last for 99 years by the British Colonial Government of the time. Presumably for economic reasons, Seltrust abandoned mining the kimberlite pipes in 1955 in favour of mining alluvial deposits in the Yengema and Tongo Fields. Operations continued until 1971, when they were effectively nationalized into the parastatal National Diamond Mining Company (Diminco) and the Seltrust of Sierra Leone ceased to exist.

Why was Sierra Leone, so richly endowed with diamond and other mineral resources, effectively bankrupt at the time of my visit? The history providing the answer to this question has huge documentation on the internet which I have attempted to summarize as follows:

It started in the early 1800s when the British government purchased land from a Temne king in order to settle freed slaves on and around what became a Crown Colony centred on Freetown, and its population became known as Krios. (Sierra Leone is made up of seventeen different ethnic groups, the two largest being the Mende and the Temne). In 1896, the outlying areas were made a Protectorate and the British dominated all spheres of life in the country. The Crown Colony and Protectorate merged into an Independent State within the Commonwealth in 1961, and even enjoyed a visit from the Queen and Prince Philip in 1962. During all that time, the Freetown-based Krios developed into a highly educated group of colonial subjects while their counterparts in the hinterland were neglected. Sadly, the British departure in 1961 and inept leadership thereafter led to a series of military coups and attacks on multi-party democracy.

Eventually, in 1968, Siaka Stevens became Prime Minister and within ten years had made himself President of a One-Party Republic beset with corruption, rampant unemployment and poverty. His retirement in 1985 was followed by incompetent appointees until 1996 when Sierra Leone elected Tejan Kabbah president in its first democratic election. Faced with the Revolutionary United Front (RUF) approaching Freetown, and likely military defeat, the government had, in March 1995, engaged the services of Executive Outcomes (EO) to help regain control. EO was a security company, headquartered in South Africa, with highly-trained ex-army personnel, its own aircraft, and sophisticated communication. It brought in about 200 armed troops and, within a year, had fought and driven the RUF to the Eastern border of Sierra Leone, creating an albeit temporary peace, and enabling the democratic election process.

Despite the progress made in 1996, previous bad governance had led to the start of the conflict in 1991 and, sadly, it resumed and continued until 2002. Horrific atrocities and destruction by the RUF, led by Foday Sankoh, coupled with other chameleonic role players who changed sides and allegiances, are widely documented on the internet, but omitted in this summary. However, the picture would be too incomplete without noting that a Peace Agreement was signed in 1999, which granted amnesty to all combatants, and a Truth and Reconciliation Commission (TRC) was established in February 2000 (though commissioners were not inaugurated until 2002). The power-sharing arrangement of the Peace Agreement collapsed in May 2000 and deplorable violence re-erupted in Freetown and outlying areas. Only then did UN armed forces intervene, capturing Sankoh and other members of the RUF, enabling the TRC to function and to reach confirmatory conclusions regarding the history such as the following:

39. The Commission found that, prior to the start of the conflict, government accountability was non-existent. It concluded that democracy and the rule of law were dead.
40. The Commission found that successive political regimes abused their authority over the security forces and unleashed them against their political opponents in the name of national security. Soldiers and police officers were reduced to playing roles as agents of destabilization.
41. The Commission found that prior to the conflict the Provinces had become totally excluded by the centralization of political and economic power in Freetown. Local government was in demise across the country.
42. The Commission found that the political elite in successive regimes excluded society-at-large from meaningful participation in decision-making, in particular youths and women.

1996 – the year of my visit – could have been the end of the civil war, and, naively, I thought it was. My assignment through WGM was at the request of Robert Friedland, in association with his brother Eric, who, in Canada, was also a diamond-related entrepreneur. I was expected to examine geologically and economically the concessions embracing the former diamond mining operations as well as certain alluvial concessions being acquired. On completion of the site visits, I had a schedule to follow which required me to meet with Robert and Eric and fly with them to Angola where I had a similar diamond-related assignment. This all worked well, my verbal opinions were accepted and in due course a thorough report was prepared and submitted to Branch Energy Ltd.

Why was I so naïve? On my arrival in Freetown on my second visit, I was met by a man in civilian clothes, who was indeed my client's representative, but who was actually a senior member of EO. Personnel and Jeeps were made available to take me to my desired destinations, which they did without evidence of danger to me. These included ransacked buildings at the former mine, a visit to the Yengema Field where numerous artisanal miners were hard at work, and several other sites that could impact my study. Only later did I learn that the peace advance failed because of lack of money and international help. EO was supposedly to be paid $1million per month (see the excellent 2016 PRISM NDU Case Study by Ismail Rashid) aided by the International Monetary Fund, but the money ran out and EO's contract terminated in 1997.

It is widely speculated, but denied by EO, that certain rights were granted to EO in lieu of payment, and that these rights were to the diamond concessions that I was assessing for Branch Energy. Additional, publicly known, use of EO by the Angola government to suppress rebel forces prior to use by the Sierra Leone Government, adds to speculation of a private link between EO and Robert Friedland. Whether the speculation is true or not, unravelling the next chapter in the diamond story of Sierra Leone is not easy. Branch Energy did acquire significant ownership, new companies came and went, changes occurred in the possession of mining rights, and there were significant influences on marketing. Today, Koidu Holdings S.A., a private company, is the current owner/operator under the control of Israeli magnate Beny Steinmetz.

Memories of the geologist (me) who visited Sierra Leone include categorizing the kimberlite pipes from explosive to one so weak that only a dyke-ring emerged, and recognizing that the few known pipes could not account for the abundance of alluvial diamonds. By contrast, dykes, extrusions and occasional blows underlie very extensive alluvial deposits such as in the Yengema and Tongo Fields. Rivers draining these fields carry diamonds all the way to the coast and have been exploited for 100 years or more by simply panning, and more efficiently by divers directing suction pipes into cracks and potholes. Remaining unknowns are the potential for recovering alluvial diamonds from beneath laterite caps, recovering diamonds off-shore, and kimberlite exploration possibilities.

Finally, one has to acknowledge the 2006 "Blood Diamond" movie in which director Edward Zwick used actual events to call attention to Sierra Leone's horrific history. One also has to acknowledge that from 1997, the UN Security Council attempted to sanction both arms importation and diamond sales that could benefit the RUF and did not withdraw the sanctions until 2010. Despite the sanctions, it is my understanding that diamonds flowed freely across the Sierra Leone border into the hands of Lebanese and Israeli buyers in Liberia and Guinea, prolonging the civil war for six years after my visit.

Strangers in the Night, *by John Paterson*

Burkina Faso was begging to be explored when Geomaque began working there in the late 1990's. The country's only gold mine had recently closed. Political problems for the last few decades, with one coup d'état after another, had discouraged foreign investment. But things were stabilizing. Being one of the first companies to apply modern exploration techniques to this almost untouched region of West Africa was an exciting opportunity.

We started aggressively with a country wide diamond exploration program but, unfortunately, didn't find any diamonds or kimberlites not even any trace minerals which might be associated with kimberlites as we sifted through the weathered sands. Zero. However, this virgin territory did show us some of her secrets as we came across numerous interesting gold prospects in the process. So, we switched our focus and began searching for gold.

I was fortunate enough to make several trips and travel around much of the country as part of the diamond program and later identifying and following up on the gold showings. Burkina is extremely poor, but from my first visit, I found the country captivating. And the people we met in the countryside were wonderful. Friendly and welcoming, they were eager to help us in any way they could. In fact, they were one of our most valuable exploration tools. When we told them we were searching for gold, they all seemed to have a cousin or an uncle who had an artisanal gold prospect they wanted to show us.

The rural population survives, largely, by growing corn. The corn is grown during the four-month rainy season from May through August. It harvested in the dry season, dried in the sun, and stored in thatched silos on stilts. This staple feeds the people while they wait for the next rainy season.

The men often leave their villages during the dry season to look for work elsewhere. A tough existence. We avoided working in Burkina during the rainy season as a precaution against damaging their precious crops.

It's easy to imagine how vastly different the lives and values of these people were from ours. Especially the people inhabiting the far regions of the country. They live in tiny villages, or walled compounds, spread across the savanna, consisting of one or more families with one communal well and a corn silo. In the north, near the border with Mali, people still used camels to get around. They had very little contact with the outside and received almost no government support for education or health care.

Burkina has one of the lowest literacy rates and highest infant mortality rates in the world. To complicate things, the official language of the country is French, but there are 69 other languages spoken and many people don't speak anything but their own tribal dialect. I wouldn't have been surprised if some were unable to tell me what country they lived in. Or really cared for that matter. Those kinds of details were low on their priority list. Somewhere way below food, water and survival.

But at the same time, it also gave these people a sense of innocence. Like an isolated tribe in the Amazon. An innocence that comes from being removed from the rest of the world. Perhaps it was this innocence that made them so likeable. Things might be different now with smart phones and internet. Perhaps not.

One gold prospecting trip took us to the far eastern part of the country, bordering Benin and Niger, where we had the opportunity to spend the night in a game reserve. It was called a "reserve," which I guess is a lot different than a "sanctuary" because people went there not only to see and photograph the wildlife, but I suspected that some went specifically to hunt game. Perhaps they were just permitted to hunt species which were overpopulated. My French wasn't good enough to find out for sure, or perhaps our hosts were skirting around the issue to keep everyone happy.

Most of the country consists of barren grassland or desert with the occasional gigantic baobab tree dominating the horizon, but the reserve was covered in mature dry forest. The shade was a welcome change from the blazing sun which brought on temperatures above 40° C. And there were birds and animals everywhere. While driving from the perimeter of the reserve to the lodge, we encountered herds of buffalo, gazelles and antelopes. There was a modest lodge and several small cabins made of corrugated steel for guest accommodation. Our group were the only visitors at the time.

We arrived late in the day, so we dropped our bags in our

cabins, cleaned up a bit, and went for dinner in the lodge. We were hot and tired from our long drive from Ouagadougou (the capital) early that morning with a couple of prospecting stops along the way. The meal, washed down with the local beer, featured what I think was wild buffalo meat, rice and some kind of corn dumpling. Again, either language was the barrier, or our hosts didn't want to share the details of the entrée's origin. But whatever it was, it was delicious. We ate at the long wooden table in a dining room whose walls were adorned with the heads of the animals that inhabited the reserve (and we were probably eating). After dinner we went back to our individual cabins which, fortunately, were air conditioned, as the heat was almost intolerable. A motor hummed in the distance which I assumed was a generator as there was no electrical grid in this part of the country.

I awoke around midnight and all was silent. The generator had stopped and so had the air conditioner.

"Perhaps the generator broke down," I thought. "Or perhaps they just shut it off after everyone goes to bed."

Either way, it was starting to get hot. As the temperature rose, the cabin creaked and groaned with the expansion of the steel. Pitch black dark with no flashlight, I lit a match to make my way to the bathroom, careful not to step on any creatures. I awoke about an hour later and could feel a tickling, like bugs crawling on my skin. It turned out to be beads of sweat running down my sides. The temperature inside the cabin continued to rise as I lay there soaking wet wondering what the story was with the generator. I was not having a good night. Then it got worse. I started hearing a series of low, "grunting" sounds. There would be three or more in rapid succession followed by a brief silence. Then the grunting would start again.

At first, I thought it might be someone trying to start the generator, perhaps with a hand crank, and either the motor or the person doing the cranking was making this guttural noise. But the engine didn't fire. And the sound went on and on. Then, my imagination took a walk on the wild side...

"What else makes a noise like that? Could it be the sound of someone engaged in passionate sex? What direction was it coming from? It didn't seem far away. Could it be coming from the next cabin where the geologist was staying?" I couldn't imagine he'd met a woman out here. And it had been going on much too long by my estimation. "What if a bunch of natives came out of the jungle and were having their way with him?" I peeked out my window but all I could see was total darkness. Scenes from the movie Deliverance started flashing in my head. I reminded myself that we were a long way from the backwoods of Georgia, still, I couldn't imagine what in God's name was making that noise. I hoped my fondness for the people of Burkina wasn't about to change.

Putting these crazy notions out of my head, I tried to get back to sleep after making certain my door was locked. Drifting off from time to time, only to be reawakened by the "grunting" and the sweat running off my chest and down my sides. Finally, a little before five o'clock, dawn started breaking. I rolled off the bed and went to the window. Cautiously pulling back the curtain to peak out, I saw strange dark shapes moving slowly through the grey mist just outside my cabin. At first the figures were unrecognizable but as it got lighter, the strangers took shape. The central area of the compound had been occupied by a troop of big hairy baboons. They were walking around the yard, and presumably communicating with each other, by making "grunting" sounds.

This was my first encounter with baboons in the wild. Their almost human-like features and actions were fascinating. The males seemed to be the noisiest, apparently telling each other what to do, while the females, several with babies clinging to their backs, moved around on the ground and in the trees. I would have guessed that the adults weighed around 50 to 75 pounds. I couldn't wait to get a closer look at them, so I quickly pulled on my jeans, grabbed my camera and went out into the yard.

I moved slowly so I wouldn't scare them, but they didn't seem afraid of me. A couple came up close to me to "check me out." I grunted at one and he responded with three quick grunts then returned to what he'd been doing. There were probably at least twenty of them. Their protruding faces were shaped like dog muzzles, with long canine teeth they flashed at each other from time to time. Olive coloured hair covered their bodies except for their butts which were bare. I quickly used my entire roll of film photographing them in the amber light of the dawn. I probably should have taken more time to get better quality photos, but I was afraid they might leave at any minute. This incredible experience made me forget all about my "night from hell" and left me feeling foolish for thinking the thoughts I'd had.

I was disappointed that no one else in our party was there to share the experience. Their rooms were farther away, and they hadn't been woken by the baboon's conversations. After a while, I returned to my cabin to shower and get ready for breakfast. When I came back out, the baboons were gone. Later, as we gathered for breakfast, I was happy to see the geologist looking well and unharmed. I told him, and the others, what I'd seen (though I didn't mention what I'd been thinking during those long hours of the night). They were shocked when they heard I'd gone outside and walked among the visitors. I was advised to be careful around baboons as they can be unpredictable and dangerous.

"Whatever you do, don't smile at them," the lodge manager told me. "They think you are showing your teeth as a sign of aggression and are liable to attack you. Their jaws are incredibly strong, and their sharp teeth can break bones!"

A little piece of knowledge, although passed on too late to help me this time, I locked away in my memory for the next occasion I wake up surrounded by a group of "grunting" baboons.

We never did find any gold occurrences that proved to be of economic interest in Burkina, but other companies did. Today, twenty years later, gold is the country's top export commodity and Burkina is one of the largest gold producers in Africa. Unfortunately, the political situation has deteriorated and gone back to military coups instead of elections. There have also been a rash of terrorist attacks, kidnappings and murders that make it unsafe to travel around the country. I hope, for the sake of the people of Burkina, that these problems don't drive away the much-needed foreign investment. And I'm happy that I was able to experience the country and meet some of the people, as well as my hairy "grunting" friends, during that era of relative peacefulness.

Botswana Fishing Stories, *by Chris Jennings*

During my 14-year sojourn in Botswana I had few opportunities to fish because most of the country has been described as "Kalahari Desert" utterly devoid of lakes and rivers.

As a boy my father had occasionally taken me on camping trips to fish for trout in the streams in the beautiful foothills of the Drakensburg mountains of Natal Province or in warmer rivers for yellow fish so I had developed an innate love for fishing which could only happen when I visited the more northerly regions of Botswana around and northeast of the Okavango swamps.

On one occasion I was searching for groundwater using an assortment of geophysical equipment in the arid far south of Botswana not far from the so-called Molopo River which only ran for a short period after exceptional rains. This had recently happened but by now the river had dried leaving a few muddy pools along its course. I decided to camp with my African geophysical crew of about eight people next to one of these muddy pools.

Soon after erecting our tents, Patrick my cook came to me saying the pool was full of fish and would I please catch some for him and the rest of the crew. Patrick growing up on the shores of Lake Malawi had grown up on a fish diet. I quickly explained I had no fishing equipment or even a net with me and Patrick departed in disappointment to cook my dinner.

One of my techniques for finding underground water was to use an electrical depth sounding technique to find basins of decomposition in granitic rocks using two battery boxes each with 25 batteries. Each battery had a 45-volt capacity so if I connected the two boxes in series I could get a near human lethal kick of 2,250 volts.

I then connected the boxes together, took a long positive and along negative lead and threw these into the water and switched on and to my surprise there was a huge churning in the water and a large number of dead barbel catfish came to the surface to the cheering of Patrick and the rest of the crew.

"Switch off," shouted Patrick, as he gathered a large bucket and filled it to the brim to supply a pleasant change from their diet of dried meat and maize meal. Not kosher but maybe easier and quieter than dynamite!

On another occasion I was camped on the edge of the near perennial Boteti River which in most years is the drainage over-flow from the fault line forming the base of the huge Okavango Swamp.

I was camped with Colin Boocock head of the Geological Survey and another of my inspiring mentors. After a hard day's work, we were relaxing on the edge of the river without any fish-ing rods, lines or hooks. Colin suggested we make our own hooks from the roll of galvanized wire all geologists kept for emergen-cies on the rough roads we had to traverse.

Using sharp nosed pliers, we cut off a short piece of wire, twisted one end into an eye and bent the other into a hook. We then used our geological hammers and beat and filed the end into a nice point. We then each cut a pole from a nearby tree, made a line from a role of string, baited our hooks and a short while later were each frying a tasty Okavango bream for supper.

I was camped on the dirt road from Francistown to Maun near a water borehole with its nearby circular storage reservoir about 5 m across by 3 m deep.

On peering in I was surprised to see someone had put bream into it and they had now grown to about three quarters of a kilo. This time I had a fishing rod with me and in no time our whole crew were having a delicious meal.

A Fishing Story, *by Hamish McGregor*

I had caught a couple of nice bream at this spot and the very next day, after plotting my work and packing up soil samples, I returned and was sitting with my line drifting slowly in the current. The water was dirty from a recent heavy rain, and the day was stinking hot. Nothing really unusual, but my chosen fishing spot was about a kilometer from camp, and I was on my own.

In Zambia when the grass is thick, one is always aware of the danger that a Gaboon Viper or Puff-adder might be hiding on your trail, and wearing gum-boots to go fishing is a wise precaution. So, I was properly booted, but it was hot, hot, hot!

There I was, sitting on the bank of a small river waiting patiently, but the fish would not bite. Sweltering, I slid forward so my booted feet were in the water, and continued to wait. Snakes were in my thoughts and how well I remembered a bridge-side stop for a swim and lunch while travelling on another hot day in South Africa.

After climbing beneath the bridge, dropping my swimsuit, undoing my belt, and letting my shorts drop to the ground, I looked down and saw a very large snake passing my sandaled feet. I froze and watched as a cobra rose before me, swaying and staring into my face. Inch by inch (or should it be cm by cm) my fingers crept down my legs until they found my shorts and slowly drew them up to my thighs. Still with my eyes locked on the cobra, I crept slowly backwards until I was far enough away to run. I still chuckle remembering going cautiously back to get my swimsuit and have a swim.

Well, today I had no plans for a swim, and I had not seen a snake. Of course, there might be a danger of a crocodile, but surely, if it was coming for me, it would drift down-stream with the current and I was a keeping an eye up-stream. Not shifting position, I turned my head and WOW there it was, not more than two metres in front of me. Lucky me! The croc was not huge and was sizing me up for attack. Like with the cobra, we stared at each other, but this time for only maybe two seconds while I dug my heels into the bank and heaved myself out of the river. The croc's tail swung at me, but fortunately not the jaws, and I escaped without a scratch.

Being a true fisherman, I recovered my line, re-baited and tossed it back in. Within minutes I snagged the croc which took off down-stream hook-line-and- sinker.

"They're Killing People Over There" *by Nick Tintor*

Mineral exploration is a fascinating business. It takes you to some of the farthest and most remote and undeveloped regions of this earth where nature, in all its wisdom, decided to put some of the largest and richest mineral deposits.

The Democratic Republic of Congo is one such place. Cursed by tribal strife, a brutal Colonial past, almost endless civil wars and banditry, it is also endowed with some of the richest mineral deposits of gold, copper and cobalt on earth. And I might add, some really good people whom I worked with over there.

In 2005, John Willet at Haywood Securities sent me a slide deck for a private Australian company that had a promising gold project in Haute Uele province in the far north and close to the Ugandan border. The brainchild behind this one was Klaus Eckhof, a man as close to Indiana Jones as you could find anywhere in mining.

Nick Tintor in front of an artisanal mine pit on the Moto property in the Congo, 2005

Congo had been in the news for the past year as the civil war was easing up. I took one look at the location and said, "John, zero interest. Gotta be nuts to go there." John came back saying,

"Did you really look at it? Look again."

So, I looked at the drilling and the sections they had and wow, this did look good. Really good. After the shell was put together with Lew Lawrick and John McBride, we listed Moto Gold Mines on the TSX, and I was Klaus's guy in Canada. Sean Harvey was also on the board and a partner in the original shell.

Now it was time to get some analysts to site to show them how promising this project was. My first call was to Haywood's mining analyst Andrew Kaip, a thoughtful, well-liked and regarded geologist.

After weeks of making arrangements in-country, I get a call from Andrew the day before we were to depart. "Hey Nick, Andrew here. I'm rethinking this trip. The guys on the desk are laughing at me, saying they're killing people over there."

"Whoa, Andrew, you can't back out now," I begged. I had been there, and the site was very remote and was never affected by the civil war. No roads, so bad guys could never get there.

Actually, after a lot of trips there, I did conclude that the only thing democratic about the DRC was your democratic right to an AK-47. But that was not the point! You needed a small plane to get in and out. That's all Andrew needed to know.

He ended up going and we raised more than $60 million in ever higher priced financings as the drills kept finding more and more gold.

After drilling out more than 15 million ounces of gold, Moto was sold to Randgold, now Barrick Gold, for $546 million in 2009. In hindsight, a steal of a price. Barrick's Tier 1 Kibali mine that now operates there, is one of Africa's largest and most profitable churning out 814,027 oz of gold in 2019.

Klaus took his winnings and flew straight to Monaco where he remains to this day. And me? I still polish a beautiful black Maserati Quattroporte Sport GTS.

What a crazy business.

A Different Era, *by Hamish McGregor*

It was very much a developing world in 1955 when I graduated and grabbed an offer of a job with Rhodesian Selection Trust ("RST" and later Roan Selection Trust) doing mineral exploration in Northern Rhodesia. A girl I had dated, who was the daughter of a senior mining official on the Copperbelt, re-assured me that the Mau-Mau rebellion in Kenya in 1952 had not impacted on them, and that Northern Rhodesia was a wonderfully uncomplicated place to live. Nevertheless, I was unprepared for "British Colonial Rule" that had been in vogue since 1924.

In South Africa, where I grew up, racial segregation was the law, and part of my reason for heading north was growing distaste for what I had sometimes seen. I duly arrived by train in the early evening, in the wrong town (Kitwe), not fully aware that nearby Kalulushi was my destination. Looking for help, I went to the first bar I found, and elbowed through a 6-deep crowd of white miners to get a beer and information. In no time, I learnt that Kitwe was an Anglo-American Company ("AAC") town, and I had to go to an RST town such as Mufulira or Roan Antelope. Not that I was unwelcome, in fact just the opposite, as a fair amount of beer passed my lips before I got a ride to Mufulira and a bed for the night.

Next day I reached my destination and learnt that I was about to head west with Cyril ("Squirrel") la Grange, a fellow geologist (and new life-long friend) to Luamata, a prospect near Mwinilunga where drilling was about to start. Within a few days we had loaded supplies into an "International" truck and embarked on a long rough ride to what was a beautiful pre-built campsite. As I recall, we stayed there for close to 3 months before revisiting HQ, getting ample food supplies locally, and keeping in radio contact.

My job was mapping the surrounding area and learning exploration, while Squirrel took care of the drilling and pitting at the prospect. Mapping was done in surveyed "blocks" containing pre-blazed compass lines. Two of these a day included collecting soil samples, mapping soil changes and any rock outcrops. My crew included a "boss-boy", a carrier and four rock-spotters who traversed the bush parallel to my line. At times, I had use of the truck to approach the work site, but there were maybe five miles walking daily and I enjoyed being very fit, then and at subsequent prospects I explored in the same way.

The Copperbelt was urban and mining, and while there were under-currents of dissatisfaction among the African leaders, white expats lived well, and locals were "labour" for households, the mines and industrial spin-offs. Bars were almost exclusively for white men, white kids went to private schools or overseas, and African kids had limited education. Rural areas were governed by District Commissioners and in such areas, local kids received most of their schooling from missionaries.

Racial segregation was the established way of life, acceptable to almost all the people despite inequality that accompanied it. Under colonialism, previously warring tribes were separated into "tribal areas" ruled by chiefs and head-men, but under reasonable laws so that (for example) a thief did not automatically get a hand chopped off. Roads were built and transport provided so that labour could reach the mines and Britain could get the metals it wanted.

Luamata was but one of many prospects identified by Canadian geologists working in the nineteen thirties under Bancroft. Without modern exploration methods, word was spread among the locals that the "Mzungus", or foreigners, were looking for green rocks and rewards were given to guides who took them to the locations. Unfortunately, Luamata and the surrounding country did not reveal economic amounts of copper and in due course Squirrel and I were assigned to exploration of other prospects.

At about that time RST, while continuing follow-up exploration of known prospects, embarked on wide-scale reconnaissance using stream-sample geochemistry and helicopter transportation. A senior geologist led a small team of juniors who traditionally were white, and were separately accommodated in tents, and Africans ranging from excellent field-assistants to camp-staff. The base-camp moved periodically and the staff, accompanied by wives and families moved with it. "Diamond", whose African name I never knew, was very capably in charge of many non-technical chores, including a daily medical clinic.

While I lived on site and became very involved in exploring different prospects, including Lumwana and Kalengwa, both of which became mines, at other times I was given charge of helicopter reconnaissance in the north-western part of the country. My relations with the staff were amicable, but I think there was more respect for the man Diamond than me, until I earned it. This happened one evening as Piet de Jong (a recently arrived geologist) and I were completing work in our office, and Diamond came in requesting help in controlling "Wireless". One of the staff, Wireless was a large, strong, man who had previously earned a living boxing. He had a happy disposition, and we liked each-other, but, unknown to me, he could drink too much and become aggressive.

The African's camp was distant enough that we (Piet, Diamond, and I) took a vehicle and arrived where a nice big campfire was surrounded by females and males, including Wireless. I called to him, he stood quickly, and I attempted to tell him to leave and go to bed. Then, as a voice from the fireside added some comment, and Wireless lunged in its direction, I grabbed his shoulder and he turned towards me. The spectators were in awe as I punched Wireless on the jaw and he crashed to the ground unconscious. The silence and the eyes around that fire were memorable and prompted only a few words from me before Piet and I headed back to our camp.

Back at our office, Piet remarked that he had never seen such a powerful, short-punch as the one I had given poor Wireless. In answer, I retrieved the paperweight from my pocket, and showed him how nicely it had fitted into my fist. Our secret! The story did not end there. About an hour later I was reading in my tent when there was a cough out-side. It was Wireless. In response to my gruff acknowledgement, he said "Bwana, I have come to clean your shoes". This he did, and thereafter was my staunchest supporter.

The Big Fish of Benin, *by John Paterson*

Have you ever heard of Benin? It's a little country in West Africa about the size of Pennsylvania. Sandwiched between Togo and Nigeria, Benin is primarily a cotton growing country. So, if you're not in the cotton business, it may explain why you are unfamiliar with it.

I can't say I knew anything about Benin until a friend passed on a fax about a gold prospect in the country and I started doing a bit of research. Benin didn't have any gold mines at that time in the late 1990's, or any other types of mines for that matter. But I found the description intriguing. The excerpt from a report by the Benin Ministry of Energy and Mines read:

DEPOSIT IN THE DISTRICT OF PERMA
It consists of 26 quartz veins spread over an area of 2 sq. km. The proven reserve amounts to 8000 kg of lode gold at a grade of 9 g/t.

A quick calculation told me that the reserves were worth over $100 million. Three times that today. It would be perfect for Geomaque which had one mine operating in Mexico and was looking for another. And, as evaluating new gold prospects was part of my job, off I went to check it out. This could be a nice addition.

Someone more skeptical might have questioned colleagues about the prospect but only a fool would go wagging his tongue about a great prospect without first securing title. Greedy, unscrupulous competition might get in my way. I was going to land this fine fish on my own.

So, without hesitation and mind made up, I boarded a plane bound for Cotonou, the Capital of an African nation I hadn't heard of a week before.

I flew overnight through Paris, all the way dreaming of how profitable this project might be. Damn I'd been lucky to come across this gem.

The government geologist was waiting for me when I arrived at the Ministry of Energy and Mines. The Ministry's offices were shockingly modest, but that was only to be expected in a country where there were no energy or mines. I spent most of the day in a small meeting room reviewing maps, drill cross sections, drill logs and analytical results. I tried to conceal my enthusiasm as I reviewed the data, taking notes and rubbing my chin while mentally calculating future profits.

The reports were in either French, the official language of the country, or Russian. Most of the work was done by Russian geologists before the collapse of the Soviet Union in 1991. Then I discovered a report in English, the one containing the excerpt I had been sent by fax.

I could hardly believe my eyes when I came to the part which quoted the "proven reserves." The reserves were quoted as 800 kg instead of 8000kg. I was sure there must be some mistake. Quickly pulling out my fax, my mouth went dry.

The excerpt I had been sent had been altered. Someone had added an extra zero! My big fish had flopped out of the boat and was quickly swimming away.

Now I know what you're thinking. Anyone in their right mind would walk out the door and catch the next plane home. Ninety percent of this potential gold mine had just evaporated and even worse, someone here, probably the geologist, was crooked enough to alter a report to entice someone to fly halfway around the globe to examine the project. And that someone was me!

And you're probably thinking that this should be the end of the story, the moral of which should be "don't look for gold in cotton country" or "if it sounds too good to be true, it's probably bullshit." But I wasn't ready to give up and decided to dig a little deeper.

I asked the geologist what he personally thought the reserves of the deposit might be. He said no one could say because it had yet to be properly drilled. At this point we were just seeing the "tip of the iceberg." I could take his word for it that the deposit was getting bigger and richer with depth. This orebody was formed over eons, by gold-rich fluids flowing from deep in the earth's crust and precipitating the gold in the quartz matrix. It was just a matter of finding the "feeder zone" and we'd see gold grades that would make the Egyptian Pharaohs blush.

You must admit he had a point. And while most people still might have written him off as a corrupt West-African fraudster and focused on putting as much distance between themselves and him, it's hard to succeed by doing what most other people would do. And, wouldn't it make sense, after coming all this way, to get a look at the property and make a fully informed firsthand judgement of the potential of the project? So, for better or worse, my pursuit of the big fish continued as does the story.

The geologist and his driver picked me up at my hotel at four o'clock the next morning and we drove for 8 hours to the project site. The countryside was flat with miles upon miles of nothing but cotton fields. Hot and dry. Like 40 degrees Celsius hot. Not surprising because we were only a few degrees north of the equator. But we rode in comfort in an air-conditioned Land Cruiser from the capital on the coast to the north part of the country. The road, which was under construction, was straight and flat and we would have made good time if it weren't for the fact that the bridges over the dry streambeds every couple of kilometers had yet to be constructed. All the way I was thinking about the "tip of the iceberg" and what riches might lie below. As we neared our destination, the hills grew bigger and the vegetation turned to jungle.

Arriving at the project site around noon, we were surrounded by several shuttered maintenance shops, an empty office and fleet of rusty earthmoving equipment which looked like it hadn't been moved since being abandoned by the Russians. This hidden gem had been kept secret for quite some time. We parked the vehicle in the yard and started on foot with the geologist and a pair of local caretaker/watchman types. The heat was almost unbearable but fortunately, the forest canopy gave us some shelter from the scorching sun. We crossed the river and started up the hill through the jungle. I imagined myself as Indiana Jones heading out to discover the Lost Ark.

Trudging up the path through the forest, we eventually came to the edge of a clearing. Perhaps a dozen artisanal miners could be seen crushing rocks with hammers and panning the fine material for gold. The watchmen said something to the geologist who held a finger to his lips making a shushing sound and telling us to stand still. The two watchmen bent down to collect several fist sized rocks then ran out into the clearing yelling at the miners and pelting them with the rocks.

The surprised miners grabbed what possessions they

could and scrambled to safety at the edge of the jungle where they stopped and yelled back at the watchmen.

The geologist explained that the miners were trespassing and knew very well that they were mining illegally, though it was obvious that they had been working the site for quite some time.

While he showed me the geology of the area, the watchmen gathered the miners' belongings. There were hand carved wooden gold pans made of sections cut from tree trunks, hammers, some basic food, and even a small vial of gold one of the miners had collected. The sun beat down on us while the watchmen dumped the miners' precious water onto the ground. This upset the miners even more and the shouting grew louder.

I looked up and the miners were waving machetes at us, yelling in some tribal language and making threatening gestures. I guess the geologist sensed that I was feeling uneasy. And I wish it was as simple as "uneasy." But in fact, I was terrified!

"They won't bother us," he explained. "They know that there would be big trouble if they did. We have to be strict with them or they won't respect us."

That response didn't make me feel any more comfortable. I wasn't the least bit interested in teaching these poor devils any lessons or gaining their respect. All I was interested in was getting out of there in one piece. I didn't have a lot of faith in my host but, at this point, there wasn't much I could do.

The way the miners made their shafts was fascinating. They would build a fire on the ground and when the rock got hot, they would dump water on it. This would cause the rock to crack where upon the pieces could be pried loose and crushed to powder to recover the gold. Then they'd repeat the process over and over following the rock containing quartz veinlets and eventually developing a shaft. Each miner had his own little work area, like a claim, perhaps 5 meters square. Some of the shafts were 5 or 10 meters deep.

While the geologist was showing me rock samples and explaining what was going on, I was keeping one eye on the miners at the edge of the forest. They had stopped yelling and were now talking amongst themselves. Unquestionably, they were working out a strategy to get revenge and regain their precious belongings. It was just a matter of where and when.

When the attack finally came, my strategy was simple: to

run as fast and far as I could. I had a Swiss Army knife in my pocket, but the tiny blade was no match for a machete. And the corkscrew attachment was also worthless, unless they wanted to share a bottle of wine with me, which wasn't very likely.

The only other thing I had was a pocket full of Central African Francs, the local currency. The plan I devised was that while I was running down the hill through the forest, I would throw the money over my shoulder and anyone chasing me would be inclined to stop to pick it up letting me get farther away. It wasn't much of a plan, but it was all I had.

When we finished looking around the clearing, I thought we would be returning to the car but the area where most of the gold was concentrated lay further ahead.

"Not far at all," explained the geologist. "Just over the hill. And we head straight back to the car from there."

As we continued through the jungle my eyes darted back and forth looking for signs of the ambush. The miners would be jumping out of trees and chopping us to pieces any minute. Sweat rolled off my forehead and into my eyes like it was raining. It seemed like we were walking for hours. If only I had done what most people would have done when they found out they'd been tricked, I'd be on my way home by now. What a mistake. A wife and two young children at home and me hacked to death in some godforsaken African Republic.

Eventually we came to the other clearing. This one was much bigger and had a lot more people working it. Perhaps seventy-five or a hundred. There was a lot of talking and a bit of yelling, but I was relieved that the watchmen refrained from rock throwing. The miners made like they were packing up to leave but I'd wager they were back working their pits as soon as we left.

We sweltered in the heat of the afternoon with no shelter from the sun. The place was dirty and foul smelling. It was painfully obvious there were no toilets. I was out of drinking water and my stomach reminded me that I hadn't eaten lunch, though food was the least of my worries at that point. So, we continued our quest. At least the geology was interesting. There were horizontal and inclined beds of white quartzite of variable thickness, up to a meter or more, which seemed to host most of the gold. Or at least that was the conclusion I drew because these were the ones into which the miners drove their tunnels. Some of the openings were so narrow it was hard to believe a man could fit inside. I wondered how many poor souls may have perished from being crushed by rock falls in these narrow caverns. It was doubtful that much of the 800 kg of gold that had been outlined by the Russians would be left in this rabbit warren of tunnels. It seemed that my big fish had been picked clean to the bone. Even if there was something mineable there, the social problem of dealing with these destitute artisans would have been formidable.

The deprived miners were skinny and sunbaked. Hardly any clothes. Their black skin caked with white powder from the crushed quartzite. I'd hate to think what their lungs were like. The only tools they had were machetes and hammers. Some didn't even have hammers, they just used big rocks to pound the little rocks. When I thought of how desperately poor these people were, I remembered that the watchmen still had their food, tools and gold. I expected them to come after us any minute.

The geologist explained that most of the artisanal miners came from the neighbouring countries of Burkina Faso and Niger to the north. During the dry season, when there was no farming work at home, any money they could make mining was better than sitting, waiting for the next rainy season. So, they migrated here and worked their pits in hopes of some meager reward. He complained bitterly because the police didn't help keep them away. I didn't care. All I could think of was getting back to our vehicle and getting the hell away from there.

We made our way down the hill and back across the river. A sense of relief swept over me as we arrived back at the office area. The confiscated tools were taken to a warehouse that was empty except for one corner where dozens of these hand carved wooden gold pans and various other simple tools were piled. I didn't see, but I surmised, that the watchmen got the food, and the geologist took home the gold concentrate.

I could end the story here by saying that I made it back to Canada unscathed and never returned to Benin again but please indulge me as I feel it is important to include one more incident.

We got into the Land Cruiser and drove to a small hotel near the town of Perma to have dinner and spend the night. The first order of business was to take a badly needed shower. Next, I opened my suitcase to find some clean clothes and was surprised to see how hot they were after sitting in the locked car for the afternoon. And I was happy to discover that amongst my clothes were two small airline bottles of gin that I had tucked in for a situation such as this. There was no ice or mix, so I poured the hot gin into the water glass from the bathroom and took a drink.

I was expecting the worst but to my surprise, it was wonderful! The heat must have activated the alcohol because it immediately started calming my frayed nerves.

A wise person once said that you learn more from your failures than from your successes. And because my trip to Benin was clearly a failure in almost all respects, I should have learned a lot.

But I didn't.

The first lesson should have been to be more skeptical about properties that sound too good to be true. But, once a dreamer, always a dreamer.

The second lesson should have been that, if you discover that the person trying to sell you something is lying, walk away. Only that one didn't take either because there are so many unscrupulous people in the business, its best to assume they are all liars and check each fact yourself.

Perhaps the only thing I did take away from the whole horrendous ordeal, was that hot gin, as terrible as it may sound, is still a damn sight better than no gin at all.

Spirits on the Hill, *by Peter Bojtos*

August 1972, fresh out of university, I arrived at an iron ore mine in Sierra Leone. Yes, I thought I knew everything but in reality, all I could do was mapping and identifying rocks along with a knowledge of geological processes and fossil identification.

Nobody had taught me about drill rigs, core logging, how to do ore reserve calculations and how to carry out exploration. But the chief geologist at the mine was a good teacher and soon I was cranking out ore reserve calculations on a manual Facit calculator. Remember those calculating machines? Three turns of the handle forward and you've multiplied by three, five turns backwards and you've divided by five. At least it was an improvement from a slide rule. When I got an electrically operated Facit a year later I thought I had died and gone to heaven. But I digress.

Mining of a massive chunk of direct shipping haematitic iron ore had originally started as a hill reduction but, by the time I arrived, had become an open pit extracting primary specularite haematite. In its original state, pre-1930's, the hill had acted as a massive lightning conductor during the monsoon storms and Africans were wary of going up there for fear of disturbing the evil spirits.

Then along came a British geologist who told the local Sierra Leonians that he was going to go up the hill and trap the evil spirits. So, on a stormy day he trekked up the hill to find the spirits while the locals waited to see what would happen. After a while he returned holding a jam jar and told the people that he had captured the spirits, put them into this jar and he was now going to take it back to England and they'll be no longer troubled by the evil spirits.

This appeased everybody and so mining started with all the relieved locals happily working on the hill. The hill was named Masaboin and the mine was called Marampa. This mine along with the diamond mine at Yengema gave the country its unofficial motto of "Land of Iron and Diamonds" that appeared on all its postage stamps in the 1960's and 70's.

Fast forward to 1972 and my arrival. Several ridges had been located close by Masaboin Hill and one of them, Ghafal Hill, was found to contain another iron ore deposit. A lot of the exploration work had been carried out a few years earlier by a geologist called Barry Padgett and I was given all his notebooks and told to follow up on a lot of his work. So off I went, trudging through the jungle for the next few months with two International Harvester BTD6 bulldozers each with a large auger drill mounted on the back, my "small" work crew of about 50 locals, and Padgett's notebooks. Among my workers was a hunched up old man, both a leader of the work force and my tea maker, who was a highly respected elder called Bokari Kamara and as a young man had witnessed the removal of the evil spirits.

Years later I met Barry Padgett at some convention or another. I seem to remember that he was working for Watts Griffis and McQuat in Saudi Arabia at the time as the firm had a contract to provide geological advice to the Saudis.

Anyway, we were swapping Marampa stories and he asked me if I had located any more economically viable deposits. I told him I had spent a long time looking and I did have his notebooks but only went to those areas that might still have promise and ignored the ridges where he had drilled and made the notation "SFA" on his drill hole notes and were therefore condemned.

"YOU IDIOT" he shouted, "SFA stands for "Sent for Assay". To this day I feel foolish when I think about it and have always wanted to build a mine and name it the Sweet Fanny Adams mine.

Another story about the mine, sometime later, in 1974 I think, I was having lunch back in my quarters when the mine whistle started blowing nine blasts, the emergency signal, a loud, shrill sound that could be heard for miles around. I could see smoke rising from the 10,000 tpd mill building.

It was maintenance day at the mill, and someone had accidentally ignited the rubber lining of the Humphrey spirals with his acetylene torch. As part of the maintenance the water tanks above the mill had been emptied earlier on so there was no water to feed through the mill by gravity and all the pumps at the bottom had been disabled.

As we all stood there wondering what to do, we were consoled by the fact that it was a steel building so there was nothing to burn other than the rubber. Then we watched the flames lick up the steel beams till they reached the roof beams. These were covered in iron ore dust which got hotter and hotter and then ignited and the flames started to crawl across the whole massive roof. The whole place was going to melt down to a pile of slag and there was nothing we could do about it.

And then the reinforcements arrived. I swear that all 3,000 of our workers, and then some, descended on the place from the surrounding villages and without any prompting they formed a long line from the tailings pond to the mill. They scooped up tailings in their hard hats and passed each hat along the chain till they could throw it on the fire to smother it. Believe it or not, they extinguished the fire in about an hour. Meanwhile, the pumps at the base of the mill were put back into service and that eventually cooled the place down.

The building's structure remained intact and the place was repaired over the next few months. But the amazing thing was that it only took about an hour for the workers to manually move the thousands of tons of tailings back up to the mill that had taken years to process out to the pond and then took months to get back down to the pond again afterwards during the clean-up. The site of those thousands of generally slow-moving Africans being driven by adrenaline was incredible.

YANKEE TALES

Texas Gulf and White Pine, *by Dave Rogers*

I came up with the White Pine Extension as a stratigraphic wildcat project for Texas Gulf. I had arranged for a tour of the underground workings at White Pine mine in northern Michigan earlier in the year without my Texas Gulf identity to get a feel for the ore bed settings and stratigraphy. In the fall of the year, we had signed an option with a large landowner and started a deep drill hole in the Upper Peninsula.

Two White Pine geologists who pretended to be partridge hunting were hanging around the Texas Gulf drill rig area. I came out of the bush with my shotgun. They asked if I had any luck. I replied that earlier I had taken a couple of sound shots but did not seem to hit anything. They paled and shortly after drove off down the road.

The White Pine chief geologist had a small plane, and he was circling the rig counting the drill rods. I stepped out onto the platform and pointed my gun at him and pretended to fire. He did not waste time skedaddling. About two years later I ran into him at the PDAC and asked him if that was his little red plane circling the drill rig. He paled and said yes. I smiled and said that was me pretending to shoot at you. We settled on a beer.

The frustrating part of this story is that Walter Holyk made me shut the drill down at about 2,800 ft which was about ~400 ft. shy of the NonSuch Shale, the host sedimentary unit for the copper deposits. I suppose I should find a financial partner to go in and finish this hole for better or worse. If anyone is interested in a 'wildcat' copper play give me a call at 613-732-8065.

Tailings, Tomatoes, and a Mining Legend, *by Peter Bojtos*

I arrived in Mineral, Virginia, in 1975 to work on a base-metal development project being run by Callahan Mining Corp with New Jersey Zinc Corp being our Joint-Venture partner. The first thing that hit me was the smell of sulphur in the air, a legacy from the Arminius Mine from the days when they mined pyrite there and roasted it to produce all the sulphur for the Confederacy during the Civil War. The Confederates imported saltpetre from Chile and mixed it with the sulphur to produce gunpowder.

On an aside note, lead was mined at the Austinville Mine in southwest Virginia and that provided all the lead both for the Revolutionary War and for the Confederacy in the Civil War. The produced lead was melted and poured off the top of nearby Natural Bridge, drop by drop, into the creek 215 feet below which formed musket balls on hitting the cold water.

Natural Bridge is also the site of the first recorded vandalism in the USA where the first surveyor in the area carved his initials in the limestone face of the arch. The initials "GW" can still be seen, left by the surveyor George Washington. The Austinville mine was the longest running metal mine in the USA before it shut down in 1979. It was named after one of its early owners, Moses Austin, whose son ran off and founded Texas. But again, I digress.

In Virginia, my boss, the mine manager, was a Canadian by the name of Jack Hambleton. Jack was the last operator at the Madsen mine in Red Lake and he always showed me an innocuous looking pyritic rock from the bottom level of Madsen that he said assayed well over 1 oz. gold per ton. I can't remember what the actual grade was, but it was a big number considering I had just come from Africa where we assayed in pennyweights.

We were using two ST2 scoop trams that we had purchased from the closed down Britannia Mine in B.C. and we were driving a decline into the Cofer Zn-Pb-Cu orebody. Easter weekend 1976 the portal timbers holding up the saprolite gave way and blocked the entrance with three miners underground at the face.

It was a very slow news day, and we were only about 60 miles south of Washington D.C. and before we knew it every single TV Network was camped out on our doorstep. "Three miners trapped," was Walter Cronkite's lead story that evening. You should have seen the disappointment on the reporters' faces a few hours later when we'd finished digging out the portal and the miners walked out who by-the-way could have climbed out up the ladder in the fresh air raise.

I'll never forget Jack Hambleton telling me that someone had come up with a new method of treating gold ores. They would take the broken ore and lay it on the ground and spray cyanide solution on it which supposedly would then suck the gold out of the rock. A dairy farmer somewhere in the eastern US, in the Carolinas I think, had come up with the idea but it didn't work well. Anyway, his dairy farm went bust and we heard no more. Jack suggested if he went broke with a dairy farm it's probably because he must have bought a herd of bulls and that accounted for his thinking that hosing down a rock pile in order to flush out the gold would work.

A year or two later talk started to reach a crescendo of news that Gene McClellan at the United States Bureau of Mines in Reno was working on heap leaching. I wish I hadn't have listened to Jack.

I had two other geo-compadres from Canada during 1976. Norm Duke, now Professor at the University of Western Ontario, was completing his Ph. D on our orebodies and his academic boss, Prof. Bob Hodder, spent three months of his sabbatical from UWO with me. I learnt more about core logging from Bob in those three months than over the rest of my career.

And then one day I was told that the Chairman of Callahan Mining would be making a visit. I tidied up my office trailer, had maps and cross-sections pinned up on the walls and I waited for the entourage of executives. At one point, following a short but heavy rainstorm, I looked out of the window and saw a Cadillac bogged down in wet, Virginian, saprolitic, greasy, red mud on the mine access road.

A little old guy in Bermuda shorts but covered in mud and his tiny lady companion were trying to walk and slither towards my trailer. I went out to help and the guy extended his hand and said, "Hello, I'm Joe Hirshorn", the legendary mining promoter from New York. Not what I had expected, but what a fun guy he turned out to be.

Meanwhile his wife was berating him non-stop and telling

me that he was too cheap to fly over to England to visit his old pal J.P. Getty on his deathbed. He never did visit him, and Getty died the following week. I know he didn't visit Getty because I asked his wife a few months later when I was at a Callahan meeting at the Hirshorn house in Greenwich, Connecticut.

What a house! It was chock-a-block full of modern paintings, with Picassos and also Rodin sculptures. Years later I saw them all again in the Smithsonian's Hirshorn Museum of Modern Art on the National Mall in Washington D.C. following Hirshorn's bequest to the Nation.

Meanwhile back at the mine we had started doing reclamation work on the sulphurous Arminius tailings. Following successful growth tests, the EPA recommended that we import treated sewage sludge and till it into the tailings as a growth medium which we did. The following year the entire tailings area was covered in a bumper crop of tomatoes since tomato seeds can apparently survive the journey through the digestive system of humans and all the way through the sewage plant. Everybody in Mineral, VA came to pick tomatoes. I can attest to the fact that they were sweet and juicy. Sometime later the EPA told us to stop people from picking the tomatoes because they had found out that Monsanto had discharged from one of their PCB plants into that sewage plant. In 1999 I had a chance to visit the area again and I was on the lookout for people, especially those in their early twenties, to see if they had three arms or eleven fingers or whatever. I didn't see any.

Howard and the Rattlesnakes, *by Dave Rogers*

Years ago, I can't remember when, I took Howard Stockford down to Arizona to examine our Blue Bell and DeSoto VMS deposits. Howard was with Jim Gill and Aur Resources and they were riding high on their northwestern Quebec VMS discovery. We decided to enter a 600 ft. adit on the north side of the DeSoto.

We had hard hats, lights and our hammers. I went first and cautioned about possible rattlesnakes. The adit was dry, dusty and small. About 6ft x 6ft but dry and in good shape. We made it into the end and made our examination.

About halfway back out, again I was leading and there was a 4 ft. rattler in the middle of the drift. We did not have a pole or two by four —nothing but our hammers. Finally, the snake moved to one side of the adit and I noted that it was stretched out full length. So, we decided that if it was not coiled it could not strike at us as we went by. Of course, I went first and made it safely. The snake did not move. Then Howard followed safely after we moved on out about 20 ft., we congratulated each other on passing the snake.

But about another 50 ft. down the adit there was another 4 ft. rattler. We proceeded the same way we had with the first rattler and made it by safely. When we got back out in the sunshine, we looked at each other and wondered out loud how we managed to walk by two rattlesnakes on the way into the adit in the first place. They must have been coiled up under the dust at the side of the adit and in some form of comatose mode. After we passed, they woke up and moved a bit. Neither Howard nor I were or are fans of rattlesnakes.

DOWN IN SOUTH AMERICA

Boulder Rolling Episode, *by Dave Rogers*

Shortly after getting into the field in Bolivia in 1962, and mapping in several of the mining areas, I realized that the tops of the hills held a large number of boulders. Now boulder rolling was a common pastime for geologists and prospectors in Canada. Well for me at least.

So, I spotted a large, round six ft. boulder perched on a hillside. It would only take about 20 minutes of digging and preparation to get it rolling. I carefully studied the slope looking for any signs of humans, alpaca herds or huts and saw nothing. So, I dug out the balance rock and gave the boulder a heave to start it on its way.

It looked like it would roll close to one kilometer. Holy crap, as soon as it started down the slope, I saw animals running, shepherds and a couple of huts came into focus. I wasted no time reversing down my side of the mountain and into my Land Rover and got the heck out of the area. I never did go back to finish mapping that area and I have no idea what chaos I had caused.

An Example of Extreme Adrenaline, *by Dave Rogers*

Chacaltaya, outside of La Paz, Bolivia was the highest lift-served ski area in the world in 1962. The road up the mountainside was a complete terror trip in the early days. The ski lift was an old slusher cable from one of the mines which was mounted on old truck tire rims and ran up and back down on the left side of the ski area.

The ski slope was on a mountain glacier. The summit was at 17,785 ft. We were skiing literally on top of the world. The views were incredible. In those days only a hardy five to 15 skiers would make the trip up the mountain to ski. I was back in Bolivia briefly in 1994 and the 18,000-year-old glacier had melted enough that skiing was no more.

Chacaltaya Ski Resort

The ski lift cable continuously twisted on itself as it ran up and down the mountain. We had a short rope with a quick release on a belt around our waist. The other end had a bent hook which you flipped over the cable and you had to keep about 3-4 ft away from the twisting cable as it moved along. I was distracted by something and suddenly realized my rope was twisting into the cable and me with it. I could not release it. One of the tire rims was coming up. Everyone was shouting to the cable operator to stop the ski lift. I was terrified and visualized being rotated into the cable and the tire rim and being literally torn in half. I was wearing a nylon pullover (latest rage 1962) which was being twisted in. I was hollering help—stop the lift. In a super adrenaline surge of strength fed by terror I actually ripped the jacket open and was able to fall out of it just as I reached the wheel. At the same time the lift operator had seen what was happening and he stopped the lift.

I carried a square of the nylon jacket with me for years inviting any strong person to see if he could tear it. I could not and neither did anyone else. It was pure adrenaline that tore it on the hill.

In the winter of 1963, we had a racing contest to see who would make the Bolivian National Ski Team and represent Bolivia at the Summer Olympics in Chile 1964. Myself and two Bolivian-German mining engineers who had studied in the States comprised the National Team. I actually left Bolivia for a contract in Chile the end of 1963 so had to forfeit the Bolivian Team. We were very good skiers, but not of Olympic caliber.

The Leper Colony and Beer Episode, *by Dave Rogers*

A group of us geologists booked a hotel resort in the tropical slopes on the east side of the Andes Mountains in Bolivia for a week's holiday at a reasonable altitude of about 6,000 ft. We had been working in the Andes mining areas located at the 12,000 to 15,000 ft altitude.

There was not a lot of tourism in Bolivia in those days and hotels only had minimum supplies. Anyhow about midnight our first day that hotel had run out of beer, wine and whiskey. One of the hotel waiters said if we drove down a back road for about 10 km, we would see white flags at the side of the road.

This was supposed to mean that they had Chicha, Bolivian beer, for sale. Well, we were somewhat pissed up and off we went. We saw a large white flag at a road entrance and drove roaring in, tooting our horn and expecting to find beer for sale.

Whoa...bad move as we drove into a clearing, we saw people hobbling off into the jungle. We hollered out "Any Chicha for sale?" One person who could not move replied, "No Chicha".

This was a leper colony. Everyone stopped breathing and we sobered up quickly. I quickly collected a pile of Bolivian money, got out and placed it on the ground then walked back to the Land Rover and we tore out of there.

Very embarrassed and sobered up. Chicha is an ancient Peruvian-Bolivian beer brewed with corn that the women chew up and spit out. Spit happens, and when it does you brew.

Underground in Bolivia, *by Dave Rogers*

I was assigned to carry out a mapping job in an operating tin-silver-base metal mine. The mine captain decided that he would walk the Gringo geologist up through the workings from the lower-level access to the top instead of driving up to the top on the mountain and working our way down. High altitude makes a difference. We suit up and he gives me a carbide lamp to set up and light. I had never seen one before and had no clue how they worked. He showed me how. On the 3 level up at a tunnel intersection he asked me to wait while he went to check out something nearby. I was feeling quite alone.

My carbide lamp started to sputter, and I did not understand how to adjust it. It died. I am in the bowels of a mountain—pitch black—and not really sure the miner was going to come back a get me. About half an hour later he came back. Another lesson in how to manage a carbide lamp and then we continued climbing up to the upper workings. He would point out the various types of workings and the ore veins etc. No map for reference. About three hours later we are at the top of the mountain and the vein system.

At least we got a drive back down in a truck. After a week I had become quite proficient and was quickly putting a composite map together of the geology and vein deposits. I was puzzled at first at their grade calculations in the stoping areas. There was no reconciliation whatsoever. Then I got the person who was doing the ore calculations to show me how he did it. Problem solved when I noted that in a column of grade intervals any blanks or low grade were discarded, and he simply added up the ore grade samples to calculate their average grade. Neat ore reserve eh!

One Fiesta Weekend, *by Dave Rogers*

$\mathbf{A}$ three-day holiday weekend came up and I did not feel like driving five hours back to Oruro, Bolivia, so I requested permission to stay in the mine site. The Indian workers and families had their private ceremonies planned but gave me permission to stay.

Then they invited me to attend the opening night festivities. Everyone was drinking Chicha beer. It was all very colourful with the ladies all dressed up in their voluminous petticoats and dresses topped off with their traditional black bowler hats. The babies and young were attached to the saddles of the decorated Burros and paraded around.

All afternoon a huge kettle of food was simmering on a fire. God knows what went into it. Dinner time and I was seated at the head table. Two giggling ladies took a large bowl and proceeded to fill it from the kettle. They giggled some more adding something else to the plate then they presented it to me to start off the meal. Right on top was a gleaming eyeball from a sheep or goat or something. My stomach rumbled and I said to myself, Rogers you have to eat it.

I pretended it was just a big oyster on the shell and spooned it with a flourish into my mouth and immediately swallowed it whole. I managed to keep smiling and did not immediately barf it back up. They started clapping and I stood up and took a bow. The party went on for three days and nights. I stayed in my room and worked on maps and my report.

One of the men's games was to put a 14" fuse in a ¼ stick of dynamite. Four to six men stand in a circle. One lights the fuse, and they toss it back and forth until the last guy decides it's time to explode and throws it over his shoulder and away. Yes, there were several maimed miners in the area.

A Resistivity Survey in Bolivia Goes to the Dogs, *by Dave Rogers*

I had borrowed a portable resistivity unit from a U.N. Geophysical Crew and was running lines to test for possible extensions of the ore veins out under the talus slope and overlying recent sediments. The locals were in audience and several of their dogs were sniffing and pushing over my pots. I re-set the pots firmly in the soil and then quickly back to the unit. I turned the unit on full power setting and waited. Sure enough, one dog decides to lift his leg and piss on a pot. I switched on the power and the dog, yelping, leaped about 5 ft. in the air. My audience sounded their applause. I stood up and took a bow. The dogs took off and I was able to continue un-interrupted with my survey.

The All-Most Canoe Trip, *by Dave Rogers*

The All-Most canoe trip into the headwaters of the Amazon River from Bolivia. This was 1962 and the Amazon and its headwaters were completely wild and uncivilized.

I had met a group of young sons of the wealthier Bolivians in a social club in Cochabamba. They told me of their upcoming 10-day canoe trip down into the upper reaches of the Amazon River system. They invited me to join them.

I arranged for time off and was looking forward to the adventure. Two days before we were to leave, the leader asked me what firearms and ammo I was bringing. I said I was not planning on bringing any. Did we need them?

He then told me it was tradition from their grandfathers and fathers to make this trip every few years. One of the highlights was hunting a rare group of Indians they called the 'pig people.' These Indians ran around on all fours most of time.

I clarified that they actually shot to kill these natives. I told him I would get a rifle and ammo. Ya right! I wired my boss in La Paz and asked him to send me a telex demanding my return immediately to La Paz for an important assignment.

He did, and I gave it to the trip leader and expressed my regrets that I could not accompany them and wished them luck. I never saw them again to find out how the trip went before I left Bolivia for Chile.

From Bolivia to Chile, *by Dave Rogers*

I took a holiday from Bolivia to the ski resort of Portillo in Chile. There I met three American mine managers on a ski holiday from Peru and Chile. My one-year contract in Bolivia was ending. A few discussions in the bar and I was hired with a 40% increase in pay over Bolivia with 95% tax free salary to come to Chile for Compania Minera Santa Fe. They were mainly direct shipping high grade iron ore to Japan. I started a copper exploration program in the north.

I was assigned as District Geologist, Antofagasta for the multi-mining operations in Northern Chile. The current District Mining Manager was about to be dismissed for various reasons. It was a dicey first month. Then he was gone, and I was District Geology and Area Manager.

More paperwork than I wanted. All in Spanish which I was becoming reasonably fluent in. My male secretary would put the various papers for signing on my desk and give me a verbal explanation in Spanish. Some I signed off on readily. Others I needed to delve into a bit more. The paperwork fell behind and I was more interested in the geology of the small mines we had in production and mapping out the potential small mines for exploitation. These were all small high grade, direct shipping iron deposits. Some we mined ourselves, but many were exploited by the local miners, trucked and sold to our shipping port at Chanaral.

I was planning to go up to El Laco Iron project in a weeks' time. My secretary came in with a smile on his face and told me if I did not sign the Police Order on my desk today then forget about going to Laco. The men are very mad at you. Please explain I said.

You did not sign lasts month's "Permisso de Putas." Here sign this month's now. The Chilean law allowed for professional prostitutes to visit remote work areas to service the men once a month. An accepted practice which I had not understood and had ignored. I immediately signed the papers and he filed them with the Police.

So, the next week I took my wife up to Laco with me. We were literally on top of the Andes Mountains and it was quite a trip. On the third day there she asked me about the two ladies who seemed to stay in one workman's cabino and then move to the next each day. So, I explained to her how the system works. She asked if this applied to the Bosses cabino as well and I smiled as I said no. Strictly for the workers.

In 1965 I had a visit in Laco from Prof. Howell Williams and well-known British volcanologist whom I had met a few years before in Sudbury where he was studying the Grenville Front for the Ontario Department of Mines. He said to me you know I was talking with Charles Park Jr., author of the just published, "Ore Deposits" and professor at Stanford University a few weeks ago. He told me that these Laco iron deposits were definitely "replacement deposits".

About six hours later after I had toured Howell over the continuous extrusive flows of iron ore and all the related volcanic flow features, he smiled at me and said David I can't wait to tell Charlie Park "you are so full of shit".

I laughed and said all the American geologists I had run into adamantly claimed the replacement theory as well. I just tell them to get out in the field and open their eyes and their brains and learn something new and real in the world of field geology.

While mapping these deposits and surrounding geology in 1964-65 I would look out over the iron oxide flows and interspersed thermal spring deposits some of which are still active in the lower slopes. I would get a surreal impression that the iron oxide flows had erupted within the past few months. Eerie. Probably just high-altitude effects. When I concluded my contract with the company, they would not give me permission to publish a paper in Economic Geology. Being a bit pissed at that I then added a second conclusion to my final report on Laco for the company.

I strongly recommended once they were in production that they run a couple of seismic lines across the main deposit for about 2km south to identify any structural zones. Then instruct the mining department to drill and set a very large blast over this structure. They should be prepared for a renewal of high-grade iron ore extruding up and onto the surface. And, that if they were swift enough, they could have installed a direct reduction iron plant to process the material into a finished product for sale.

About one year later I heard that my added note had

caused much laughter by many people and completely pissed off at me by others in both the Santiago and New York head offices. C'est La Vie.

Blown off the Mountain in Chile, *by Dave Rogers*

It was 1964 and Induced Polarization surveying was becoming popular and the thing to do for porphyry copper and other disseminated mineral deposits. I met Peer Norgaard who was pioneering I.P. in Chile. Peer later became President of Geoterrex Surveys based in Ottawa and we have been best friends ever since. We were surveying the Santo Domingo 'Mantos' type Cu-Ag. deposits.

We had extended the grid up a high, steep hill area and Peer had stepped up the electrical charge to maximum to get results. A man called Olivares was the straw boss of the field assistants who laid out the electrodes. Orders were all hands off the electrode contacts before Peer could hit the power switch. Olivares gave the all-clear signal. Peer hit the power and we watched, as in a silent movie as Olivares was hurled up in the air and down the hillside. A silent movie. He survived – lesson learned. I drilled off two small high-grade Cu-Ag deposits which were subsequently mined.

Santo Domingo Shaft and the Quake, *by Dave Rogers*

I was mapping in the western part of the property. Our property records were sketchy. I came across a shaft opening which was well timbered and looked to be fairly deep. I was alone and stupidly decided to work my way down the shaft if it was solid. I left a note of where I had gone in my truck. The timbering was first class and in perfect shape. I climbed down about 400ft to the bottom. All was well so I started to reconnaissance map the drift off the shaft. Eureka!

The weathering oxidization process had clearly outlined a very pervasive and high-grade copper-silver sheeted fracture system cutting the volcanic flows over about a 45-foot width. This provided an extra dimension to the normal flow top and interflow mineralization. I was ecstatic and I had just observed the nature and extent of the mineralization in this type of "mantos" flow top volcanics. The sheeted vein system measured 40 feet in width and about 500 feet in length of ~4.5%Cu + 5 oz. Ag/tonne = Excellent ore grade in Chile in 1965.

My euphoria crashed when a very strong earthquake hit, and I was 400 feet underground. I quickly moved back to the base of the shaft. Some fine rock was trickling down but the lower-level timbers were in good shape. I realized that often it was the aftershocks that triggered collapse. So, I gathered my courage and moved up the ladders level to level as fast as I could climb until I burst out onto the surface. I had made it. What a relief and realized how stupid I had been to go down in the first place. Hey, I solved the mantos geology-ore geometry and would be able to apply it when drilling of and modelling the other 2 deposits indicated by the I.P. survey.

A Hoax and One Million Dollar Scam, *by Dave Rogers*

In November of 1965 two Armenian promotors approached the owners of Santa Fe Mining. The owners were 3 Hungarian Jews who had come to Chile after WWII and started in the mining and purchasing of high-grade iron ores which they shipped, at a nice profit to Japan and Europe. The Armenians claimed to have an old trunk full of geology and exploration targets written up by a prominent German Mining Engineer before WWI.

It was all hush-hush, and they provided a couple of copies of supposed iron ore deposits in southern Chile. All of the names, places and identities were blacked out. The owners only showed this material to the Chief Geologist and asked him to have a read through the files and then do a quick field check on one large deposit reported as east of Puerto Mont. He asked if I could join him in this evaluation. The bosses said no just you. The majority of the supposedly, direct shipping iron and copper ore deposits were located on islands in the offshore area southwest of Punta Arenas at the bottom tip of Chile. The company then paid the Armenians a US$100,000 (approx. 1 million dollars today) for the full, uncensored mining reports. With a closing balance of US$900,000 due in three months' time.

The chief geologist and I were assigned to check out the validity of the reports. In January 1966, we rented a 75 ft. long schooner, just built, by the Alverez brothers out of Puerto Natales in the Chilean Patagonia for the 2.5-month voyage chasing down this hoax. The Patagonia in Southern Chile was a wild, and inaccessible area in the 1960's.

Unfortunately, the Armenian connection who sold Santa Fe this project also had some deal/connection with another foreign company. When we sailed out of Puerto Natales on the second day, we noted that we were being followed. Therefore, instead of being on our own and able to examine the various islands with reported mineral deposits we had to stake them first so that the other group could not jump our efforts. This turned out to be very frustrating because none of the reported rich copper, gold and iron deposits supposedly discovered and described by the German Mining Engineer before the First World War existed in fact. Totally bogus. We saw some nice geology and had an interesting two months sailing the Chilean Archipelago but to no avail regarding ore deposits.

Sea Urchins & Facing Death in Southern Chile, *by Dave Rogers*

Some Sea Urchins are edible, and I had eaten them in restaurants in Chile. I was in a dory well up a fiord accompanied by a local Chilean guide and an Indian worker. We were having a snack of the edible portion of some sea urchins. Some can contain allergic portions. Suddenly I felt a flush in my body, throat and head. I spit out what was in my mouth and rinsed with fresh water. Then I sat absolutely still as I felt my whole throat swell and close shut. I was able to breathe through my nose quietly. I was terrified. I thought this is the end.

I had left my wife, Jule with two baby girls, the latest only three weeks old, back in Ottawa living with her mother while I went off on this southern Chile exploration escapade. Was I going to suffocate to death in a dory or live? My life passed before my eyes. I fought the mental effects in order to stay calm. Sit it out and hope. Praying was not going to help the likes of me. I had sinus problems from an early age and hardly ever was able to breathe through my nose. However, when I had taken a one-year contract in Bolivia the year before it was only a few months living and working in the higher altitude that I realized my sinus problems had basically gone away and I was regularly breathing through my nose.

I sat frozen for about one hour still breathing through my nose. Then very slowly I felt my neck and throat muscles starting to relax and within about 30 minutes I was breathing normally through both my throat and nose. I had survived.

The Tornado Effect on a Lake, *by Dave Rogers*

April 1966, I was examining a purported a high-grade porphyry copper prospect as recorded by a German mining engineer. It was located on the southeast shore of a very large lake (can't remember the name of it.) I had traversed back and forth over the whole rugged area for a whole day. There was no semblance of a porphyry copper in the area.

Taking a break and enjoying the rugged Patagonia vista including the northeast end of a large lake. I noted a storm blowing in quickly. I had no time to get back to my taxi driver guide location. The wind was already blowing sand grains and trash. I scanned the hillside and spotted a crevice part way up the slope. I quickly climbed up and into it. Just big enough for me to fit and held my extra jacket over the opening. Now small stones and cobbles were being thrown about by the wind and the area around me was literally being sand blasted. Then a huge tornado like cloud swept in over-the-top end of this large lake. It literally picked up the top 3 or 4 ft. of the lake water and hurled it down the lake. No boat or canoe would have survived the fury. About 10 minutes later it was all over.

Flash forward to the '80's or '90's and I heard a report that a Cominco field crew were working down in that same general area. A four-man crew were living on a small but sturdy boat and surveying on the same lake I believe. The party chief was seasick and lying in his bunk below deck. The others were on deck with life jackets on. They reported that a sudden tornado like storm had come quickly down the lake and it turtled the boat. The crew floated free and made it to shore. But the party chief went to the bottom with the boat.

Another firsthand lesson in why you never underestimate nor ignore Mother Nature and her warnings. After all, most all of the great fossil collections found today are the result of storms or other calamities of and by Mother Nature.

My Infamous Landlocked Salmon Dinner, *by Dave Rogers*

As mentioned, I had checked into a very up-scale tourist hotel which catered to the very rich in this Patagonia Wilderness. Can't remember the name or place specifically. However, I had to find transportation to the three locations described in the Germans report to see if anything of either interest or reality actually existed. After a few questions around town, I located a taxi driver with a four-wheel-drive vehicle and a complete outfit for his clients to enjoy fly fishing. I hired him for the week on the spot. We laid out my objectives on his map. Then he told me about the various fly-fishing locations in the same general area.

So, we laid out the days ahead so that I could enjoy some terrific fly fishing for speckled and brown trout and a location he said held spectacular land locked salmon. It should be noted that the American mining men who flooded into the Andes of Chile and Peru in search of and opening up of rich silver and copper mines back in the 1930's and '40's quickly cottoned on to the beautiful streams, some lakes and rivers. They managed to transplant trout and land locked salmon into most of the waterways. They also did a fair bit in the Patagonia area in the south end of Chile and neighbouring Argentina. I was about to experience some of the fruits of their labour.

My last day out examining barren rocks was finished and my guide drove us to the location for the salmon-trout. We drove over a rise and before me was about a 35-acre lake. The surface was green. Completely covered with green algae. My guide smiled and said follow me. We had on chest waders. He gave me a good spinning rod with a single 4" silver spoon attached. Follow my footsteps exactly he said. We walked out through the green algae up to our waist. He slowed, looked left and right and moved about 8 ft. to the left.

He indicated a line of a steep drop off which we were standing beside which was covered by the algae mat. Do not walk forward. He handed me the spinning rod with the silver spoon and directed me to start on the left and cast and reel in slowly and repeat until I had a bite, or I reached the right-hand side. I cast from left to right and back again varying my retrieve somewhat. I caught and released a number of nice, speckled trout and a couple of small land locked salmon. Then I caught two magnificent 3 lb. salmon trout which we kept. One for him and one for me. He cleaned them and wrapped them in damp moss. What an experience.

It was midnight before we got back to the hotel and the kitchen was closed but the door was open. I put the salmon on a plate in a refrigerator and attached a note to the chef telling him what I wanted and would speak with him at breakfast time.

The hotel dining room main seating area was a spectacular semi-circle overlooking a smaller three table circular dining area below. All views were out over the ocean. After breakfast I spoke with the Chef and Maitre'd and explained what I had in mind. They loved it and of course embellished the whole scene. The hotel was not allowed to serve land locked salmon as no commercial fishing of it was allowed. I had mentioned that I was having no lunch and that I would like to eat the whole fish....one half at a time. He set me up at the central table on the lower level.

I then went into a local town and found a clothing store. I purchased a snowy white fancy shirt with cuffs a large collar and fitted shoulders with a red cravat for the open neck. Plus, a pair of jet-black pants. I looked quite dashing in my opinion. All week the guests had been less than friendly towards the gringo geologist (me) for what reason I did not know. Anyhow on my final evening meal in the hotel with the help of the Chef and the Maître'd I was going to do it my way.

When I came into the dining area the upper area was filled. Only one table was set below with one seating and the head waiter seated me there. I faced out over the ocean view. It was spectacular. First, I was served a small shrimp salad. Then the head waiter and his assistant wheeled in a serving table. The oven baked salmon was covered. The vegetables were tiny potatoes, and asparagus. With a flourish and pizazz, the waiter removed the cover and proceeded to peel the top half of the salmon whole onto my plate then added the vegetables and a small dish of quartered fresh lemon. There was much discussion going on in the upper level.

I kept my eyes on my plate and out front to the ocean. Of course, a half bottle of Unduraga White was consumed with the first half. When I had finished the two waiters came in and cleared the table and re-set it with a flourish. Then they wheeled out the remaining half salmon and fresh vegetables. This time small green peas and pan-fried potatoes. Plus of course a new ½ bottle of Unduraga White. The upper levels got a bit noisier. I completely ignored them and polished off the second serving. Again, the table was cleared, and they brought me a small dish of Flan Flambé for dessert.

When I finished my meal, I stood up and facing the upper level I gave a small bow. Remember this was the era of the "Ugly American". I turned and walked out the front and down to the beach area for a short walk. Then back to the hotel and bed. I left early before breakfast to catch a plane back to Puerto Mont and then to Santiago where I handed in my reports. Said my goodbyes to my friends in the office and took off to the airport and flights back to Miami and Toronto.

Adventures South of the Equator, Ecuador 1965-68, *by* *Ian Thompson*

In 1965, for English-speaking geologists anyway, the sum total of known geology of Ecuador was represented on a single legal-size sheet; a brief overview paper by an unknown American geologist, possibly the late W.C. Stoll. The Geological Survey of Ecuador had, I am told, a single geologist. And, while Ecuador was normally a constitutional government, it was then under Military Dictatorship [1963-1965], making importation of foreign goods very difficult and travel within the country challenging.

Those were the conditions that greeted us when Duncan R. Derry Ltd., with the assistance of German mining engineer Bill Hesse, convinced the client, Triangle Conduit & Cable of New Brunswick, New Jersey (the world's largest manufacturer of jukeboxes) to finance exploration of the Obras Concession in Ecuador for porphyry Cu- Mo -Au deposits. Despite these odds, by the time we completed work on the project, we managed to bring in a full working geochemical lab from Ottawa and had assembled a remuda of 70 highly flatulent mules for transportation and cartage.

Old Bill Hesse, the German mining engineer, returned to Duncan Derry in Oct 1964, following our escapades at Blow River, YT earlier that year. He had acquired an option on a granted Ecuadorian Exploration Concession in the Cordillera Occidental named OBRAS [Obras Civilises y Mechanizada S.A.]. for the Ecuadorian construction /contracting company.

Located in Cotopaxi Province, west of the provincial capital, Latacunga, and 50 miles south of Quito in Central Ecuador, the 1,000 sq. mile concession covered a mixed terrain of grassland, moderately arable farming territory, and jungle. The extensive property began in the high Paramo (grasslands) at about 10,000 ft. ASL in the north, descending down the east flank of the Andes into jungle at about 1,200 ft. ASL. in the south.

Two copper-zinc-lead -silver -gold VMS deposits in the vicinity - Macuchi and La Plata - had been originally mined in the 1930's by Cerro de Pasco of Peru. These were considered, in the 60's, as typical Japanese Kuroko mineral deposits which were, and still are, important producers in Japan. The concession was thought to be generally underlain by volcanic and intrusive rocks, including the noted Kuroko deposits, however, there was no record of any exploration. Hesse's client, Triangle, was searching for a copper source and, Duncan R. Derry Ltd., was chosen to execute the program in exchange for good professional fees, but no property interests.

We built our program on stream sediment geochemical exploration, a then relatively newly-developed applied science, since it was the quickest and most efficient means of evaluating essentially unknown terrain. We had developed expertise in this field in Tipperary, Ireland, where Derry and I had discovered the Gortdrum Cu- Ag-Hg orebody in 1964. And, I had previously carried out Bloom Tests for Zn in the field, [as developed by Prof. Howard Bloom of the Colorado School of Mines], in a field program near Bathurst, New Brunswick for Dominion Gulf Co. in 1955. This measured readily-soluble Zn adsorbed on the surface of stream sands and silts.

At this time Dr. Ron Holman of the Geological Survey of Canada (GSC) had developed a similar field test for readily soluble [weakly-extractible] copper in soil and alluvium [GSC Paper 63-7]. This method had worked in tropical and mountainous terrain in Borneo and in Zimbabwe, and in Norway.

To support the program and keep costs in line, we needed to build a field lab on site in Ecuador and we were fortunate to purchase one from the GSC, plus an allowance for Holman's time, which the GSC considered a good technological investment. The lab contained sufficient quantities of Reagents - Thymol Blue Solution, Dithizone in Benzene - and Buffer solutions for 1,000 samples or approximately two years' operations.

The Military Dictatorship had challenging protocols on importation of foreign goods, including all processed [canned] foods, and bringing in material directly from Canada was out of the question. Our solution was to ferry the geochemical lab from Ottawa to Panama, and then charter a shorter and slightly less-scrutinized flight from Panama to Ecuador. With the help of our field manager, Kevin R., a Canadian and former U/G Supt. at the Cerro de Pasco mine in Peru, the plane landed at our field site [10,000 ft ASL], off-loaded our cargo, including the lab (now dissembled into numerous wooden crates) and paid thousands of US dollars in cash for negotiated fines and duties. Our unexpected willingness and preparedness to make this on-the spot-transaction blew their minds, since such an approach had never been tried before. With that stroke of luck, we saved many months of negotiations with the Ecuadorian military.

We hired Ecuadorian university graduate chemists to operate the lab and also to act as the geochemical sampling crew, assisted by locals. They were glad to gain such experience as employment was scarce for professionals. A team of Canadian/American /English/German geologists, with at least minimal capacities in Spanish, began to work under my field management. Mapping and sampling proceeded in unison. The base maps were poor topographic copies and lacking in any sort of validity, however, detail mattered only if Cu anomalies were detected.

Mapping/prospecting followed a seat-of-the-pants approach as the teams were working in unknown and rugged terrain. This required fluency in geological thinking, but we had the right mix of talent. Swiss Altimeters and Brunton compasses provided some degree of control. And, since helicopters were reserved for the Military, trains of continuously farting mules following rutted mule tracks – what passed for roads in the Highlands - supported our team. These were the worst-possible surface exploration conditions I had ever encountered; food, what there was of it, was almost inedible to North American and European tastes. This was because the Ecuadorians liberally saturated the food with a nauseating spice, no matter what they cooked. Imported food in cans was prohibited.

We were working with people from the Highlands, the paramo, at 3000m. They also grew potatoes which I could eat right from the pot before any spice was added. Of course, we all had the trots. I had Amoebic Dysentery and Malaria as well.

Cigarettes kept us going. The chemical engineers, glad to have a job sampling, somehow had their own food and, being in their early twenties, could endure anything. People were friendly, the sample assistants were local and Spanish speaking, but the Quechua Indians were rarely hired as they had their own language which made communication difficult.

The Military were a big presence and nuisance and on the main highways all expats had to carry bricks of Sucres to pass the roadblocks - never complain amigo. With traversing in severe terrain, it was normal to lose 30lbs in a month.

With the rapid turnaround from the lab, we located anomalous Cu in 1966 in the central part of the concession. Confirmatory soil and rock sampling and prospecting outlined unfortunately only weak Cu-Mo-Ag mineralization in andesite and minor intrusive rocks.

As a result, we then shifted exploration to the southern La Plata mine area for the next two years, which was really the main reason for choosing Ecuador as an exploration target in the first place. We completed detailed soil sampling and drilled six non-wireline holes tracing extensions of the mafic volcanic tuff. On several holes, we cut encouraging, stratabound, Cu, Pb, Zn, Ag mineralization. An extensive and shallow yellow volcanic ash of Recent age blankets the area which had to be excavated to obtain soil samples.

In 1968 our program was wound up when OBRAS lost the concession to the BRGM of France for their research purposes. Such was business in Ecuador. The final report was written by a German geologist on the team, in Spanish, for Ecuador's Government Mines Branch, then translated into English for Triangle Conduit & Cable. I returned to Ecuador in the 1970's for the Banco de Londres y Montreal to examine a proposed mining plan for La Plata during the next period of Military Government from 1972-1979.

Our work represented the Pioneering Phase of Exploration where success cannot be assumed. Indeed, various unsuccessful attempts to develop La Plata and the Macuchi Kuroko deposits have continued to take place over the past 50 years. At present a new company, Toachi Resources Inc., has started a detailed drilling program to extend the ore -grade mineralization we located in 1967, thus, I consider our exploration as worthwhile and representing the Pioneering Phase.

1994 Bolivia –A DPR–Noranda-Geoterrex Story, *by Dave Rogers*

I put together a J.V. package between myself and Geoterrex to fly their "GEOTEM" Electromagnetic and Magnetic system over a huge area in northeastern Bolivia. Geoterrex had an arrangement with the World Bank at the time to subsidize worthy projects, world-wide, where the host country was a participant. We then approached Noranda Mines and they agreed to the project. So, Clarence Logan and I flew to La Paz, Bolivia to meet with the appropriate officials of the Bolivian Government to make our proposal.

In advance I had cautioned the Bolivian connections to the necessity of secrecy for this project to get off the ground and to succeed. We had a successful meeting and basis of agreements with the top Government officials. Again, both Clarence and I stressed the importance of keeping the project secret initially while all aspects of the project could be put in place. Most important would be the Government to grant the J.V. an agreement covering the pertinent area of interest for the mineral rights before any announcements. They agreed and said it would be put in place soonest. That evening we were guests of the assistant mines minister at a public meeting and dinner.

Of course, the "Latin Way" overcame and the minister, in all his fluent, elaborate way, proceeded to announce publicly that "A very important group of major mining companies together with the World Bank were going to carry out extensive airborne surveys and ground exploration in the particular area. The T.V. cameras and reporters were on the story like a dog on a bone. Clarence and I just looked at each other. We quickly left and we caught the plane back to Miami and Toronto in the morning. The project died in the minister's announcement. Clarence handled the cancellation of our proposal. Once again I was short-circuited by 'well-meaning idiots'

Bolivia, *by John Paterson*

The first time I went to Bolivia was with Geomaque when we were considering a merger with Orvana Minerals. We went to look at the Don Mario gold deposit, jointly owned by Orvana and a company controlled by the ex-president of Bolivia, Gonzalo Sánchez de Lozada, familiarly known as Goni. We flew to La Paz, then to Santa Cruz by commercial airlines.

From Santa Cruz, we flew east in a small single engine Cessna for a couple of hours, over the rainforest, to a site on the edge of the Pantanal. We were almost at the point where Bolivia, Paraguay and Brazil meet.

The little plane was vibrating like crazy, likely because it was packed with supplies and working like a son-of-a-bitch to keep us airborne. I breathed a sigh of relief when we landed on a gravel strip that had been carved out of the rainforest. The project was at the underground bulk sample stage. Good gold grades but talk about remote. We spent the night in the tent camp which was where I saw my first "dessert-plate-sized" tarantula. I was with Neil Hillhouse and Phil Walford. It was supposed to be a dry camp, but Neil produced a bottle of rum from his bag and I forgot all about the creatures around us.

The next day we flew back. It was a bit unnerving because we were flying over miles and miles of jungle where there was nowhere to land if there was a problem with the plane. The little plane vibrated so furiously that some knobs fell off the control panel. Unfortunately, the knobs rolled under the seats, out of sight and out of reach so we couldn't retrieve them to put them back on. It turned out they weren't crucial to our landing in Santa Cruz, so all ended well.

The second time I visited Bolivia, I was with Aurogin and Neil Gow and I went to look at some silver projects. The La Paz airport is at 10,000 ft. and the first project we looked at was a small operating mine uphill from there. Above 12,000 ft. Spectacular scenery. Pretty thin air. Typical narrow vein underground operations turning a small profit but no reserves to speak of.

Then we went south to the Altiplano looking at some other old silver mines and prospects. This time we flew in relative luxury in a twin-engine turboprop charter from La Paz to Uyuni, beside the huge salt flats, where the indigenous women all wore colourful dresses and bowler hats. From there we drove around the area looking at some exploration projects, not too far from where Butch Cassidy and the Sundance kid were finally killed. Llamas grazed in the hills like cattle. Fascinating country.

Don't Poke the Bear, *by JJ Elkin*

In the 1980's there was a Vancouver Stock Exchange-listed mining exploration company with large land holdings in Brazil called Treasure Valley (TVX). Brazil was considered unstable, bankrupt, a Third World investment No-No and in spite of its mineral prospects, not a place that investors, even speculators, considered.

At that period South Africa, though the world gold mining leader, was a pariah because of Apartheid. Anglo American, however, was accepted in Brazil. The enormous Anglo Empire, with the DeBeers inclusion, true to its roots, was a rough tough group which did "whatever they had to do" in Africa and in Brazil, to retain their power.

As TVX's CEO I had to raise drill money for our large Brazilian land package. I thought South Africa might be a possibility as they understood gold mining, had the approval via Anglo's interest in Brazil and there was gold mining money there.

I got in touch with "Golden Dumps", a new successful South African mining company led by Lukis Parulis. By telephone we agreed to meet, and I flew to Johannesburg.

Lukis knew a thing or two about rough whatever and had had the tough job of mining foreman in Anglo gold mines. Lukis figured out there was lots of gold in the large amount of Anglo's tailings. So, he left Anglo, bought the Anglo tailings and through his public company called Golden Dumps, thereby made a fortune.

When I went to Lukis' home he was like a young kid, excited by his latest venture. He figured DeBeers had missed a Namibian coastal area which had spewed out large amounts of diamond stones onto the ocean floor Stupid Anglo and stupid DeBeers. Accordingly, Lukis had spent a fortune on building a modern diamond dredge.

The morrow was the commissioning of his dredge. We would meet afterwards and discuss the deal of Lukis investing in our Brazilian properties. We had a set time. I went to Lukis' office. It was strange. He had not shown up. Several hours went by. Finally, I badgered someone into telling me what was going on.

With a pained face the chap told me. Last night the dredge

had mysteriously sunk and was ruined. I understood. I packed my bags and booked the next plane back to Canada. And so ended Lukis Parulis. I never heard from him again. Incidentally, Anglo and DeBeers are still in business.

Fogos, *by Kerry Knoll*

I'm in Andarai, Brazil in 1989 trying to get our little diamond mine going. It is the night before some kind of festival and a neighbor knocks on the door and says I better move my pickup truck, or it could get wrecked. I didn't understand what he was talking about but did move it into my backyard.

The next day a procession came down the street about noon. All women and children dressed in white, singing hymns. It was very beautiful. Then came the men, mostly hammered out of their skulls, with a huge log hoisted above them, maybe 60 feet long. There were about 100 men. It clearly weighed a lot, I couldn't believe they could keep it hoisted up. Apparently, some tradition going back hundreds of years to Africa (most of the people in the town were descended from slaves). That's why the guy told me to move my car.

Sorting diamonds in Andarai, Brazil, 1989

Once that was over the party started in the town square, a band playing, all the ladies in their traditional costumes selling food from little carts. People drinking more and more. Then the fogos came out. Brazilian's love their fireworks and make most of them at home. A fogo stick, which translates as fire or cannon, was a paper tube stuffed with some combination of toilet paper, gunpowder and God knows what else. They would set it on the ground and light it and it would go rocketing around the square, forcing the mass of humanity this way and that to get out of its way. Kids, old men, it was kind of scary. A well-made fogo lasted about five minutes.

I was sitting at a bar under a big tree and moved my chair beside the tree so I could hide behind it in a hurry. One of the fogos went screaming by me and into the open door of a bar. The place emptied in a big hurry, and just after the last person escaped, the rocket came buzzing back out the door and into the crowd. Like something from a roadrunner cartoon.

NORTH OF '60

Alien Mining, *by Kerry Knoll*

In 1992, we bought the Grew Creek deposit in the Yukon Territory for Wheaton River, with the idea of shipping ore to our Ketza River mill. It was advertised to have what they called "preliminary reserves" of about 800,000 tonnes grading 8.8 grams of gold, and it had credibility because it had been drilled off by Noranda only a few years before. It had been discovered by tracking the gold up the hill from a stream where a handful of prospectors lived, panning gold in their little sluices.

We went to visit the site, and when we were walking around with the former Noranda geologist we had hired, a very grizzled prospector with only two or three teeth left in his mouth walked on over to say hi. He lived year-round in a trailer by the creek, surrounded by broken down trucks, old refrigerators, tires, you know the kind of place.

"You know," he said after the first round of small talk. "There's no more gold here. The aliens have been coming at night and they've mined it out."

We did our best to keep from laughing and asked him what these aliens looked like.

"I can show you if you want, I've got a video of them. Come over to my trailer and have a look." It was starting to sound like the opening scene of a horror movie, and it was getting late, so we declined.

We mobbed the drills a few weeks later and started some infill drilling to get met samples. We sent out the core and the holes all came back dusters. Almost no gold at all. We drilled some more, same thing. WTF? We went back to the site with a few geologists that had worked on it in the past to try to figure out what was going on. Maybe we drilled in the wrong place? The old prospector came by once again.

"Didn't find anything, am I right?" he said smugly. "What'd I tell you?"

Blow River Gold, Yukon Territory, 1964, *by Ian Thompson*

The Dew Line station operator at Shingle Point on Yukon's Beaufort Sea coastline, was telling us to piss off. It was late April, 1964, and I was a passenger on a Norseman flying out of Inuvik. The pilot had attempted to land on the delta of the Blow River but badly heaved ice and snow drifts made that impossible.

My partner on the trip, the late Francis Mergus, had been a 7th-ranked heavyweight Canadian boxer, took the radio and managed to talk us down onto the Dew Line landing strip. After we landed, we got our gear and headed out as quickly as possible. I had met Mergus back in February of that that year. He and his German backer, the late William [Bill] Hesse, P.Eng., had shown Duncan Derry and several colleagues a big bag of gold nuggets that apparently had come from the Blow River. Mergus had been the operations manager of one of the most westerly DEW LINE stations "BAR 2, Shingle Point", located about 10 km northwest of the Blow River delta.

It would be fair to report that none of us, beyond Hesse, had any direct experience in placer mining, merely general knowledge of that industry. In 1964, with the discovery of the Kidd Creek orebody near Timmins, no one was paying much attention to placer deposits. But, the nuggets were impressive and Bill Hesse, at 70 and not in the best health, was putting together projects like Blow River and other enterprises to make up for losses he had suffered.

Bill, a well-known and respected mining engineer, had prospered in exploration in the Labrador Trough in the 1950's. A run of ill health had drained his assets, prior to any Canadian government health plan, forcing the sale or abandonment of his claims in the Trough which, more bad luck, later became a site of one the Labrador Iron ore mines.

Hesse asked if Derry would help finance and organize the staking and exploration program of placer gravel deposits of the Blow River, assumed to be the source of the gold nuggets. Derry was known to be a prospector's friend and financed a number of grub-stakes. Derry, of course, also had excellent connections with senior management and wealthy entrepreneurs.

The backers raised $100,000, for their Arctic Gold

Syndicate, sufficient to pay for staking and a summer drill program, with Hesse and Mergus holding a combined 25% interest in the properties staked. The Canadian government assessed the syndicate $10,000 for staking and recording costs based on the sketches we provided and on available air photographs.

We laid out six extra-large placer claims to cover the Blow River gravels from the headwaters to the large delta on the Beaufort Sea. As planned, Mergus and I flew to Edmonton to buy and inscribe the mandated 4x4 inch x 8-foot-long claim posts, two for each claim.

He was the Arctic expert, and I was the field geologist, only five years from graduation. Sled dogs were not available, so we loaded the Norseman with a skidoo, sleeping bags, a tent and food. After our illegal landing and quick exit, we drove east directly to the headwaters of the Blow River where we staked our first claim. We built a small cairn around the post at each site and took pictures of each other at the posts for proof.

We moved rapidly down the river to stake the next 4 claims, the largest one on the delta. Even in April, the days were already surprisingly long, however, by now it was nearly dark. Mergus was nauseous from inhaling gas fumes and motor's racket so we shut down the skidoo for a rest and food.

That was a mistake. We could not restart the engine.

Ordinarily, we would have made camp for the night and started back in the morning but, in our haste to leave the Shingle Point site, where we had landed illegally, and with the poor snow and ice conditions early in our trip, we had lost most of the tent poles from the support sled towed behind the snow machine. So, we decided to walk out.

The snow looked like frozen waves and was unsuitable for snowshoes. We left them behind. With each step we would break through the crust of the snow slightly. This was hard going. I wore my usual light-weight winter clothes and wind protection and carried my Army .303 rifle for polar bears. Mergus was wearing a full warehouse-type winter suit and boots.

In his late-forties and out of shape, he tired quickly and wanted to quit. I motivated him to keep going but eventually I had to hold him up hard and push ahead. I gave him credit for still being tough enough. Helped by a beacon from the Shingle Point Site, we finally arrived at 5 a.m., with a spring blizzard whipping up several hours later. Two days later we flew out and on to Toronto.

In the summer we hired Jack Theissen, an expert placer engineer from Yuba City, to drill four tiers across the Blow River with his Keystone drill. Results were negative, with zero gold detected.

The syndicate members and Hesse were shocked, and we finally learned the true story from Mergus. As manager of the BAR 2 site, he had purchased gold over the years from travellers passing through Shingle Point from Alaska to Inuvik. But, over time, he came to believe that the source of the gold was the Blow River and so convinced Bill Hesse.

We now understand the problems with traumatic brain injuries, so it is probable that his earlier experience as a heavyweight boxer may have compromised his judgement somewhat. I do not believe he was running a con because there would have been nothing in it beyond a few months' good wages.

We then checked all our sources at the Geological Survey in Ottawa concerning glacial patterns along the Yukon Coast and learned that there had been a distinct glacial advance from the northeast that pushed inland for up to 25 km along all the coast from Inuvik to Herschel Island to the west. Any pre-glacial gravels that could have been preserved, as in the placer deposits of the Klondike district, had been pushed out by these glaciers.

Hesse came to Derry a few months later with a proposition to explore for porphyry copper in the Cordillera Occidental of Ecuador. Another fabulous story. I also saw Mergus once or twice over the years as I was leaving work late at our office in the Bank of Commerce building.

He was a Brinks guard, still tough, and he thanked me for helping us find our way back on the Blow River, Yukon Territory, in April 1964.

Adventures on Baffin Island, *Story assembled by Ross D. Lawrence*

Murray Watts was successful in establishing a prospecting syndicate in 1962 called British Ungava Explorations Ltd. Members of the syndicate were Anglo-American Corp., Madsen Red Lake Mines, Asbestos Corporation, Falconbridge Nickel Mines, Duncan Derry, and John Buchan, 2nd Baron Tweedsmuir. Buchan was the Hudson Bay Company clerk in 1937 at Cape Dorset, while his father (the 1st Baron) was the Governor-General of Canada from 1936 until he died in 1940.

Exploration was focused on certain areas along the Cape Smith-Wakeham Bay Nickel Belt in Ungava. But Murray was interested in exploring further north along the Melville Peninsula and onto Baffin Island.

Ron Sheardown was the pilot, and ultimately the co-discoverer of the Baffinland Iron discovery at Mary River. Like all good pilots, Ron kept a detailed daily diary. His diary forms the basis for this account.

Ron was born in Bolton, Ontario on 8 August 1936. He went to school in Bolton and Brampton and yearned to become a pilot. He learned to fly at the Toronto Flying Club at Malton Airport, near Toronto and on 1 June 1953 won his license (age 17). His first job was flying for L&L Dredging in Barkerville BC. In 1956 he joined World Wide Airways and flew DC-3s and C-46s from the supply and fuel base at Frobisher Bay to supply the various DEW Line sites that were under construction. In 1958, Murray Watts hired him to fly Norseman CF-FOX to support the newly discovered Asbestos Hill project.

Our tale begins in July 1962. Murray was itching to get prospecting, and Ron got the aircraft and camping gear organized to go. The daily entries are taken from Ron's diary, with comments added later in square brackets. The aircraft owned by Murray Watts was a Cessna 180 CF-ORO equipped with floats.

July 15, 1962 -- Arrived at Hall Beach on Melville Peninsula. Murray Watts and Lord Tweedsmuir had flown to Hall Beach on Nordair.

July 16, 1962 -- Flew south on Melville belt and camped on a lake at N67°03' W83°42', large gossans area. No visual mineralization. Saw one caribou.

July 17, 1962 -- Moved on down the Melville belt to N67°07' W84°25'. Very nice camp site, old Inuit campsite. Prospected for several hours. Then flew to Hall Beach for fuel and inspection on aircraft.

July 18, 1962 -- Worked on Murray's 16mm Bolex camera, which had fallen in water. Got it working. Prospected and then flew a reconnaissance flight of the area. Old Inuit camp at N67°02' W84°52' looked about 50 to 75 years old. Murray and John saw three caribou, I saw one.

July 19, 1962 -- We prospected and then flew to Repulse Bay [now Naujaat – is about half way from Hall Beach to Rankin Inlet]. The Priest asked us to pick up a sick Inuit man at a camp about 50 miles northwest of Repulse [which we did]. Later we picked up Murray and returned to camp for the night.

July 20, 1962 -- We continued to prospect the area and then in the evening I flew to Hall Beach for fuel. returned to Melville camp for the night.

July 21, 1962 -- Moved camp to Grant Suttie Bay on Baffin Island N69°50' W70°42' We had a DC-3 on skis leave fuel here in 1957. Good camp site.

July 22, 1962 -- Flew on search for Al Wright NSO [Northern Service Officer] from Igloolik NU. He was lost in Foxe Basin walrus hunting. One RCAF Lancaster, Rocky Parsons with his Lockheed 10, DHC-3 Otter from Wheeler Airlines (pilot Al Folby) and myself flying CF-ORO. He showed up in the evening. Apparently, he got caught between ice flows and ran out of gas. Lord Tweedsmuir and Peter Green were with me for the search.

July 23, 1962 -- Flew around Barnes Icecap with Murray. Very interesting falls 150' high, goes under the ice on west side of icecap about one third from north end on west side. Picked up Lord Tweedsmuir in evening. Almost two weeks of CAVU weather and hot - up to 80° F.

July 24, 1962 -- Flew with Murray and Lord Tweedsmuir to Inuktorfik Lake N71°07' W78°37' [now known as Angajurjualuk Lake, about 15 km south of Mary River] Had lunch at Gravity Survey of Canada camp; Dr Hans Webber in charge. Geological Survey of Canada working from same camp; George Falconer in charge. Then flew northwest following the geology between the Paleozoic and the older rocks to the north and east. [There were no geological maps available for this area.] Saw several gossans near contact and landed at N71°33' W79°12' and prospected new serpentine belt. Looks good near large black magnetic hills. [Erratic compass]. Then to Arctic Bay and the Texas Gulf camp [Nanisivik]. Had lunch with Hugh and Mary Clayton. Then flew to Pond Inlet. Water rough so landed behind iceberg and taxied to shore. Dropped Murray and John with gear and flew south to Utuk Lake and secured aircraft. Helicopter for Geological Survey picked me up and took me to Pond Inlet. Spent the night in Pond with Bob Pilot [RCMP] and other people including the Hudson Bay factor [Jim Haining or Bob Cummings?] and Father Latomb? We used 4 10's (40 gallons) of INCO avgas at Utuk Lake. Sent telegram to INCO and arranged to have replaced.

July 25, 1962 -- Lord Tweedsmuir, Murray and I flew south to Mingo Lake, South Baffin looking for Tweedsmuir's cryolite prospect. Did not find it.

July 26,1962 -- We flew around old Amadjuak trading post and on to Cape Dorset. Returned to Mingo Lake for the night.

July 27, 1962 -- Flew to Frobisher Bay [Iqaluit] to get Lord Tweedsmuir onto Nordair to Montreal and BOAC [now British Airways] to London for a board meeting. Murray and I returned to Grant Suttie Bay camp.

July 28, 1962 -- Weather out, prospected most of day.

July 29,1962,We flew to Hall Beach for supplies and did 50-hour check on aircraft. Paid Knobby Clark at Nordair $25 to sign out inspection after I completed the work. Spent the night at Hall

Beach.

July 30, 1962 -- Flew to Grant Suttie camp and then flew north to a lake at N71°19' W79°18' [this is now known as Sheardown Lake] to prospect the large black magnetic hills. Murray and I walked up in rain. One hell of a day (lousy weather) near top I found hematite float in the frost boils, very high grade. We found very high-grade massive hematite. Looks like it could be a new discovery of importance if all of it is as high grade as we saw today. We both returned soaking wet. [Now known as Deposit No. 1].

July 31, 1962 -- Got rained out of our tent, so decided to move down to Gravity Survey camp on Inuktorfik lake Dr. Hans Webber is a Swiss glaciologist and happy to have company. [Inuktorfik means flesh eater or cannibal. One year the caribou did not come through and the husband starved to death and the wife and children ate him.]

Aug. 1, 1962 -- Flew northeast to George Falconer's camp on Raven River N71°46' W77°03'. Then northwest to N71°55' W80°00'. Large low-grade iron formation. [These coordinates are iffy. Borrowed two air photos from George Falconer. The story that we absconded with these photos is absolutely false.]

Aug. 2, 1962 -- Murray and I went to N71°19' W79°18 to look at high-grade showing we found on 30th July. Climbed hill 2500 ft. ASL east of landing lake [now Sheardown Lake] two miles. Put up cairns every 500 feet; starting station "A" approximately 1000 feet from south end. Looks like about 8 to 10,000 feet long with widths from 200 to 500 feet. I returned to camp with 80 pounds of sample and Murray went 3 miles east to look at second showing [Deposit No. 2]

Aug. 3, 1962 -- We flew to our old cache at Grant Suttie Bay for supplies and returned to Inuktorfik for the night.

Aug. 4, 1962 -- Murray and I landed on Glacier Lake - a small lake 15 miles east of main showing and we walked 3 miles north to see iron outcrops, mostly low grade (with high-grade in frost boils). Then to Gravity Survey camp for the night at Inuktorfik Lake.

Aug.5, 1962 -- We flew to N71°27' W79°50', prospected and found high grade iron striking east west [now known as Deposit No. 4] about 100 feet wide exposed. Murray and I followed it about one half mile east then we separated, and I went about another one-half mile southeast and found some low-grade iron. Then I went back along main showing and worked west. I found an outcrop of specularite about one half mile west of main showing. It widens out to about 350 feet and then I lost it in overburden.

Aug. 6, 1962 -- Murray and I staked 16 claims on Deposit No. 1. My NWT license number 232. Then we continued chip sampling.

Aug. 8, 1962 -- Rained like hell all day, stayed in tent. What a hell of way to spend my birthday 26 years old, five thousand flying hours in 9 years and 3 months. Started June 1st, 1953. [Started my mining career with L&L dredging Barkerville BC June 1954 as a student].

Aug. 9, 1962 -- I flew to discovery and about 15 miles northwest staked 6 claims at N71°55', W79 52'on a showing on north side of small lake. [I referred to it as Deposit No. 3, but it is actually Deposit No. 4 as No. 3 had not been discovered until later that day.]. The showing can be identified in outcrop and float for 100 to 350 feet wide and 1.5 to 2 miles long. A lot of specularite.

In the afternoon Murray not feeling good so he stayed in camp. I packed into Murray's high-grade outcrop [Deposit 2] on north side of low-grade outcrop in place and staked 10 claims. Found extension about a quarter mile west of main showing. Just one outcrop. Later found more high-grade showings on south side of low grade showing. (Deposit No. 3 and 3A)

Got back to camp at 2 am. Murray made breakfast. I packed more than 20 miles today and returned with more than 50 pounds of chip samples.

Aug.10, 1962 -- We loaded what turned out to be 280 pounds of chip samples in the floats ahead of the center of gravity as we had plenty of weight with our gear in the rear. Visited George Falconer at the GSC camp at Inuktorfik Lake and then to our cache at Grant Suttie Bay. Then flew southeast to Flint Lake. Prospected the area. Weather low, 100 feet ceiling, not so good for flying. Flint Lake area looks like a good prospecting area. INCO has a Beaver airplane on floats from Saskatchewan Government Airways based at Piling Lake. This geologic belt runs from Baird Peninsula to Clyde Inlet. [Mid Baffin Belt]

Aug.11, 1962 -- We continued to prospect in the morning. Later we decided to move on south. INCO Beaver flew over us. I tried to make contact on VHF and HF but no contact. [I spoke later at PDAC to Hank Vorey and he said he was prospecting the same area of Mid Baffin that year and saw us, but his radio was not working.] We flew south to Basin Lake for gas left by Shoran station in 1957. Then south over the Great Plains of the Koukdjuak. Saw thousands of geese. This is the largest breeding ground for waterfowl in the world. Then crossed the Hudson Straits via Cape Dorset, Salisbury Island and Nottingham Island. Hit south shore near Cape Wolstenholme and on into Sugluk. Father Verspeek still here. Clare Wright is the school teacher and Ed Spackling is Hudson Bay Manager. New NSO and his wife.

From August 12th to October 13th, Ron was busy (1) with the British Ungava prospecting crew around the Gerido Lake area, (2) in the Sudbury area where Murray had some iron prospects and then (3) in Toronto, where CF-ORO was winterized.

Oct. 14, 1962 -- Murray and I left Toronto with CF-ORO on new Fli-Lite wheel skis headed for Mary River. The plan was to meet Jack McOuat in Hall Beach, and take him to look at the iron discoveries, which would allow him to write a qualifying report and stake some more claims. Got as far as Nakina ON. Overnight. Weather out at Churchill MN, snow and rain.

Oct. 15, 1962 -- Took off at 2pm for Churchill. Ran into weather 18 miles north, so headed for Red Lake but weather out, so went to Kenora for the night.

Oct. 16, 1962 -- Left Kenora at 2pm - weather out in morning. Unable to get to Churchill due to weather. So, went to Ilford strip but rough so went on to Thompson, MN for the night.

Oct. 17, 1962 -- Left Thompson at noon for Baker Lake. On instruments from Henick Lake to Baker Lake. Andy Quinn (DOT), Boyd and Teddy Pilgrim of HBC (was at Sugluk in 1958). Murray and I had a nice evening with Boyd and Teddy talking about old times in Ungava.

Oct. 18, 1962 -- Weather out in morning. Left Baker Lake for Hall Beach, ran into weather and icing around Wager Bay. A lot of detouring cut north of Repulse at east end of Douglas Harbour. Landed at Repulse for the night. Spent night with Mr. and Mrs. Henry Voisey of HBC. Henry was clerk at HBC Sugluk in 1932 when Murray and Mike McCart were there for Cyril Knight Prospecting. That was 30 years ago. I always thought when Murray talked about 1932 it was centuries ago. It was only 30 years. [Now it's 2021 and that was 89 years ago!]

Oct. 19, 1962 -- Left for Hall Beach in morning. White out most of the way, on instruments. Met with Jack McOuat who came to Hall Beach on Nordair. Murray and I left for Mary River in afternoon. Weather out so we landed at Inuktorfik Lake and camped out for the night on the ice.

Oct. 20, 1962 -- Took off at 11am for Mary River. Weather bad, so landed at Sheardown Lake. Left Murray to set up base camp and tried to get back to Hall Beach, weather bad so returned to Sheardown Lake and spent night with Murray.

Oct. 21, 1962 -- Made one try today but had to turn back at south end of Erichsen Lake due to weather fog. Running low on fuel. Overnight at new base camp [one Mount Logan tent].

Oct. 22, 1962 -- Took off at 8.30am for Hall Beach; weather out so tried to find fuel cache at Inuktorfik Lake. Unable due to weather so returned to base camp. We decided to radio for an aircraft to bring fuel. 10.45 am talked to Coral Harbour on 5680 and gave him our position and ice conditions at 12 to 14 inches of ice. Good for wheel landings. Not much snow, mostly bare ice. Asked him to pass our message to Jack McOuat at Hall Beach.

Oct. 23, 1962 -- Talked to Coral Harbour at 10.05 am and passed our weather as 2500 and 10 miles, wind southeast at 5 mph. He said RCMP Otter CF-MPY had left Frobisher and was estimating our location at 13.00 EST. Radio working very well. Still have about 10 gallons of fuel in tanks. Otter CF-MPY arrived over our lake at 12.30 noon and landed under white out conditions. Sgt Jack Austin is pilot, and Glen is engineer. They brought one drum of fuel and our groceries from Frobisher They decided to stay for the night. I left for Hall Beach and arrived 4.00 pm. Met with Jack McOuat and decided to stay for the night and try tomorrow.

Oct 24, 1962 -- Jack McOuat and I took off from Hall Beach at 11.05 am for Sheardown Lake base camp. Just south of Igloolik I talked to CF-MPY who was still at our camp with Murray. Jack Austin said the weather was below the hills and two miles visibility. So, I told him I would land at Igloolik and wait for the weather to improve. I looked at the ice and upper airstrip at Igloolik. Talked to Bill Calder (HBC) on his frequency. He said there was 10 inches of ice on the bay and they had been cutting ice blocks for the village. We decided to land on the ice. Touched down at 11.40am, taxied till 11.47 when the ice gave way under us about 150 feet from shore. Jack and I left in one hell of a hurry but still got real wet and cold (Temp is -20° F.). Bill Calder helped Jack out of the water as his door got stuck in the ice. I made it out on my own as I had opened my door before taking off my seat belt so it would not jam in ice. I immediately asked for some planks to put under the wings to stop it from going down to the bottom. Then we went to Bill Calder's house (HBC) to get dry and change clothes. Spent most of the day with Al Wright (NSO) and Bill Calder and some of the Inuit, thinking of ways to raise the aircraft out of the ice and water. We checked the ice and found no more than 6 inches of ice. Also got a message to the RCMP to have CF-MPY bring Murray Watts and his gear to Igloolik.

Oct. 25,1962 -- Spent the day doing inventory of equipment and writing incident report. Spoke to several local people to get ideas of what was available and any ideas of how to raise the aircraft off the thin ice. Jack and I had dinner with Al Wright.

Oct. 26,1962 -- Sent telegram to RCMP. Jack McOuat suggested we use the tide to raise the aircraft if bottom was shallow enough. Cut hole in ice and measured to bottom, about 12 feet. Decided that we could lift aircraft with about 3-4 tides, by putting two timbers to bottom vertically on either side of propeller with cross-member on top. Hired some local Inuit to put two 18-foot 3"x12" timbers vertically to bottom and installed cross member and tied rope to propeller hub at high tide. On each tide we had to block wings and wait for next tide. Had dinner with school teachers, Ann Emmet and Ruth Schepfer.

Oct. 27,1962 -- Jack and I spent the day around the aircraft blocking and raising it out of the water.

Oct. 28,1962 -- Finally got CF-ORO out of the water and planks under it. Let ice freeze under it. Otter CF-MPY came in at noon with Murray Watts, Sgt Jack Austin and Glen. They took our load of gear to Hall Beach and returned. Had dinner with Rod Warneaks.

Oct. 29,1962 -- CF-MPY took Murray Watts and Jack McOuat, ORO engine and propeller to Hall Beach. I took wings off and got aircraft ready to take to Hall Beach by dog team.

Oct. 30,1962 -- Left Igloolik this morning with three dog teams and 60 dogs. We have three komatiks (sleds.) Koulout is leader with three other Inuit. Crossed Hooper Inlet to mainland (not much ice; no more than 5 inches) A lot of ice was sinking under komotiks. Stopped at N69°09' W81°35'; built an igloo and spent the night on the trail. We had a lot of fresh snow and the komatik with fuselage was very heavy and tough sledding. One wing on each other komatik was not too bad and moved a little better.

Oct. 31,1962 -- Got up at 6am fed people and dogs and on the trail at 8am. Traveled until 11pm. Got to Foster Bay at 4pm and water still open so had to travel further into Foster Bay. Almost to Deep Bay on the north side. Then along flow edge. Ice very thin and not very safe. Koulout really knows the ice. Sure scared the hell out of me, almost 10 miles along flow edge after dark. This would be OK in the spring but with no more than 6 inches of new ice in the fall it was very risky. Finally found an old Inuit shack at N68°54' W81°38' and put up for the night, thank Christ.

Nov. 01,1962 -- Up at 6.30am and left at 8.00am. Crossed ice to Nugsanarsuk Point. Then on southeast to Hall Beach. Arrived at

4.00pm. Base manager for Federal Electric (Ruddy Hubner) met us on road to base with a rifle. The base was on full alert due to the Cuban Missile Crisis I had met Ruddy several times and he was OK once we identified ourselves. We put the aircraft pieces in the hanger. Took undercarriage and struts off and got aircraft ready to ship to Montreal on Nordair. Issued Hudson Bay wage order for $250 for Igloolik to pay Inuit and for clothing.

Nov. 02,1962 -- Took off from Foxe Main (Hall Beach) Nordair flight 44, DC-4, CF-JIR for Frobisher 8.00 am. Met Murray and Jack in Frobisher and off-loaded CF- ORO except for radios and instruments. Then to Montreal and Toronto.

Postscript from Ron Sheardown:
I remember two things that Murray said at the time when we were sampling and staking:
"Look around, do you see anyone?" I said "no" and he said, "Watch how many people will tell you they told you about this discovery." There were many.
"It will take ten to fifty years to develop a mine here." It is now more than fifty years. Ron Sheardown now lives with his wife Karin in Anchorage and Phoenix.

Maple Floors – Worth Every Penny, *by Richard Hogarth*

I visited Pine Point in the early '60s while on a fishing trip with my cousin, Don Paterson from Winnipeg. Each summer we would fly Don's amphibious Grumman Widgeon to the North West Territories and fish the pristine lakes for trout.

The Consolidated Mining and Smelting Company of Canada, which was later renamed Cominco Ltd., had recently started mining on the south shore of Great Slave Lake and direct shipping lead/zinc ore to its smelter in Trail B.C. My boss, Sandy Richardson of T. A. Richardson was a long-time follower of the public company, dating to the 1930's. So, Don and I decided to drop in and check out the company's new development.

We flew in unannounced to the private airport nearby. Someone called the mine manager who picked us up and showed us one of the open pits. The high-grade lead/zinc ore was truly remarkable. He subsequently, took us to his home for a drink and conversation. I noted that the manager's residence had beautiful maple floors and thought this was a bit extravagant when he told us they had only three years production left. Perhaps there was a possibility of adding reserves? Anyhow, the visit piqued my interest and I started to look for other companies with potential orebodies in the vicinity that Pine Point didn't own.

A couple of years later, a company called Pyramid Mines was working in the area and the rumor was that they'd been having some success. I purchased 22,000 shares of Pyramid @ $2.00/share. It was all I could afford at the time. An announcement was to be made on the weekend.

That Saturday, I went downtown to buy a pair of summer shoes at the Owens and Elmes store. I had just walked in when I heard a clerk call out, "Is there anyone here by the name of Hogarth? "

I went to the phone and it was one of my colleagues shouting excitedly, "They've struck it!"

I went back to the salesman, and said, "Give me a pair of your best quality summer shoes."

The stock closed the previous Friday at $4.00 and opened on Monday at about $8.00. It was ultimately taken over by Pine Point (Cominco) @ $18.00. The Pine Point operation continued

for another 20 years so it seems that the cost of the mine manager's maple floors was justified after all.

Disappointment, *by Kerry Knoll*

Leon La Prairie had been promoting his big gravity anomaly up on the Arctic coast for at least a couple of decades and had managed to get a total of one hole drilled (and it got lost short of the target). I got involved in 2009 and raised him $8 or $9 million to finally get it drilled properly, after getting a $2 million lead order from Chris Beer over at RBC.

But the program turned into a shit-show and none of the holes made it through the overburden. Finally, in about 2013 or so, I could see that Leon, who was in his mid-80s, was fading fast and I looked around for a new president, settling on Jamie Levy after an introduction from Tommy O'Bradovich. He had been working over at Pinetree Capital and sounded ready to cross the street, as it were.

We hired a geologist named Jacquelin Gauthier who recommended we do a program of magnetotellurics, a geophysical technique. When he brought it up, I had to admit I had never heard of MT, much less ever used it. The first step was a trip to the town of Paulatuk, population 275 (and ice-bound 10 months of the year) to introduce ourselves to the local first nations. We chartered out of Yellowknife and landed at the tiny airport near the end of April. Even though it was sunny it was still about minus 10 and the snow hadn't even thought about starting to melt.

When we landed and made our way to the community centre for the introductions, we saw nothing but a whole lot of sad faces. It was strange. What had we done to make this people dislike us?

As it turned out, when we had announced we were coming and the local leaders saw the list of names, they thought that Jamie, Jacquelin and Kerry meant three women were coming. They had been excited because they seldom had women visitors from the south. That got things off to a bad start and many in the town opposed our program.

We also met the Inuvialuit leader Nellie Cournoyea, over in Inuvik on that same trip. She is a remarkable lady who had been only the second woman premier in Canadian history. She was an astute business woman and had been managing the Inuvialuit's finances for a few decades as the president of their corporation, with considerable success. She also managed the first land claims settlement in Canada. She over-ruled the locals and let us complete our program.

CROSSING THE RIO GRANDE

Encantada, *by Ed Thompson*

In the early 1970s my main efforts involved looking for acquisitions and managing three public companies: Lacanex, Pure Silver and Tormex and a 50 %-owned private company with Dupont of Canada, Ducanax.

Lacanex was exploring in Canada and the U.S.A., Pure Silver was developing four silver-gold mines at Guanajuato, Mexico and Tormex was exploring in Mexico. Originally our U.S. activity had been completely through the Cordex syndicate which was managed by John Livermore and Pete Galli. Lacanex was one of four junior companies that subscribed for US$50,000 per year for the basic budget. Once a substantial project was discovered, a separate budget was generated. John and Pete found the Pinson gold zone in Nevada in the first year, but it would take 10 years and a lot of effort before it reached production in late 1980, following a boom in gold prices.

We hired Peter McCrodan, an ex-McIntyre Mines engineer, to work with me on evaluations, and one of our first projects was the Encantada silver-lead property in northeastern Mexico. The area was remote with no facilities. A rich rancher was developing the mine and the workers lived in caves on the property. Some of the mineralization graded 20 oz. silver per tonne and 20% lead – high enough to be shipped directly, hauled by small trucks, to a rail line to the Peñoles smelter at Torreón. The people at Peñoles had examined and sampled the property but could not come to terms with the rancher.

Our Mexican staff examined the property and recommended we acquire it, so McCrodan and I flew to Mexico City, then to Chihuahua, followed by a six-hour ride on a dusty road to the property. We later constructed a dirt airstrip at the mine. McCrodan and I cooked our meals over an open fire and slept in the back of a half-ton truck for a couple of nights while studying the property. It's amazing how many stars you can see when you sleep under them.

To get underground, we had to stand on the edge of the bucket that was used to haul up ore and waste and then hang on for dear life. For some reason we didn't have hard hats or regular miners' lamps, only the old tungsten-carbide variety, and we could hear the falling stones as we were lowered down the shaft. The type of mineralization, geologically known as pipes and mantos and completely oxidized, was unknown to me. It was crumbly, orange-to-red-to-yellow in colour, and impossible to differentiate by eye from low-grade ore and waste.

Fortunately, Peñoles, under the direction of Pedro Sánchez Mejorado, had done a great job sampling the various zones. What Pete and I had to do was a preliminary feasibility study. That involved calculating the mineral inventory, estimating capital and operating costs, considering the mining methods, predicting silver and lead prices, calculating net smelter return royalties, and so on. This information, in turn, would be used to determine what we might be able to pay. At that time, the calculation of mining taxes, profit sharing, income, and royalties was complex. And as Tormex had little in its treasury, we would have to convince a bank to lend us the money.

Pete and I went back to Toronto and started cranking the numbers. There are always many permutations and combinations in evaluation work and this one was above average in that respect. There were no facilities available and neither Pete nor I was familiar with this type of deposit. However, after a lot of discussion with our group and with Peñoles, who would become our Mexican partner, and bearing in mind that foreigners could own a maximum of 49% of a Mexican mine, we agreed on a price of US$2.5 million. Our Mexican staff, consisting of Harvey Sobel, Antonio Alvarez and Bill Shaw, started negotiations.

The rich rancher was not too impressed by our offer. He had money and liked the romance of owning a mine. I remember sitting in his lovely living room and discussing matters with him. Tormex needed a project and our idea was to use the profits from the mine to pay for exploration in Mexico as none of the original properties in the company looked economic. Negotiations dragged on until someone had the bright idea of adding some cows, as he seemed to value his herd. I believe the number was 20 or 25, but it could have been more, and the deal was done. We borrowed part of the money from Pure Silver and part from DuPont via Ducanex, and Tormex was the proud owner of the Encantada property.

Little did we know our problems had just begun.

This remote area of Mexico is a geologically monotonous

sequence of limestone beds that have been pushed up into high ridges and intruded by small igneous dikes, sills and plutons. These intrusives generated the mineral solutions that, when contacting the limestone beds, precipitated out their metal values.

As the water table is quite deep, the original sulphide mineralization was oxidized and the metals moved around, sometimes concentrated and other times dispersed into the limestone beds. Exploration was difficult as the zones generally did not outcrop and had few geophysical signatures. We thought that with detailed geologic mapping of the range front, it might be possible to differentiate the limestone beds and that certain beds would be more favourable for mineralization.

It was now October and winter was coming in Canada. I thought of my old friend Fred Sharpley from my Teck days. He was now consulting and probably not too busy. Some conversations you forget in a week while others stay with you all your life. My conversation with Fred was of the latter type. He had a Saskatchewan-slow style of talking and usually called me by my last name. After I tracked him down and made my pitch about working three months in Mexico rather than freezing his ass in northern Canada, he said: "I don't know, Thompson; aren't there a lot of bandits in the hills?"

He had seen a couple of Pancho Villa movies about life in northern Mexico at the turn of the century. I assured him that this was not the case and that I had been back and forth and that we were building a guest house where he could stay and work. Although he wasn't fully convinced, he hadn't received any better offers, so he agreed to fly to Mexico City and then out to the mine site. I was confident Fred would do a good job.

By this time, I was also running the exploration program in Canada that entailed going to Newfoundland to look at some properties Dennis Happy was promoting. After a few days of being wet and frozen after looking at unimpressive showings, I was happy to return to my warm office in Toronto. I was just settling in and catching up on my mail when the telephone rang.

"Thompson?"

"Sharpley?" I replied. "Where are you?"

I knew there was no phone on the property and all I expected from him were written reports.

"I'm in Mexico City."

"What are you doing in Mexico City?!"

"They came with guns and chased us off!"

His worst nightmare had come true and our worst imaginable problems had started. It's a good thing I was sitting down. A fleeting thought crossed my mind: is this a joke? But Sharpley was not a joker.

The story, as became clear over the next few days, was as follows:

Tormex had bought both the "A" and "B" shares from the rancher and was planning to resell the "A" shares to Peñoles as our Mexican partner. As Peñoles was partially foreign-owned, it was necessary to sell them 60% in order to ensure the mine was 51%-Mexican owned. The A shares were to be temporarily held in trust by our general manager in Mexico, Bill Shaw, who was a Mexican citizen. Somehow the shares were not properly signed off. Bill Gross, the President of Tormex, blamed our young Toronto lawyer who had been sent down for the closing and the lawyer blamed Gross.

Shaw said he had been promised a bonus by Gross and that Gross had reneged so he took the A shares and control of the mine. Just as Sharpley feared, Shaw arrived with a couple of pistoleros and chased off our people.

The justice system in Mexico is slow at the best of times and in the early 1970s it was very slow indeed, not to mention uncertain. Our major partner, DuPont, was distressed but pitched in admirably, and its representative, Art Baker, was a brick.

He went to Mexico and helped organize the legal teams and saw the fight through. Regretfully he was to die from a heart attack a few years later. Great guy.

Tormex and our group of companies were between a rock and a hard place. We had borrowed $2.5 million to buy a mine we now did not control and had to come up with more money to pay legal bills and overhead costs. Meanwhile Mr. Shaw was mining some of the high-grade material and using the profits to pay his lawyers.

The battle got vicious. Death threats were issued, and shots were fired through windows. Gross told the story of how he had contacted a Mafia group in Florida and taken out a policy such that if anything happened to him, Shaw would be taken out as well.

We were never sure if this was true, but it certainly served as a warning to Mr. Shaw.

The case went through all the court levels in Mexico for almost a year and though we had the law, Peñoles and DuPont on our side, we finally had to buy off Shaw. The problems soured DuPont on mining and Mexico and prompted their exit from both.

The Encantada Mine would produce silver and lead intermittently for the next 45 years.

Mr. Fields? He's Probably Dead - The Tale of Arturo Campos, *by John Paterson*

One great thing about the mining industry is its colourful cast of characters. People who might not fit well into other sectors often thrive in the mining business. One such individual who stands out in my memory is prospector by the name of Arturo Campos. A lot of exploration drilling had been done at the San Francisco Gold Property in Sonora, Mexico before we optioned it in 1992. Nearly all of it around an abandoned shaft that led to a warren of derelict tunnels.

Most of the known reserves were close to the shaft, but Peñoles, the Mexican company from which Geomaque was buying the property, had also found gold on some nearby claims. This separate property called "La Chicharra", was about one kilometer to the west. It had been under option from a third party, but unfortunately, Peñoles had dropped the option.

So, the claims reverted to the original claim holder, who, according to the records, was one Bertin Arthur Fields. Our company was working on a feasibility study for the project when it became apparent that without the additional La Chicharra reserves, it was going to be impossible to reach the critical mass required to justify the initial capital to build the mine. So, I set out to find Mr. Fields. Unfortunately, it seemed that he had disappeared off the face of the earth.

I asked around but it appeared that no one knew anything about any Bertin Arthur Fields. Finally, I tracked down the Peñoles geologist who had managed the drilling program a few years earlier and asked him.

"Oh," he laughed. "You mean Arturo Campos. That's the name he goes by when he's in Mexico. The Spanish translation of "Arthur Fields." Good luck finding him though. He's a crazy old prospector who goes off by himself into the mountains or the desert, sometimes for months at a time. I haven't seen him in years. Probably dead."

I hoped he wasn't dead, and I asked the geologist to check Peñoles' records to see if he could track down any way of contacting him. A week or so later, I received a fax with the name and phone number of a lawyer in Hermosillo that Mr. Fields had used when he first made the option agreement with them. I called the lawyer and explained who I was and asked if he could give me an address or phone number for Mr. Fields, or Sr. Campos or whatever name he was going by.

"I don't have any way to contact Mr. Fields," he answered. "He would come by my office once a year to pick up option payment cheques from Peñoles. But I haven't seen him since they dropped the option. He might well be dead by now."

There was that "dead" thing again, and it didn't sit well with me. "Why did people keep saying that?"

"Was he sick?" I inquired.

"No, not that I was aware of. But travelling through the hills alone like he did can be dangerous. People grow marijuana up there and don't like unexpected visitors. Prospectors have been known to disappear."

"So," I asked just in case, "if he were dead, what would happen to his claims?"

"They would be passed on to his heirs."

"Would you know who his heirs might be?" I asked.

"No señor. But I remember he had a young Mexican wife. Unfortunately, I have no idea what her name is or how to contact her. Sometimes I run into a young man who knows Mr. Fields. If I see him, I'll ask."

It didn't sound too positive. Meanwhile, the clock was ticking. Our agreement with Peñoles required us to complete a positive feasibility study on the project by the end of the year. And it was already September. I had instructed Kappes Cassidy, the engineering company doing the study to continue their work under the assumption that La Chicharra was part of the project, but if I couldn't get a deal with Mr. Fields, we were screwed.

I followed a few more leads and came up dry. It seemed that most people could care less if he were alive or dead. And even if he were alive, didn't care if they ever saw him again. Then I got an idea. Make them care. Offer a reward.

So, I made up a fax and sent it around.

$200 Reward Offered
For information leading to contact with
Bertin Arthur Fields
(Arturo Campos)
If you have any information that might help

please call collect to
John Paterson
Geomaque Explorations Ltd.
in Canada at 416 555-5555

I knew it wasn't a very big reward but didn't want to look desperate. A couple of long weeks later we still hadn't heard anything, and I was thinking it might be time to increase the size, when one day, the phone rang.

"Hello John?" the gravelly voice said. "This is Bert Fields calling."

The kid that the lawyer knew in Hermosillo had tracked him down and Bert had called me from somewhere in Northern Mexico. I explained that I would like to talk to him about making a deal on his La Chicharra claims. He said he was heading up to the U.S. and suggested meeting in Tucson on the weekend to discuss the issue.

Bert picked me up at the Tucson Airport around noon on Saturday. He looked pretty well as I imagined he would. Tall, thin, weathered, perhaps around sixty years old. Seemed like an okay guy if you didn't pay too much attention to the slightly crazed look in his eyes.

So, I got in his old pickup truck and we headed off to find some lunch. We found a restaurant where we could keep an eye on Bert's truck from our table and ordered something to eat. It didn't take me long to realize that Bert loved to talk. Perhaps he'd spent too much time alone in the desert and was trying to catch up. Maybe it was why no one else went prospecting with him. Anyway, I had a return flight booked for Sunday morning so needed to work out a deal today. But every time I tried to get him focussed on business, he would go off in another tangent.

"You like Mexico?" he asked.

"Of course," I answered. "Great people, great food. Great place to do business."

"Yes," he replied. "And great women too."

He told me he was on his way to California where he had a young Mexican wife. When he explained that he'd had several young Mexican wives, I started wondering if he was some sort of weirdo or was making up stories.

"I marry them when they're teenagers," he went on to

explain. "I find someone who's ready for a change. They may not love me, but they marry me so they can leave their life in Mexico and get a "green card" in the U.S. Eventually they leave me too, but then I just marry another."

"Oh shit," I thought. "Am I going to spend the whole day listening to this sick son-of-a-bitch go on about his deranged love life?"

I just wanted to make a deal and assumed so did Bert. But it seemed that he wanted to share the tales of his exploits first. Some guys are like that. He likely realized that he had a captive audience and was prone to exaggeration. So, he talked, and I listened through lunch and into the afternoon. It turned out that besides young girls, he also liked dogs.

"What about you? Do you like dogs?" Bert asked.

"Of course, love dogs. We have two at home," I answered, thinking that this could be a subject with which we might have more in common. But I turned out to be wrong again.

"I like to build a strong bond between myself and my dog," he explained.

He said he would take a newborn puppy from its mother before its eyes were open and feed it milk from a baby bottle. When the puppy finally opened its eyes, it would think Bert was its mother and go through life that way. There seemed to be a troubling pattern forming here between Bert's fondness for young women and young dogs. I wondered how much more of this I would have to listen to. I desperately wanted to do our business and be on my way. But I didn't want to say anything that would piss him off and jeopardize our deal.

I had booked a couple of rooms at one of the hotels along the airport strip and suggested we check in, thinking that a change of scenery might also lead to a change of subject.

On the way to the hotel, when I thought that our conversational subject matter had reached an all-time low, he surprised me once more.

"You have a dog now?" I asked.

"Until recently," he said. "Went with me everywhere. Followed me through the hills. Protected me at night when I camped out. Best friend a guy could have. Better than any human. But got old like dogs do and died a couple of weeks ago."

"Sorry to hear that," I said, while Bert looked out the

windshield and seemed to be somewhere far away.

"Part of the reason I'm heading back to California," he continued. "Couldn't bear to bury the poor beast in Mexico where I wouldn't be able to visit the grave, so I cremated him on a barbeque and am bringing his ashes back home."

At this point I could see the "wacko meter" needle going into the red. "Who cremates their dog on a barbeque? And carries the ashes around in the box of his pickup truck? What did he tell US Customs when he crossed the border at Nogales?"

If it wasn't so critical that I got this deal done, I would have told him, "Either we do the deal or not, but I'm not listening to one more of your weird ass stories, you crazy old man!" I used to think sixty was old when I was in my thirty's.

Anyway, I checked us in and paid for the rooms and we parked around the side of the hotel near the side entrance. I only had a small overnight bag, but he had all his prospecting gear and said he was afraid to leave anything in the truck in case it was stolen. So, we hauled it all up to his room on the second floor.

Including his dog's ashes which were in a knapsack weighing about 30 pounds. Which I carried up for him thinking that it must have been one big dog. Hopefully, a dog, not an ex-wife or some unfortunate hitchhiker he'd talked to death.

Well, if this was a test, I guess I passed, because now Bert was ready to sit down and talk business. Peñoles was obligated to pay him $100,000 to complete the purchase of the property before they decided to drop their option. So, I told him we would make the same payment, but in three installments, $10,000 today, $40,000 in six months and $50,000 in one year.

Our company didn't have the money for the next two payments, but I figured we could raise it if the feasibility study was positive. I didn't complicate things by sharing this detail with Bert. He said that those terms were fine with him, so, I quickly wrote up an agreement before he had a chance to change his mind. We both signed it and I wrote him a cheque for the $10,000. The whole deal went as smooth as silk.

We ate dinner together that evening and he told me about numerous other prospects around Mexico that might be of interest to our company. This conversation was much more palatable than the ones earlier in the day. I think he liked doing the deal for $100,000 and was now working on how he might repeat the process. The next morning, Bert insisted on driving me to the airport and even coming in to see that my flight left on schedule.

He probably had some more stories up his sleeve in case of a delay. After carting all his gear and ashes back down to his truck, we headed back to the airport.

In those days, you could walk through security without a boarding pass to see someone off. So, he took his .22 calibre pistol out of his pocket and put it in the glove box. He made sure that I noticed he had been carrying a gun all this time, and grinned as he gave me that slightly crazed look again. He walked with me to my boarding gate and fortunately, my flight left on time.

I don't think I ever saw Bertin Arthur Fields/Arturo Campos again. Now, like they would say almost thirty years previously, he's probably dead. But, over the next few years, our geologist, Phil Walford, went on numerous burro expeditions into the hills looking at Bert's other prospects throughout Chihuahua, Sinaloa, and Durango. Phil had a lot more patience than me.

With the addition of the La Chicharra reserves, we were able to produce a positive feasibility study and get the San Francisco Mine financed and built. Our study anticipated a five-year mine producing 150,000 ounces of gold but the mine produced double that before closing in 2000 due to low gold prices.

Timmins Gold reopened the mine in 2010 and operated it until 2019 producing another 800,000 ounces. It was recently purchased by Magna Gold which plans to bring it back into production once more.

CENTRAL AMERICA AND THE CARRIBBEAN

The Tailor of Guatemala, *by John Paterson*

"The Tailor" translates to "El Sastre" in Spanish. This story is about developing the El Sastre Gold Mine in Guatemala. We never found out how the property got its name, but I believe some wag gave it that name because of the ruthless thorns on the scrub brush covering the property that resembled the large sewing needles of a tailor.

It was the spring of 2003 and I had been running Aurogin Resources for a little over a year. The company was started or renamed in the late 1980's by Dave Rogers and Bob Ginn to explore for gold. They used the Au for gold the Ro from Rogers and the Gin from Ginn to come up with the name Aurogin.

Dave Hutton, Hank Reimer, Ed Thompson and Norm Paterson were directors, but the founders had moved on by this time. I was subletting a small office from Roscoe Postle Associates at 55 University Ave. in Toronto.

We'd been exploring in Canada, currently working on a property we optioned from John Lee Carroll, a mining entrepreneur from New York, near the Rambler Mine in Newfoundland. John's family had a royalty on the old mine, and he was trying to get it up and running again. We were following up on airborne anomalies from a survey flown by Wally Boyko's AeroTEM system.

Bill and Susan Scott were managing the fieldwork. We'd had some drilling success with a few targets giving us interesting copper grades, but our share price was still around a dime and financing was difficult and dilutive. I remember trying to talk resource investor Sheldon Inwentash into buying our stock, but he said he wouldn't touch it with a barge pole because it was too illiquid. And it was true.

The share price chart looked like the square teeth of a pumpkin. Most of our money came from flow-through funds and, as is often the case with flow-through, the shares would be right back in the market after the 3-month hold period.

I'd been thinking about getting back to work in Central America, but it would mean raising hard dollars. I was talking to Simon Ridgeway from Radius Gold at a convention one day and he mentioned that he'd come across some smaller but attractive gold deposits in Guatemala. I liked working in Central America and loved small gold deposits, so off I went to look around.

There wasn't a lot of mining activity in Guatemala at the time. I met with the Director of Mines and he was eager to help. I asked if he could point me towards some local prospectors that had gold properties and might be looking for partners. He put me on to a geologist and businessman by the name of Jose Manuel Lemus who had a surface showing which justified drilling. Trying to save money as much as possible, I thought that sharing the drilling cost might make sense.

Geoff Evans, Jose Manuel Lemus and Dave Hutton

Every couple of weeks during the summer, Ed Thompson and I would go out at lunch time and grab a sausage from the cart on Wellington Street. We'd eat in the park behind Roy Thompson Hall and shoot the breeze and admire the scenery. I told Ed what I was thinking, and he said he'd be keen on a joint venture through Consolidated Thompson-Lundmark Gold Mines. This was before Ed made his deal with Stan Bharti and Gerry McCarvill to develop the Bloom Lake Iron Mine.

Dave Hutton, who was living in Costa Rica, met me in Guatemala. Geoff Evans, an ex-Placer Development geologist and friend of Ed and Dave came along to help spot and drill a couple of holes. Unfortunately, we didn't get much encouragement and dropped the project.

Next, I travelled to the Lake Izabal area in eastern Guatemala with Geoff who was retired and also living in Costa Rica but still had exploration in his blood and liked getting the occasional contract. Geoff was a fun guy and knew what he was doing. We hiked up rivers and through the rubber tree plantations south of the lake looking at gold showings and prospecting around hot springs.

"What we're looking for is "mondongo,"" he would say. Mondongo is what they call tripe (a cow's stomach) in Spanish. It's available at most butcher shops in Central America and used to make soup but looks like a weathered hydrothermal quartz stockwork. We didn't find much mondongo, but we had an interesting trip and enjoyed the fresh fish from Guatemala's largest lake.

The third project had been under option to the Goldfields/Radius joint venture and recently returned to the owner, again, Jose Manuel Lemus. Jose Manuel wrote me to tell me he got the property back and I went down to check it out. The property was ideally located just 30 kilometers outside of Guatemala City. On my first visit to the property, I became sorely aware of the thorny bushes as they savagely tore through my clothing and skin. The few emaciated cows and horses wandering around the property had devoured everything except these vicious bushes and a few venomous serpents snoozing in the trenches. There were a couple of old tunnels, apparently developed by the Spanish or perhaps the Mayan Indians, which we made a point of staying out of.

The joint venture had drilled eight holes on the property and encountered values of a couple of grams of gold over a few meters in some of them. Fortunately, the JV decided the property didn't meet their threshold and walked. I found the property interesting because it had a lot of multi-gram near surface mineralization exposed in trenches. The trenches were on a hillside and there were good gold values in several other spots around the same hill. It looked to me like there could be a flat zone several meters thick, cutting through the hill and outcropping on all sides. The JV drilling indicated that it could be continuous through the hill. And the Spanish tunnels looked like they had been driven into this zone, who knows how far? On top of that, the rock was weathered, and the mineralization oxidized which would likely leach well. The property was called "El Sastre."

Then came the challenge of making a deal. Jose Manuel,

or "JM" as his friends called him, also had a partner in the property at the time. And getting them both to agree on anything was difficult.

But naturally, they agreed they would like a lot of cash up front and that a big, carried interest would also be nice. The problem was, Aurogin didn't have any money.

So, I was going to have to scratch for anything we paid and wanted to keep it to a minimum. The other problem was that JM had quite a temper and was known for getting mad and walking out of meetings or dropping out of deals if he felt like he wasn't being dealt with fairly. I found this out early in the negotiations and was careful about what I said from then on. JM and I spent a lot of time together, mostly visiting the property and driving back and forth.

Guatemala City has a tangled web of roads through the sprawling home of four million people, so you can imagine how bad traffic was. But it gave us lots of time to talk and get to know each other. I also discovered that he liked Chivas Regal scotch, so each time I visited I would pick him up a bottle at duty free. Eventually, I discovered that he also had a desire to be a mine operator.

I'd been involved in the development and operation of a few heap leach operations by this time. And I had recently visited several small operations in China for Lee Barker's Sparton Resources, and Gang Chai's McVicar Resources, where I'd learned some new tricks on how to minimize capital and was eager to try them out.

"I bet we could get El Sastre into production for $1 million," I said. "How about you put up the property, Aurogin puts it into production, and we go 50:50 on the operation?"

JM thought for a bit and said, "You have a deal amigo."

And we did, basically on those terms. Aurogin was to finance the project through to production and be the operator, and if the capital cost exceeded $1 million, JM would pay back his half out of profits. I knew a 50:50 deal had potential for problems, but it was the best I could do. At least our interests were aligned and having a Guatemalan partner might help with permitting. This was in August 2004.

It was around that time that RPA was growing, and Lee Barker and I got squeezed out of their office. So, we rented an office upstairs and shared it between Aurogin, Spartan and McVicar.

The market wasn't interested in the Guatemalan acquisition, and financing continued to consist of piecemeal private placements, mostly at a dime. In September, we carried out a 38-hole, air track drill program at El Sastre that Geoff Evans helped supervise. We also sent a bulk sample to the Dalhousie University Minerals Engineering Centre for column leach tests. It turned out that the gold was extremely fine and leached easily with extraordinarily little cyanide consumption. We got an astonishing 97% recovery in 15 days!

We now had enough data to calculate a resource. So, while we continued working at Rambler, I got my friend Toren Olson, a mining engineer whom I'd previously worked with, to build a block model and together we assembled a 43-101 report. We had about 50,000 oz indicated and 120,000 oz inferred grading 3 to 4 g/t. We released the results in March 2005, but the market didn't give a damn.

It was then that I realized that the only thing the market likes less than a mining company without a mine, is a mining company with a small mine.

By this time, I'd already invested quite a bit of money and three years of hard work trying to get Aurogin moving and was getting frustrated. But I knew the Tailor of Guatemala could be a money maker and might be the catalyst I needed to get the Company off dead center, so I pushed on. We hired a consulting company in Guatemala to do an Environmental Impact Study and submitted it in May.

It was around this time that I met Rick Adams, another mining engineer from Queen's University, who graduated a few years after me. He was enthusiastic and had good business and market sense.

Rick lived near Campbellville and I lived near Carlisle, so we both commuted to Toronto on the GO Train from Milton which was the end of the line. During our train time, we developed a plan to build value into the company. To make it into something more attractive for merger or acquisition by increasing the reserves. Rick was not a quiet talker, quite the opposite in fact, so I'm sure everyone else for several seats around us on the train also became well aware of our plan.

JM had two other properties adjoining El Sastre called "Lupita" and "Bridge." Lupita was big with lots of mineralization, although lower grade and not oxidized like El Sastre. We figured that if we could put together the complete land package, we might get to the magic 1-million-ounce mark and the market or perhaps a mid-sized producer would take notice. But all this was going to take money.

The share price had dropped to 6 cents by July, but I was happy to get Rick and his friends some cheap stock to get their foot in the door. So that's where we did the financing. Units for 6 cents with a full warrant at a dime. We planned to raise about $100,000.

I then called Farmer Tom Toth, whom I'd known for several years. Tom liked to play the market, had been following the company and was already a shareholder. And as anyone that knows Tom would agree, he's also good at spreading the word.

"Tom, I just wanted to let you know about an incredible opportunity to make a bucketload of money," I said.

I told him the details and he said, "Put me down for $10 k minimum but I'll get back to you to confirm the amount."

Well, he got back to me alright. First to say his sister Kathy would like to get in. Then he called back to say he wanted to increase his own piece. Then he got back to me to ask if there was room for his brother-in-law from Alberta. Then a friend. Every time the phone rang, someone else wanted to subscribe. By the end of the day, between Rick and Tom and their contacts and family jumping in, we were at $275,000 where we cut it off.

With more hands to do the work and more money available, we kicked things into high gear. In August 2005 our EIA was accepted, we received our environmental approval and Rick joined the company as Vice-President Corporate Development.

In September we made option deals on both Lupita and Bridge. These deals were more conventional as we had a bit of cash to pay up front. In October we hired Darren Koningan, a mineral processing engineer and classmate of Rick's as Vice-President Engineering. We also hired Michael Farrant, another Queen's grad, as CFO around this time.

Mike is currently CFO at Judy Baker's Argo Gold. It wasn't by design, but we now had four Queen's grads running the company. We leased a larger office of our own in the same building.

At first, Darren was skeptical. He'd never heard of 97% recovery in a 15-day column test. Nor was he familiar with the Dalhousie Test Centre. So, we sent another sample to SGS Lakefield and this time ended up with 98% recovery in 14 days. Darren came around.

Of course, we were going to need more money. So, I went to see Don Ross at Jones Gable and Company. Don hired an engineer to review the data. But it turned out that Darren wasn't the only skeptic. The engineer told Don that he believed the data to be fictitious and that I was running a scam. I was infuriated but moved on.

Bob Buchan had just left Kinross and had hung up a shingle in an office in First Canadian Place called Quest Securities. I went to see him, and he liked the project. In December, he brokered a $1 million private placement at 10 cents with a warrant at 20 cents, with a group of his associates.

It probably didn't hurt that he was also a Queen's Mining grad. He later donated $10 million to Queen's and they named the mining department after him. Now the stock was getting into the hands of some players and started gaining a bit of traction. Buying in the market began increasing when the deal closed in January of 2006.

In February, we filed another 43-101 Report, this time on Lupita. We announced an inferred resource of 518,000 ounces. So, with the El Sastre resource, we were now at close to 700,000 ounces total and more to come at Bridge. It was around this time that we hired Neil Gow as VP Exploration.

In early April, the company announced the start of construction at El Sastre. The mine was to produce 20,000 ounces per year starting in the fourth quarter. We hired a contractor, Sococo, who I had worked with previously in Honduras and did a great job at a reasonable price. Later that month we did another private placement. This time we raised $1.1 million at 22 cents with a warrant at 36 cents. This time Don Ross also participated.

By mid-May the earthworks for the leach pad were complete. I would visit the project at least monthly but the visit in late May 2006 was especially memorable. JM picked me up in the morning at my hotel in Guatemala City and we drove out to the site. I don't think I'd ever seen him this happy and could tell he was pretty excited to show me the progress.

It was a big change going from an exploration project in the scrubby, thorny brush covered hills to a construction project with a significant amount of earthmoving. We needed a flat area for the leach pad, so we'd taken the top off a hill and had exposed an area perhaps 150m in diameter. He drove his big old Mitsubishi 4x4 up the newly constructed road to the leach pad. From there, we could see almost the entire El Sastre property. The mine area, plant site and leach ponds.

He parked in the middle of the pad and we got out to look around. JM opened the hatchback and pulled out two deck chairs and set them up on the pad. Then he pulled out a cooler and we sat down. He reached into the cooler and produced a bottle of Chivas Regal, two glasses, a can of smoked oysters and a package of crackers. It was still before noon but that didn't stop us from celebrating our progress and toasting The Tailor of Guatemala. It was a moment I won't forget.

In July, the government issued the operating permit or "License of Exploitation" which was the final step in permitting El Sastre.

Darren did a great job of designing and building the plant. It was simple but everything was first class. His father, an electrical engineer, even came down from Canada for a while to help with the wiring and instrumentation installation. When it was finished, it looked great and ran like a charm.

In October, we announced the completion of construction and that we had now loaded 20,000 tonnes on the pad. It wasn't long after the release went out that the phone rang. It was the Ontario Securities Commission. They wanted a meeting. Now!

So, Rick and I headed over to their office on Queen Street beside the Eaton Centre. The analyst had a copy of the release on his desk.

"I think we are looking at a serious disclosure issue," he barked. "I don't see any record of you filing a copy of the feasibility study for El Sastre,"

"No, we didn't," I answered.

"Why not?" he asked.

"Because we didn't do one," I replied.

"Why not?"

"Didn't need to," I said.

"Of course, you need to," he snorted. "It's a requirement."

"Where does it say that?" I inquired, though I already knew the answer. I had thoroughly researched the matter before we announced the start of construction. I was actually expecting to hear from the OSC sooner and was surprised it took them until after construction was complete to notice what we were doing.

He looked feverishly through the regulations, and finding nothing, closed the book went back to the question and answers. I explained that it was a very simple project and that an internal evaluation was all that was needed to make a production decision. We'd kept the public up to date with two 43-101 Resource Reports, and press released each step of our progress and I didn't see where the problem was. He finally let us leave and said he'd get back to us.

A week or two later, I was in Costa Rica with my wife and we were driving along the Inter-American Highway over the top of "Cerro de Muerte," the "Mountain of the Dead," when my cell phone rang.

The signal was bad and the person on the other end of the line sounded upset, so I stopped the car in front of a restaurant called "Everest." Cerro del Muerte is the highest point of any highway in the country and I was surprised I had any signal at all. From the peak at 3,400m, on the rare occasion that it's clear, you can see the Pacific in one direction and the Caribbean in the other.

But there was no time for sightseeing today. It was the OSC's Chief Mining Consultant on the line and she had me on her speaker phone with who knows who else in her office.

"Where are you?" she demanded.

It seemed like an odd way to start a conversation, but I answered, "In Costa Rica."

"Why?" she asked.

I didn't know how to answer that one or see the relevance of the question, so I said, "What do you mean?"

"You have an extremely serious disclosure issue that must be dealt with immediately."

She was furious and demanded that we publish an independent report on the feasibility of the El Sastre project to protect the public. I told her I didn't know how that was going to protect the public because we had already finished construction and were now operating the mine. This didn't sit well with her and we had some more to and fro.

Finally, we left it that the Company would release the internal calculations on which the production decision was based so everyone was dealing with the same knowledge base.

Later that month we released our internal calculations and estimates. In summary, the capital cost was estimated to be $2.7 million, with a footnote that construction had been completed at an actual cost of $1.7 million. The estimated operating cost was $177/oz. of gold and the payback period, based on $550/oz gold price, was less than a year. Gold production of 20,000 oz was expected to commence in the fourth quarter and continue for at least five years.

Tom Toth and his sister Kathy came to Guatemala and visited the mine around that time. We'd gone out for dinner and were walking back to the hotel in the evening when we passed a billboard featuring a flashy BMW. Tom pointed at it and said, "Hey Kathy, there's your car!"

And it was. Kathy had bought a white 2006 BMW 325xi with some of her profits from the stock. Apparently, the car sported personalized license plates with our stock symbol "AUQ" on them.

We poured our first gold on December 5, 2006. A total of 825 oz which we sold in January for $619/oz.

In 2007, we merged Aurogin with Chester Miller's Morgain Minerals which owned the El Castillo Mine in Mexico to form Castle Gold. Castle was subsequently purchased by Argonaut Gold (2010) for around $1.25 cash per share or about $140 million. It seems that the new operators didn't like being 50:50 partners with JM because they sold him back their interest in the Guatemala properties for $1.5 million a few months later.

I've kept in touch with JM over the years. When he got the property back, he bought his own trucks and excavators and continued to operate El Sastre for several more years. Then Lupita and Bridge. I spoke to him recently in 2020 and he was still producing gold from the operation.

The Tailor of Guatemala, that used to support only a couple of skinny cows, had worked out well for everyone. Especially JM.

Mitchell, Can You Get Me Another Cold Beer? *by Tom Toth*

And so, it was about 15 years ago I was out working in a hay field and Mitchell, one of my four boys, came running into the field yelling at the top of his lungs, "Dad, there's a guy on the phone called John Paterson and he's been calling for the past hour and says it's very important I call him back pronto."

I asked Mitchell what day it was, and he told me it was Friday and nearing 5:00 pm, so I thought yes, this might be important, so on the way back to the house I asked him to grab me a cold bottle of beer. While I was dialing John's number, Mitchell came running in, popped open the bottle and handed it to me. By the time JP answered his phone, I had already slugged down that refreshing bottle and motioned to Mitchell to please go and get another cold one.

So, John filled me in on a private placement Aurogin Resources was doing to raise a bit of money for a gold project in Guatamala and he figured as a current Shareholder in Aurogin I would probably be interested in participating in the financing.

As he continued to brief me on the deal, Mitchell came running in and already had popped off the cap and handed the bottle to me and that's when I noticed there was a bit missing. I figured he ran so fast that he probably spilled a bit of it. Or maybe he had a sample for his efforts? Needless to say, 15 years later, he always has a supply of beer in his shop or his camping cooler, and he doesn't mind if I borrow one or two once in a while!

After John finished his "pitch" on the El Sastre Property, he was quick to ask if I would be interested in taking part at $0.06 with a full $0.10 warrant, good for 2 years. I had already finished off the second beer and a fuzzy feeling came over me and then I remembered that I hadn't eaten anything all day, save for some cereal and a coffee earlier in the morning.

Without hesitation I replied, " Sure John, put me down for $5,000". To which he countered, " You can have more if you'd like, possibly your sister or your parents ". So, I said, "Sure, why not. " Make it $10,000 then and that should be pretty good ", to which he replied, "You can have more if you'd like since you are a great current shareholder". So once again I said, "Why not."

By now I was feeling a little more fuzzy in the head, but I managed to make my raise up to $20,000, and at that point I asked JP when he would require the funds.

Fortunately, he said he would give me three weeks to come up with the dough and with that window of opportunity, I decided to up the ante to $30,000, to which he remarked, "You can have more if you'd like".

In the meantime, Mitchell sat in a chair beside where I was standing, listening to my conversation, and noticing a certain degree of giddiness coming forth from my speech. So once again, John offered more and I didn't let him down and so we hit the $40,000 mark and by now I was half looped and I said, "Let's just make it a clean $50,000".

Easy figuring and I can split it up in $10,000 lots. But then he came back with a Finder's Fee option. I would receive a percentage on any amount of the financing not in my name. So I figured what the heck, I'll go for an extra $5,000 and make it $55,000 in total.

I would end up with a portion of the Financing and also get a cheque for the Finder's Fee and with that money, I would buy some more free trading shares at .06 a share. I was now sitting on the counter looking for something to eat, and John came back with the big enchilada.

"Tom, make it $60,000 and that way you will have one million shares at $0.06 with one million warrants priced at $0.10 and therefore you will end up with two million shares at an average price of .08!!!" Wow I thought to myself. This might just turn out great!!

Great, and so our call ended with some laughter and good cheer and I hung up the phone and looked at Mitchell and he kind of laughed as he questioned me, "Did you just buy $60,000 of stock???" "Yup,", I remembered saying and straightaway I added, "I better get on the phone and see who wants in on this deal," because I fully knew well I could never come up with that kind of money in three weeks.

Sure enough, I ended up with a third of the $60,000 and my sisters and parents came in for the other $40,000, from which I received a Finder's Fee cheque from Aurogin for I believe it was $3,200 and with that I bought another 50,000 shares to add to the totals.

Within three years, those 2 million shares we paid $60,000 for were bought out by Argonaut Gold and we all lived happily ever after. Oh, we did have to deal with one-for-two reverse split, but we still ended up doing very well.

The math was, $0.16 for a million shares and we were bought out at $1.25. I'll take that any day and with a good portion of my winnings, I began buying Virgin Metals (VGM) and it has become Minera Alamos (MAI) and I have retained a large position in the stock. Finally, after a little over 10 years, my investment has come to life with the Santana heap leach gold project , the La Fortuna gold project and the newest gold project just acquired in Zacatecas State, all three Projects located in Mexico.

This MAI gold stock is fast becoming my winner chicken dinner #2 and as it happened, it all boils down to those two cold, frosty beers that Friday afternoon some 15 years ago. Thank you Mitchell and thank you John, it's been a blast!!!!

Opening Up Cuba, *by Sethu Raman*

In 1991, I flew to Managua, the capital of Nicaragua. The Contra War had just ended and the Sandinista Party defeated in recent general elections. As the President of Holmer Gold Mines Ltd, my aim was to investigate any new mining opportunities. Dr. Steve Ogryzlo was my partner and director of the company. We have been working on reports submitted to the Toronto Stock Exchange for listing requirements since 1986.

In Managua, I met Romero Bermudez, Director of INMIN (the Nicaraguan State Mining Company) and visited the mining camps at Bonanza in the north and La Libertad in the east. At Libertad, there was a small 100 ton per day gold mining operation dating back to Rosario days. Weather was good, people in the countryside were friendly. Mining here is still controlled by Sandinistas. Dealing with some of the defeated Sandinistas in the mining town was difficult. I had to listen to the demands by the Sandinistas who wanted bribes in millions of American dollars. I did not want to be part of any bribery which, in my opinion, always ends up badly. I had a breakfast meeting with Daniel Ortega, the opposition leader of the Sandinista Party (FSLN) at Hotel Intercontinental in Managua. He became wealthy by diverting the military shipments sent to Nicaragua from the Soviet Union and selling them to the dictators in Chile. He confirmed his future plan to recapture the presidency. In fact, he became the President in 2006 after losing three straight elections. Ortega, now 74, is in his fourth term as President.

After several weeks of field work in the La Libertad mining camp, Kilborn Engineering, an independent consulting group, prepared a Feasibility Study to build a heap leach mine at an estimated cost of US$18 million. Ned Goodman agreed to provide funding for the project. The INMIN insisted on a bidding process to sell 100% interest. There were no other bidders in the first round. In the second round held in 1991, another Canadian company Greenstone Resources, led by Ian Park, apparently using some of our metallurgical data, won the bid to acquire 50% interest in parnership with mine workers holding 50% interest. In March 9, 2000, Greenstone decided to wind down the operations. All directors and officers resigned.

Romero Bermudez, Director of INMIN became a good friend of mine and showed me a large (4 x 8 ft) mineral map of Cuba showing all prospects and deposits. This map was the result of a $100M program over a period of ten years involving several hundred geologists from Soviet Union, Cuba and Eastern European countries. It was apparently the only copy outside Cuba. I was blown away looking at the details. I recognized a fantastic opportunity to discover base and precious metals. When I expressed my interest in visiting Cuba, Bermudez was willing to contact officials within GeoMinera in Cuba on my behalf and arrange a visit to Cuba.

My letters of interest to the Cuban Trade Commissioner in Montreal led to an investigation and a personal interview by a CISIS official who work closely with CIA on Cuban matters. I was questioned about my proposed visit to Cuba.

Early in 1992, we received an invitation letter and visas to visit Cuba. Steve Ogryzlo and I planned a one-week Sunday to Sunday only trip to Cuba. Two local geologists, Pedro Vega and Armando Simon from GeoMinera S.A. (the Cuban State Mining Company) greeted us at Havana Airport. We visited five mining camps spread over 1100 km and reviewed reports in Spanish on more than 50 projects. We had time to visit only few projects. In each camp there were over 50 to 70 geologists, engineers and support workers sitting idle following Soviet collapse but ready to work. Amazingly, we travelled on a four-lane divided highway across most of the country with little or no traffic.

During my first trip to Cuba, I saw a once-in-a-life opportunity to cherry-pick from advanced exploration projects with excellent discovery potential. Soviet-led exploration had included heavy emphasis on exploration for industrial metals such as iron, nickel and copper, but not on precious metals. They had never used airborne or ground EM systems . It seems that Soviet geologists were not exposed to or were unaware of modern geological concepts like VMS models. Above all, it seemed that there were far less indicators of corruption in Cuba than countries in Latin America.

Another advantage was that Canada has had a long history of diplomatic relations with Cuba. With American Embargo in place, we didn't have to compete with American companies. In my first meeting with our Canadian Ambassador, I asked why there are no significant Canadian businesses in Cuba. I was told that Canadians generally follow Americans in foreign countries. In Cuba, there were no Americans to follow. I was advised to be careful not to get involved in local politics and that the CIA was always watching.

After the Soviet collapse eliminated Cuba's main benefactor and subsidizer, the economy had hit rock bottom. The country was going through a crisis known as their "Special Period". That meant long lineups for food along with frequent blackouts. There were two gas stations in all of Havana that were open to foreigners only. Long road trips meant carrying a 20-litre tank of gas in the car and essential food supplies like peanut butter, sardines, crackers and SPAM.

Sethu Raman with Cuban Vice-President Dr Carlos Lage at the Loma Hierro Silver Project in 1998

Steve and I visited the San Fernando property previously explored by a team of Soviet and Cuban geologists but abandoned in 1991. Checking the rocks near an old collapsed shaft, we noticed banded cherty felsic and altered mafic volcanic rocks with quartz veins including pyrite and chalcopyrite. I also saw a rusty outcrop which looked like a supergene enriched zone representing the leached cap of the sulphide zone. The geological setting and altered lithologic units were comparable to those at Waite Amulet mine in Noranda, Quebec. In 1971, while working for Noranda Exploration, I spent the summer mapping the alteration pattern associated with the eroded VMS deposit at the mine site.

Our first visit to Loma Hierro property was difficult because of poor road access and heavy tropical rains. After a long walk through a thick forest, we reached the top of this mountain covered with lateritic rocks and soil that go along with hot tropical areas. Through a translator, we understood it was an iron deposit (20% Fe) that had been fully explored and bulk sampled. Recent drill hole tested an IP anomaly intersected sedimentary rocks with some galena veins. I noticed someone digging a pit to get kaolin clay (alteration ??) to whitewash his house. It became apparent to me that no one assayed for gold or silver. Lateritic rocks were very similar to the gossan I mapped at Caribou VMS deposit near Bathurst, New Brunswick while working for Anaconda American Brass in 1970. I believe Anaconda was the first company to apply the volcanogenic concept to exploration and to discover a VMS deposit. I took a sample from the outcrop near the pit back to Toronto. I was not surprised to see the sample assayed over 15 ounces of silver per ton.

We returned to the Hotel Triton in Havana late in the evening on a Saturday. At my request, Armando arranged a meeting with officials at 10 p.m. to discuss a possible deal on the properties we selected. We started with a strong Cuban coffee and ended by negotiating a Letter of Intent at about 3 a.m. The agreement covered the two most promising prospects- San Fernando project in Central Cuba and Loma Hierro project in Eastern Cuba. Steve was very tired after a long working day and fell asleep at the office for an hour or so while I continued the negotiations.

We returned to the hotel, packed our luggage and took the early Sunday morning flight in an old Russian aircraft. I noticed a strong cold draft coming from the floor of the aircraft and I reported it to the hostess. She said "no problema" and returned with a cup of water and poured it over the vent. Voila! The water froze and no more cold draft.

After 18 months of negotiations, Holmer eventually signed the Final JV agreement with GeoMinera in the summer of 1993. Holmer set up offices in Pinal del Rio and Santa Clara. Cuban operations were supervised by Jose Preciado. Mr. Preciado had over

25 years of Canadian and Latin American experience in mineral exploration, development and production.

Systematic exploration programs at the San Fernando project in Central Cuba proved successful with the first drill hole in 1994 intersecting stratabound mineralization assaying 18.54% Zn, 7.93 oz/t Ag, 0.08% Cu, 0.32% Pb over 10.7 ft . Subsequent drilling confirmed that what was originally thought to be a vein-type Cu-Zn deposit was instead a volcanogenic massive sulphide deposit with extensive foot wall alteration. Old underground workings reached within 60 feet of the massive sulphide zone.

Following the silver discovery at Loma Hirro in Eastern Cuba, initial drilling established a high grade silver gossan deposit which was previously reported as a low grade iron deposit. It is tabular in shape and flat-lying, less than 75 feet deep and readily amenable to open pit mining. Average grade estimated at 10 oz per tonne.

Holmer spent a total of $1.5 million over a two-year period in Cuba. Two significant mineral discoveries have been made in each of those two years – a silver deposit and base metals.

By 1997, Holmer was already well-established as a leading exploration company in Cuba and by that time, more than 13 other Canadian junior companies were competing.

Palmitas, *by Kerry Knoll*

We were sitting in a fine restaurant in San Jose, the capital of Costa Rica. I was with Franz, a local mining engineer who was our managing our Bellavista gold project and the president of their little mining association. He may have been the only native Costa Rican mining engineer, certainly the only one I ever met.

Anyways, I saw on the menu that they were serving a salad with hearts of palm, or palmitas as they called them. I had grown to like them while living in Brazil, so I ordered it. While we were waiting for our food, Franz told me that the heart of palm served in this particular restaurant was illegal, different from the variety that we bought at the supermarket. It was much tastier wild breed that grew high up in the protected cloud forests. It was illegal because you had to kill the tree to get a few servings of it. Poachers were cutting them down in the national parks, since most of the ones outside of the parks were long gone. The trees that were farmed for palmita, by contrast, keep on giving for years. Now I felt bad.

Then Franz said, "See that guy over there. He's the Minister of the Environment. Have a look at what he is eating." Same salad. It was delicious.

Cobra Panama, *by Ed Thompson*

In the 25-year period from late 1991 to early 2015 I was a director, president, or chairman of some 20 exploration/development/mining companies. Of the 20, four eventually became major mines, Adrian Resources, Cobre Panama, Consolidated Thompson, iron in Quebec, Chariot Resources, copper in Peru, and International Gold, Bibiani mine in Ghana.

Six companies developed one or more medium-sized mines, Aurogin, Dakota Mining, Geomaque, Golden Queen, Minera Rayrock, and Orvana. Freewest's large chromite deposit remains undeveloped. Three of these companies were subject to takeover battles, and I was the chair of the special committee negotiating these takeovers and another four were involved in mergers. It was a very exciting, interesting, and rewarding time.

Adrian is one of these stories.

In July 1993, I joined the board of Adrian, of which Chet Idziszek was president. The company's main project was Petaquilla, in Panama, which was found to contain two copper-gold porphyry deposits with a geological resource of about 1 billion tons grading 0.5% copper plus a little gold. At that time, the company was initiating a $4.7-million exploration program and feasibility study at Petaquilla, as well as general exploration on four other areas.

The shares were around $2 and the directors received options on 120,000 shares at $2. I mention this to make the point of how fortunes come and go in our industry. In 1995 and 1996, with high copper prices and negotiations for a takeover, share prices reached $6 to $7 and I only sold a few shares as we expected higher prices.

Later on, after Teck had spent more than $20 million on a feasibility study and the price of copper declined below $1 a pound, the project went on hold and share prices drifted downward, remaining stuck in the 10-to-20¢ range for many years. Sic transit gloria mundi . . . and your money too.

In reviewing my old files, I was reminded of the heady times we had for a couple of years. At the time of our listing on the Toronto Stock Exchange, in early 1994, we were busy raising money, drilling away in Panama, getting exciting results, and finding several new deposits. Yorkton, our main broker, was pumping the stock. It was an interesting time in Panama as well as the U.S. was starting to pull out of the Canal Zone.

Our initial studies, based on dollar-per-pound copper, looked positive and everyone thought we had a winner. As usual, we had a beauty contest with various financial advisors to determine who would advise us on the sale and get a big fee. They all suggested we sell on the basis of much higher copper prices in the range of $1.25 per lb. Teck, which had some weak rights-of-first-refusal, agreed to fund a feasibility study. The amount of paper generated by all the regulatory filings, audit committees, and various business dealings was enormous – something I hadn't realized until I started cleaning out my files.

The feasibility study did not get completed properly by the end of 1996 and the capital costs had escalated to more than a billion dollars, so suddenly the numbers didn't look too promising. The size of the operation kept increasing -- from 60,000 to 70,000, even to 120,000 tonnes per day -- in an attempt to improve the economics.

In January 1998, engineering firm H.A. Simons completed the final feasibility study on behalf of Teck. It showed an after-tax cash flow of US$2.1 billion with a net present value at 10% discount of US$364 million using long-term prices of US$1.10 per lb. copper and US$375 per oz. gold. Daily production was pegged at 120,000 tonnes. According to these assumptions, the project had a 14% rate of return and a payback period of under five years. Total mineable reserves were estimated to be 1.47 billion tonnes grading 0.47% copper and 0.08 gram gold with a stripping ratio of 1:1.

But copper and gold prices were crashing, and in mid-1998 Teck decided to postpone development of Petaquilla for a year. Adrian's shares gradually declined and by 2000 they were in the 10-to-20¢ range. Then the emerging economies of China and India started powering new consumption and the copper price rose steadily to around $1.50 per lb. in 2005 and to $4 per lb. in 2008. However, in 2003, we had sold a block of stock to a new group at 15¢ and, after several months of discussion, turned the company over to them. Adrian eventually lost the option and the shares became worthless.

In 2011, Inmet Mining started to develop the property.

The company was acquired in 2013 by First Quantum for $5 billion and first production was in June 2019 at a total capital cost of US$6.5 billion. Projected production was 72 million tonnes per year by 2020, increasing to 100 million tonnes per year by 2022 (about 285,000 tonnes per day), making it one of the largest copper mines in the world.

Current reserves are listed as 3.2 billion tonnes plus another one billion tonnes as inferred, grading 0.38% copper, 0.07 grams of gold, 1.3 grams of silver, and 0.006% molybdenum.

Before leaving the Adrian saga, I have a little adventure story to tell.

In 1996 the company invited some brokers, analysts and directors to visit the property. It was only accessible by helicopter, so four choppers were leased to move about 20 people from Panama City westward to the property, a flight which lasted about half an hour. I was in the last chopper with a broker and two employees and was all set to enjoy a pleasant visit to the property, where I would examine core, and so on. I had on a set of headphones and could hear the conversation between the pilot and the control tower. We were just picking up altitude and getting ready to head out over the jungle when I sensed something was wrong and the chatter took on a tone of urgency. The machine lost power and the pilot auto-rotated down into an open field. We crashed with a bump (not much more than the shock from a fender-bender), but the tail rotor snapped off and whirled across the field and there was a cloud of smoke and dust and the smell of gas.

A woman employee went a little hysterical and we all scampered out of the machine and ran away in case of an explosion. However, nobody was badly injured. Fairly soon, a vehicle found us and drove us back to the airport. The broker and I waited for an hour and went on to the property when one of the other helicopters arrived. We were fortunate because in another minute we would have been out over the jungle and auto-rotating down into the rain forest. As Churchill said, "There is nothing more exhilarating than to be shot at and missed." The rest of the tour was uneventful.

AIRBORNE

Last Chance Airline, *by Dave Rogers*

I was visiting a drill camp site. A geologist was loading a Cessna 105 at the end of a beaver swamp for his last trip out. It was a good landing site in the winter with the dead trees cut down at both ends. But summer heat made it dicey. He had agreed to give me a ride out. So he tied the pontoon to a tree stump at the take-off end and told me to chop the rope when he got the engine revved up and signaled from the pilot's seat. I was to quickly walk back up the pontoon and into the back seat position.

I made a quick decision and when I chopped the rope I dropped down on the log as he took off. He barely cleared the trees and if I had been on board, I suspect we would not have made it. So, I walked the 8 miles out on a messy drill road and lived for another day.

Flying Memories, *by Chris Jennings*

Early flying memories include flying to the UK on BA Comets up Africa circling Mt. Kilimanjaro to see Africa highest snow-capped mountain. Comet flying was discontinued when wings fell off several of these newfangled passenger jets while crossing the Mediterranean Sea with all passengers lost.

Before this, my wife Jeanne's grandmother was flying just after the end of World War II from the Vaal River south of Johannesburg. She flew in some of the earliest planes to the UK all the way up Africa in flying boats which landed and refueled in some of Africa lakes like Malawi and Victoria, then on to the Nile, Mediterranean and finally the UK.

While on one occasion while flying from South Africa to Rhodesia, now Zimbabwe, in our small twin engine plane, we ran into a series of typical summer thunderstorms that at first we were able to avoid.

Eventually the plane's radar showed no way through and our pilot said, " there's no longer any way round and I cannot get high enough to fly over them so buckle up and hold tight". Then followed one of the most frightening flights of my life with our plane dropping hundreds of feet then abruptly rising similar amounts with our experienced pilots struggling to control our plane . To this day I don't know how we survived that storm.

On another occasion and without our normal charter flight pilot, we again boarded our six seater plane and our young pilot got in and we set out for a remote airstrip in central Botswana. As we started to get close to our destination and having fortunately visited there many time by tracks through the bush, I tapped her on the shoulder and told her she was 50 miles off course.

At first she hotly denied this but when I insisted she corrected her flight path and we landed safely at our destination. While camped there that day, I noticed she walked with quite a limp. The next day we set out our for another air strip in North Botswana and again I had to correct her for being well off course. I later found out that she had some time back lost her way, crashed and broke her leg in the process! But for my knowing my way on the ground in these areas I too may be walking with a limp or worse!

On another occasion I was visiting a remote uranium prospect with my Falconbridge team in Namibia when I heard a warning siren go off in the pilot's cabin only metres from where I was sitting. The pilot seemed calm with this until I realized as we touched down and broke our propeller while skidding along the runway in a huge cloud of dust. We had made a wheels up landing fortunately without the plane flipping and catching fire!

Crashed Beechcraft Baron, Namibia, 1974

One memorable flight was from Maun, Botswana on the southern end of the Okavango swamps in a small twin-engine plane . While deep into the area, one engine started to make strange sound with our pilot breaking into a heavy Giuliani-style sweat. He finally switched off one engine and we limped back safely to Maun. I found out later that day that he had consumed at least half a bottle of brandy the night before.

While working in Rhodesia during the troubled days before Ian Smith's resignation and the Robert Mugabe takeover and the creation of the new Zimbabwe, we would fly up to the small but lucrative Falconbridge gold mine near Gwanda. As we crossed the border into Rhodesia our pilot would fly at 200 mph just above tree level so that rebels with ground to air missiles or AK47's would not have time to pinpoint us.

Another time, I wanted to visit the huge Camafuca-Camazambo kimberlite pipe in Angola's Lunda Norte Province during the peak of the war between the government and Unita's communist backed rebels.

All bridges to the area had been blown up or the approaches to the remaining bridges land mined so there was no road access. There were also no scheduled flights to the area, so I hitched a ride on the Russian cargo planes supplying food and fuel to the alluvial diamond mines in the area.

The plane on which I had hitched my ride was delayed about six hours in the boiling Angolan sun so I eventually sat on a cargo of smelly semi-thawed frozen fish on the way up and stood between huge diesel tanks on the way back knowing that the Russian crew were consuming huge amounts of beer on the flight. At least it wasn't vodka!

I was being taken to the pipe in a government vehicle when a local woman hailed our vehicle and told us that there was a Unita ambush waiting for us not far ahead and over a rise. When we asked her if she wanted a lift away from the ambush she declined and said she had friends nearby that she needed to warn as well.

The fancy pink diamond on the left sold for $50 million in 2018. A beautiful rough pink is on the right.

Incidentally, while with SouthernEra, we later acquired rights to explore this pipe and were going to mine the pipe lying under a swampy area by dredge when our mining engineer was murdered in an ambush either by Unita or some other group. This pipe, still unmined to this day, is likely to be the source of the beautiful pink alluvial diamonds found nearby of which I had personally seen many pink microdiamonds when looking at micros extracted from our core. This same pipe features as the Camafoza pipe in Mathew Hart's newly published brutal novel, "A Russian Pink" and is the source of the huge so called "Russian Pink" diamond around which the novel is featured.

During the Rhodesian bush war I would sometimes fly by commercial South African Airways flights to Harare or Bulawayo. On takeoff, the planes never left the airfield in the same direction but would veer off in odd directions and at varying ascent angles. This all to evade the possibility of being shot down by a ground to air missile.

"Don't mess with me!"
– an angry lion in Kalahari, Botswana

Years later in a long and friendly conversation with Tokyo Segwale, a very senior African National Congress member and at one stage a prime candidate to be president of South Africa, he told me that he was one of the people manning those ground to air missiles which did succeed in shooting down at least one commercial flight. He ended up becoming a successful South African businessman.

A Flying Lesson, *by Dave Rogers*

In northwestern Quebec four of us flew into the Lac Inconu area for a week's staking job. The pilot was Art Fecteau out of Senneterre, Quebec, who was a well-known Canadian bush pilot. As we came into the lake over a large poplar tree and all in bloom, he came down and smacked the top of it with his floats and landed the plane in the lake with a satisfied grin on his face.

"That scared the shit out of me", I said. "By the way, why did you hit the tree with the float? It's kind of dangerous and you have paying passengers?" He just looked at me and said, "You want to be picked up in a weeks' time, right?" "Yes sir", I said. He got in the plane and took off.

One week went by and no plane. By the second week food was running low. Eating fish three times a day and we were waiting for the plane that did not land for us. No Fecteau airplane for our camp. So, another week later he flies over and radios down, "Are you ready to come out?" I replied, "Yes sir." He landed we packed up without another word spoken and he flew us out.

Lesson learned do not piss off the pilot. Especially if he owns the air service

Flying High, *by Kerry Knoll*

I'm pretty sure it was Tom Ogryzlo who told me this story. Back in the early fifties, he got a job as a student with a junior company to spend part of the summer prospecting in the Yukon. He and his co-worker flew to Whitehorse and went to meet the float plane early in the morning.

The pilot showed up three sheets to the wind, maybe four, apparently having been drinking all night. Being young naïve geology students, they weren't sure what to do so they loaded the gear, got into the plane and took off. After they had been flying for about 15 minutes, they looked over and saw the pilot had passed out. Again, not sure what to do, they thought it best to just sleep for the two hours it was going to take to get to their destination.

When the job was finished, they waited for the guy to pick them up again, but he never showed. They waited day after day, getting a little nervous as the days were getting shorter. Finally, another plane showed up. The pilot told them that their the original guy lost his pilot's license for flying drunk. It wasn't until about a week later that somebody thought to look at his schedule book and found that these two young students were scheduled for a pickup, and the location.

Flying Canoes, Snakes and Guns – Nakina Style, *by Dave Rogers*

I was on the first float plane out of Nakina, in northwestern Ontario with our field Party Chief heading to our camp site. A first for me. It was a very hot and windless day. Standing on the shore beside our pilot, having just unloaded, I was watching our second plane with our second canoe tied on to the pontoon and struts coming across the lake.

I said to the pilot, "Wow that would make quite a sight if the ropes broke and to see the canoe tumbling down crazy like." He whirled on me just about to clip me on the side of the head. "Sonny it doesn't work that way. The rope breaks and the canoe shoots up into the wing, damaging or tearing it off and everyone dies in the crash."

Dead silence. Then he said I lost a good pilot buddy last month in that type of accident.

Early Sunday morning and I get jarred awake by a gunshot from a .303 rifle. I'm camped on a small island near a couple of returned veterans who were prospecting in the area. I walk over expecting they had shot at a bear. But No.

One guy is sitting on his bed holding the rifle and laughing his fool head off. His partner is standing by his bed cursing a blue streak. The guy with the rifle had wakened up to see a very large garter snake coiled up on top of his partners sleeping bag. His partner was snoring away inside the bag. He blew the snake into pieces and guts all over the bag and the tent wall.

And all I could say was, "Hey fellas, got any coffee?"

More Flying, *by Chris Jennings*

While looking for diamonds in Venezuela on one occasion we were to fly in a chartered fixed wing plane from a part of the country to an area in the jungle to the north where alluvial diamonds were being mined.

We had arranged for a helicopter to pick my wife and myself at a remote strip and take us on to small clearings in the jungle inaccessible to a fixed wing plane. As is usual in some countries, our fixed wing was very late in picking us up and as we approached our destination our pilot told us that our helicopter pilot had grown tired of waiting for us and taken another charter.

By good fortune, we were able to find another helicopter and we proceeded to land at a number of small clearings to observe work mining gold and diamonds. We noticed that while on the ground the pilot would keep the chopper running and not switch it off. On enquiring why, he replied that he wasn't sure he could start it again if he switched off.

After several stops, we returned to the chopper and our pilot replaced his headphones and was startled as he received a message that our original helicopter had crashed into a river with most people dead.

We took off, rounded a huge tepui one of those magnificent flat topped circular mountains projecting way above the dense jungle, we came across the kilometer-high sheer drop of the Angels Falls and went on to drop us at the small resort at the mile plus wide   Falls before going on to a rescue mission for our crashed helicopter.

Incidentally, most helicopters we hired in Venezuela had no seats, no doors and no seat belts. We sat on wooden boxes! Most pilots scared the hell out of us by flying just above jungle canopy and straight at the occasional huge tree protruding above this level and would then flip over the tree at the last moment.

On one occasion we had Joe Reed, new CEO of Superior Oil, visiting some of our newly discovered kimberlites near Tshabong in Botswana. Just before our small plane was due to takeoff we had a heavy thunderstorm which turned the dirt strip into a mud strip. As Joe had only a few hours to catch his return flight from Johannesburg, he told the pilot to take off despite his protests.

Anyway, we started the takeoff but because the thick mud we could not get up enough speed so the pilot aborted the flight and we prepared to get off the plane and drive but Joe again commanded the pilot to take off. This time we barely made it and just became airborne before the end of the strip.

Terra Firma Never Felt So Good, *by Ed Thompson*

In the period from 1992 to 2016 I was a director, president, or chairman of some dozen and a half junior companies. In late 1993 I joined the board of Denver based Dakota Mining Company (then Minden Gold). The company had interests in three marginal heap leach gold operations, Gilt Edge and 40% owned Golden Reward mines, both located near Lead, South Dakota, and Stibnite in Idaho.

The August board meeting in 1995 was held at the mine offices at Stibnite, Idaho, an old mining camp and led to an unusual experience for four of us. As access to the mine was difficult, we flew in that morning in two small Cessna planes and landed on the mine's small gravel strip. We toured the property, held our board meeting, had a nice lunch, and left around 2 o'clock. There was a little concern about the winds as the runway was short and surrounded by hills but both planes got off okay. I was in the second plane with Martin Quick, VP of operations, who was in the co-pilot's seat. Allen Bell, president, and I were in the middle seats, and Stan Dempsey, director, was in the back.

It was a beautiful summer day over central Idaho and as the pilot got the plane up to our flying altitude to go to Salt Lake City, he turned around and yelled, "Anyone got any Tums or something. I don't fell too well." And indeed he looked as white as a ghost. A minute later he threw up and slumped over the controls. Some concern. Martin held onto the dual set of controls while Bell and I tried to rouse him with shakes and slaps. No luck. Martin said, "I think he's had a heart attack and is dead. Does anyone know how to fly this plane?" He looked at me and although I had lived in these small aircrafts for many years doing exploration in northern Canada, I had never taken lessons. "Not me," I replied; "how about you, Allen?" He gulped and looked back at Stan and repeated the question. None of us had.

Then we decided to try the radio to contact the base or someone to get instructions. We couldn't even get the radio to function. I remember thinking that I must be in a dream and would wake up any second. But it wasn't a dream. I'm sure that all of us thought that we were about to meet our maker.

Martin suggested that one of us move up with him into the

pilot's seat, but what to do with the pilot as there was little room in the small Cessna? We discussed just opening the door and pushing him out. Martin was grimly holding onto the controls to keep the plane steady while we discussed strategy. If we could get near an airport, could they talk us down like they do in the movies or could we survive a crash landing? As we tried to move the pilot, he moved, groaned, and slumped over again. Well, at least he wasn't dead. We waited.

A couple of minutes later, he moved again and we shouted, "Can you land this thing?" Someone remembered a large abandoned US Air Force base nearby. Now this was the dangerous part, circling down, because if he passed out again, Martin was unlikely to be able to straighten us out and he certainly couldn't land it. A long five minutes before we were bumping along the gravel strip. Within seconds of stopping we were all out into the loveliest summer day on record in central Idaho. We kissed the ground and took pictures. The pilot stumbled into the bush, shedding his clothes and puking away. Martin and Stan tried their cell phones with no result and I lit up a cigar and sat under a tree.

About a half hour later, the pilot wandered back out of the bush, half naked and looking half dead. He must have been around 65 but looked much older. He said, "Well I feel a little better and think I can make my base. Does anyone want to come with me."

It was one of those moments you remember forever. We looked at each other and simultaneously replied, "No thanks, we'll wait for the replacement pilot."
So we sat and talked and speculated whether he would make it and what his problem was. A couple of hours later, a replacement plane arrived and took us all to Salt Lake City without further incident.

Later we learned that, despite extensive medical tests on the pilot, there was no explanation. The suspicion was food poisoning although we all ate the same lunch. He was relegated to flying mail. Bell and Dempsey took flying lessons but I decided that it was my first bad experience in 35 years and probably wouldn't happen again (and it hasn't). Dakota Mining was forced into bankruptcy in 1998 due to environmental delays.

OFF THE BEATEN PATH

From Canada to Siberia, *by Hamish McGregor*

No question, I have had more than my share of good luck in Canada. Most memorable was being offered a job by Bill James a year after emigrating from Zambia in 1967. My first assignment was to program exploration for a small group of companies in the Findathoran Syndicate, managed by Bill.

Initially, this was most of what I did, but, when needed, I did field work on other assignments and learnt about the Canadian Mining Industry. The firm James and Buffam consulted mainly for senior companies such as Falconbridge, Abitibi Paper and the Bank of Commerce, and while Bill was their mining brain, he became my mentor and friend. I owe him a lot including my becoming a P.Eng. and a member of the Tuesday Club.

So often, exploration results in discoveries that are either too small or too low grade to be mined profitably. Such was the Findathoran discovery at O'Hearn Brook in New Brunswick where some 30,000 tons of very high-grade Cu-Zn-Ag ore might have been mined by resueing, and shipped to the nearest smelter, but it did not happen. In time, Findathoran was wound up.

Fortunately, every now and then there's an exciting major discovery and consultants are called in for their opinion. One I enjoyed in the company of Bill was Tara in Ireland, which we visited upon its discovery in 1970 and confirmed its worth to the company's executives.

Another was Mattabi, discovered in an airborne EM survey by Mattagami M.L. encroaching over Abitibi land. Deciding terms of an agreement with Abitibi to jointly explore and develop it was a challenge for the executives and Bill, their consultant. Suggested acquisition of Mattagami by Abitibi, before it merged into Noranda, was considered, but Abitibi executives were too occupied at that time with their pending merger with the "Price Company".

After Bill was persuaded in 1973 to move to Noranda, I tried consulting on my own, but without connections, it was too tough for me. So, I accepted a two-year posting with CIDA in Botswana, mostly to help the government negotiate a contract with De Beers for mining one of the world's greatest diamond pipes, Jwaneng, and for me to learn about diamonds. Then back to Canada for another brief struggle as a consultant before being hired by Abitibi-Price to manage their small Mining Division.

The metal mines in which Abitibi-Price had major interests, Buchans in Newfoundland and Mattabi in Ontario, gradually ran out of ore and when management decided to focus on their paper industry, logical steps were taken, and the Mining Division closed in 1985.

I had met Jack McOuat and Ross Lawrence from time to time and was highly flattered when, soon after I left Abitibi, they invited me to join Watts, Griffis and McOuat ("WGM") as a Senior Geological Associate. Of course, I accepted, and then enjoyed a remarkably active association which continued for almost 20 years, and has never terminated.

It was truly wonderful for me to be assigned in October 1990 to head up a team that would complete a full assessment of the mineral exploration opportunities in Zambia, the land I had reveled in before coming to Canada. With a deadline of March 31, 1991, it took little time for me and seven professional staff to embark and get to work across the country.

We had invaluable help from numerous other professionals and completed the projected work on schedule. After compilation and editing, the WGM report, available through Zambia Consolidated Copper Mines Ltd ("ZCCM") is dated August 31, 1991.

Among other remarkable assignments was a technical evaluation, in Russia, in 1993, of the diamond mining and processing operations of Almazy Rossia-Sakha, the state-owned company. Amicable meetings with executives then led to organizing an on-site study tour of the mines and workshops for a group of Canadian geologists in Russia, and a similar group of Russian geologists in Canada. This was followed by editing a unique WGM publication "Diamonds of Yakutia, Russia: Extended Abstracts". Vivid memories remain of my visit: extreme cold, carpet-covered walls in bedrooms, filtered beer with straw-remnants, a "memory tree" decked with pieces of clothing apparently torn on-site by visitors, too much vodka, and my seeing Russia's largest diamonds, still uncut, and preserved in Moscow.

I had often visited Buchans in Newfoundland when with Abitibi, so was eager to accept a surprise request to rush to St. Johns and examine some core from a supposed new discovery.

The company was Diamond Fields Resources Inc ("DFR"), and, although I did not know all this at the time, two prospectors, one of whom, Chris Verbiski, I knew was from Buchans, had been grubstaked by DFR. They had identified a promising base metal outcrop near Voisey's Bay in Labrador, completed surface sampling and magnetometer and horizontal-loop EM surveys and followed up with four diamond drill holes.

On November 3, 1994, Diamond Fields announced the discovery of the Ni-Cu-Co mineralization. On completion of the drilling, the core was shipped to St Johns and hidden in a warehouse until my core examination on Nov 7.

After examining the core, I called Robert Friedland, President of DFR, with my very positive opinions. Logging and core-splitting followed and complete assay results for the four holes were released by DFR on Nov 17. Although I revealed my opinion only to DFR and WGM, Lionel York, a friend and fellow member of the Tuesday Club, got wind of the discovery and my involvement. He called me for some verification, and when I did not deny DFR's merits, he recommended acquisition by the club. It turned out well!

Turkish Gold – Nevada Style! *by Ian Thompson*

Of all the places to work for a geologist trained in the Canadian Shield, Turkey was by far the most complicated. The country is the meeting point for two tectonic plates and the resulting geology is fused, folded and rotated and generally mucked about. For three months over the summer of 1991, using a rusty Lada Niva 4x4, a young Turkish geologist, whose father was a General, and I scouted the essentially volcanic /sedimentary eastern half of Turkey, searching for gold and copper. We were supported by a Turkish exploration company based in Ankara.

In 1991, I had re-located to Vancouver from Toronto. At the time, the mining industry was, once again, in the midst of recession, however, that spring I was approached by a retired Canadian senior mining executive, who wanted to explore in Eastern Turkey, via his new Turkish company. His partner was a Turkish mining engineer.

I decided to apply for a summer term position of Senior geologist/prospector. Pay, in U.S. dollars, was extremely generous for experienced and imaginative geologists, plus a 10% Net Profits Interest in any claims or mineral rights so granted. This was to be rigorous field work, traversing rough and mountainous terrain, thus demanding a good fitness level.

The rationale was that certain geophysical characteristics – inferred structural, gravity and magnetic trends – typical of the geology and copper deposits of Nevada and Utah -- could also be found in East Central Turkey. This program was proposed by a hefty, asthmatic, 60-year-old, Reno-based geologist, who was to be my cross-shift. There was also a Reno Professor, a porphyry specialist, particularly on microscopic identification of key alteration minerals, but too large to contemplate hiking up the mountains. Eastern Turkey was selected, since Western Turkey, being as modern and as attractive as Greece, was considered to be too well explored, offering less chance of discoveries.

We followed a series of postulated magnetic, structural, gravity trend lines that would indicate prospecting areas. Detailed geological maps of eastern Turkey may have existed, but were not available, and the military maintained an embargo on releasing any road maps in the less traveled areas. We used ragged old topographic maps that had been photocopied numerous times. It was fortunate that my Turkish geologist was able to plot our routes through this hideous, mountainous terrain.

I was always driving as young Turk men never seemed to get enough practice in driving, let alone a four-wheel drive vehicle. Our actual field work was to be as secretive as possible, as was the custom in exploration. I posed as an American mineralogy, paleontology professor in talks with the leaders of small villages we passed through. Everywhere we went found evidence of small-scale mining and smelting by the Romans who had been there earlier. They mined copper, but also silver, lead, gold and iron. In some cases, this likely went back to the Bronze age, so at least we were following our prospecting noses correctly. We also found rare examples of prospecting by Cominco, which was active in Turkey then.

We were jailed briefly, scouting too close to the old Soviet border but thankfully the General got us discharged after buying a big dinner for everyone.

We cut samples wherever we noted hematization, kaolinization, brecciation, veining, deformation, and rarely sulphide mineralization. Samples were sent to Vancouver and routinely assayed for copper, gold, silver, plus other noted mineralization. Results were disappointingly too low to be of commercial interest.

The Reno-based geologist was to continue my work, but I was not party to the results.

During our work we toured the majority of the Cappadocia region, but it became quickly apparent that this was the wrong area to search for gold deposits. The landforms such as the fairy chimneys of younger volcanic tuff were fascinating, but the area had been better developed as a refuge from Bronze-age, Roman and other incursions, as evidenced by the numerous underground caverns, galleries and Orthodox Christian churches. So, we took a brief break from work and enjoyed the alternative geology.

To succeed in mineral exploration, one needs time to build relationships and a solid technical base, and then you might get lucky. It is not possible to assume initial success. Where gold is involved, faith often overtakes firm science reasoning, particularly when times are poor, and we did not locate any significant gold or copper deposits as a result of this program. The secretive approach, based on hunches and ignorance, was by then out of fashion.

WILD CRITTERS AND EXOTIC PETS

"If You're Gonna Shoot – Shoot!", *by Nick Tintor*

Have you ever awoken suddenly at night in a daze to realize that something not very good is happening around you? That feeling where you go from a dreamy sleep to an instant state of awareness and consciousness?

It was my first ever field job as a summer geology student in 1977 working for Western Mines, the predecessor company of Westmin, west of Baker Lake, Nunavut. This was the wild, wind swept barren lands of Farley Mowat, who in later years while working in the tundra, I learned the geologists referred to as Hardly Know It.

I was in a small fly camp with four people managed by our party chief, Marie Michaud. A fly camp is almost like a quick re-action team, usually a helicopter ride from a larger base camp, that goes to complete a specific exploration assignment in a re-mote area.

In the summer there is no night when you go to sleep in the tundra. At midnight in June, it's still quite bright and I would pull my head under my sleeping bag to make it lights out.

That's when in my dreamy sleep I heard a large bang. I turned over in my sleeping bag and then another loud crack. And that one woke me.

I was on the right side of a 10 ft x 12 ft canvas tent, really a palace for one person. I turned to my left and looked up and could see the blue sky and a few white clouds drifting by.

Then I really snapped awake. "What the hell?" my woozy brain registered. You shouldn't see the sky in your tent.

"Bang", the third time now and I know it's the camp .303 rifle firing. And there, about three feet past my shoulder, is the large reddish-brown hump of a Barren Land Grizzly taking its time to amble away from my ripped down tent wall.

"Marie..." I yell, "Where the hell is that thing? Did it walk around to my other side?" I shouted. "No, it's going to the kitchen tent."

Picture this. I'm in my underwear, sitting up in my sleep-ing bag and holding my 8-inch Buck knife, which by the way, is one of my most prized possessions to this very day. I start to get dressed and think about running into the lake. But it's still got ice on it.

With no real plan if the grizzly decides to come back, you do what anyone else would do, grab your camera. I had one of those crappy Kodak Instamatics and took one snap that shows a grainy brown blob walking away from my tent with the wall gone.

Eventually the bear walked away over a small hill and disappeared. I ran to the tent where Marie and another person were and asked, "When did you see that bear?" She says, "About an hour ago. The dog woke me up."

"Are you kidding me? You watched it walk over to my tent while I'm a sleeping and tear the shit out of it with me in it?" I couldn't believe it. She explained she was scared and didn't know what to do except finally start shooting in the air when it was on my tent. "Marie, if you're gonna shoot, then shoot before it goes into my tent, not after!"

Must have been like 3 or 4 in the morning so we had to wait for base camp to wake up for the scheduled 7 am radio call. While we waited, I said I'm holding the rifle. No Yogi is going to chew on me today.

Then one of the funniest responses I have ever heard comes crackling over the radio from Ernie Nutter, the senior geologist on the program. Ernie went on to become one of Canada's most respected base metals analysts at Royal Bank of Canada and then the Capital Group.

"Ernie, a grizzly has attacked our camp," Marie reports. "One tent wrecked, kitchen tent damaged and we think it's coming back. What should we do?"

Long pause on the radio and Ernie radios back, "Just piss on it. Over."

Piss on it? Is that what he just said? That's it? Son of a bitch, I'm sending that bear to his goddam tent!

But Ernie did end up sending the chopper to pull us out back to base camp.

And from that day on and for the next four field seasons, Nick Tintor packed a Marlin 336C loaded with 200 grain 35 Remington rounds and his Buck knife and vowed never to feel so naked and helpless again when sleeping in a tent.

And that was also the very last time I ever saw a Barren Land Grizzly bear again in the field. I did have to shoot a black bear one summer, but that's another story.

Pets, *by Hamish McGregor*

In my novice time at Luamata, word of our exploration spread among the locals and people dropped by with things to sell. Mostly these were foods, but one day a vendor unrolled a package containing two tiny mountain leopards. Squirrel and I could see no easy course of action to save the beautiful little beasts, so we bought them – one each. We quickly devised bottle feeding supplemented with whatever they could be persuaded to eat, and they survived. Our barricaded tents were the home where they grew and played, often in our absence as work came first. One terribly sad day we returned from work to find our pets had torn apart a pair of socks and consumed part of the material. Poor Squirrel, he had to endure the death of his pet, while mine, that I had named "Spike", survived.

Spike learnt to sleep on my bed and come and go around the camp as he pleased. I purchased a 16 gauge shot gun which I used from time to time to hunt ducks, partridge and guineafowl, and supplemented Spike's diet with doves. At whatever camp I was located, I would walk in the early evening with Spike trailing behind me like any lazy domestic cat, until I saw and shot a dove. Then he would pounce and eat it all except the bird's crop. He accompanied me on the necessary trips to HQ and loved meeting and playing with all the urban people and their dogs.

After about nine months, Spike was semi-independent – able to head into the bush for the day and return in the early evening as I sat in the shade and waited for him. At the time, I was looking after a drill on the Solwezi Dome, but far from the town of Solwezi. A radiometric survey had revealed a strong anomaly that I located easily on the ground after dropping a toilet-roll from a plane window as my hand-held Geiger-counter peaked. Tracing uranium mineralization into potentially economic quantities proved impossible as the ground was highly fractured, but a couple of holes were drilled, nevertheless.

It was the end of that project and I was about to return to university which was the first of several returns using accumulated leave to further my education. Perhaps I should have taken Spike to a Game Reserve, but I did not. I left him in a delightfully isolated rocky terrain along with a few chickens released in the woods near-by. Did he survive? Back at university and maybe a month or two later, I received a letter from a co-working geologist who told me he had returned to near my old camp in a jeep. As he pulled to a stop a leopard emerged from the bush, jumped onto the hood of the car, looked at him, and then returned to the bush. I hope it was Spike.

Dogs were always company for us in the bush. Owners commonly left their pets in the camps when away on holiday, or as I did, returning to university. In one area that I was mapping the usual two cut lines a day, in flat country with beautifully open bush, we had the pleasure of two dogs to keep us company. One was large and easily ably to do the traverses and the other was large by the standards of its breed, but, being a Dachshund, limited in the length of its legs. On the trails, big-dog veered off chasing other animals that we disturbed quite frequently, while small-dog stuck to the trail even when I veered off to examine an outcrop called in by one of the rock-spotters.

A call one day from one of the rock-spotters was that he had seen a wild pig up ahead and soon after we saw them too. As the dogs took off after them, with small dog yapping constantly, we dropped everything (except my geological hammer) and ran in pursuit. Wild pigs have stiff necks and trouble running as the snouts sag and snag, and within half a mile or so, we caught up. Big-dog was side-lined with his throat cut by a boar while small-dog, firmly attached to one of its hind legs, was being whirled and dragged in circles. It was easy to hit the boar on the head with my hammer, carry it back to the trail for a later BBQ, and resume operations. Big-dog received a good wash in a near-by stream, and fortunately was not injured severely.

At this same camp, a week or two later, I bought a small wild pig, presumably caught after a hunter had killed the mother. I named him "Emperor" after P.G. Wodehouse's famed Empress of Blandings. Emperor grew up thinking he was a dog, free to roam, eating bacon scraps and competing with the dogs in camp for our attention. He saved us one night with a huge commotion when a fire threated to engulf the camp, and on another occasion chased a dog in-heat all over the open plain in front of my campsite until the dog came to me exhausted and desperate. Emperor travelled with me to HQ where he was accepted by other humans and dogs for the unique companion he was. The ending of this story was, once again, my return to university to further my education. Emperor was given a home at a friend's house in Kalulushi, but not long after my departure, his life was ended, and his body consumed with relish.

Moose Encounter, *by Dave Rogers*

It was 1960 in Northwestern Ontario in the Sturgeon-Metionga Lake area mid-September with my senior assistant, and we had finished our field mapping and were scheduled to fly out the next morning. There were a lot of moose running up and down a swamp across the river and we were hollering at them.

We had finished supper and were polishing off a bottle of medicinal rye and feeling mellow. We had a nice tent set up parallel to the lake shore with a large cedar tree leaning out over the lake. Picture the tent opening up to a fire pit with a nice bed of coals and a large, curved log reflector behind it to give us some heat in the tent area. My assistant stepped off into the bush left of the fire to take a leak.

Loud snorting, cursing and the assistant jumped back in and over the fire pit and straight up the cedar tree hollering "Heads up! A fucking moose!"

I was sitting in the tent opening enjoying the heat and doing up the final day's notes. I did a back flip into the tent and under our bedrolls.

The moose, snorting, landed feet first in the fire pit. Then with a roar crashed through our log heat reflector and took off down the shoreline. My assistant came down the tree and we finished off the bottle quietly and went to bed. Who would have thought, almost trampled by a moose!

Moose on the Beach, *by Dave Rogers*

One junior assistant was a runner in track and field and after a day of traversing in the bush, if we were camped anywhere near an old logging road or a stretch of beach, he would go running for 45 minutes. One evening I heard him calling. He was running down the beach back to our camp and yelling "help!" A moose was chasing behind him.

As he got closer, I hollered to him to pass me and then jump off the beach into the camp area. I had spotted a fairly large dead spruce leaning out over the beach. Four strong swings with the axe prepared the tree and as he passed me, I pushed the spruce down on the beach in front of the Moose. It snorted, turned around and took off back up the beach. Would have been great if we had someone on a movie camera.

Snake Encounters Around the World, *by Chris Jennings*

As a young boy riding my bike on a narrow path in Natal province, South Africa, I suddenly came across a fat puff adder lying across the path. Puff adders are notoriously fast strikers, but my reflexes prevailed and I lifted my feet up to the handle bars and flew over and by the adder unscathed.

While with the Bechuanaland Geological Survey, I was driving slowly on a bush track, to show senior mining company officials from South Africa the outcrops that became the large Selibe- Pikwe nickel copper mine. Suddenly a huge cobra, with hood raised, rose up next to my open window. Both of us, startled, briefly looked each other in the eye before we were carried slowly forward and out of range by my jeep.

Also, while in N. Namibia trying to find another fabulous Tsumeb Mine for Falconbridge, a huge black mamba reared up next to my open window for a brief terrifying moment before that killer strike could happen. (Tsumeb probably produced a more spectacular variety of magnificent museum specimen minerals than any other mine. It was always a pleasure and exciting to visit underground there.)

While working for Corona in Nevada, I suddenly became aware of a nearby loud rattle (which of course came from our famous rattlesnake). I stepped aside quickly and we each went quietly about our respective business.

On another occasion about six years ago two little girls from a neighbouring house in Topanga, CA where my son lived, came to visit our two granddaughters who were out at the time. They were not in any hurry to leave and had been chatting happily with us for 15 minutes or so when one of them casually said, in passing, "Oh by the way we both stepped over or bye a small (but still poisonous) rattlesnake lying on the stairs" apparently not at all concerned about their safety.

Early this year while at our game lodge in S.A. I opened the lid to the quite small seed container of our bird feeder and out popped a 1.5-metre green boomslang. I got such a fright that I fell on my back amongst some hefty rocks, lucky to miss all of them, while the snake escaped into the tree above us. A boomslang bite produces a venom yield of 8 mg but only 0.09 mg are required to kill an adult . When compared to the black mamba, long regarded as Africa's and one of the world's most venomous snakes, it has a bite venom yield of 300 mg, but 15 mg are needed to kill an adult.

We often have visits from Mozambican spitting cobras investigating the frogs in our fish pond but have never had them enter our buildings because of the screens that our son, who was our architect, had installed in all the windows and external doors. Other game lodges have had fearsome bites from these reptiles biting guests while asleep in their beds. Apparently, if you can slide a finger under your door this aperture is big enough for a two-metre cobra to enter.

On another occasion my wife and were travelling on a track in the central Kalahari in our trusted one-ton Chevy pickup when we rode over a +3 m black mamba gliding right across our soft sandy track. On stopping to check it appeared that neither our vehicle nor the mamba had suffered any damage as it had disappeared into the bush.

Chris' Chev pickup truck in deep sand tracks in Kalahari, Botswana

On another occasion while driving our five-ton Bedford truck in Botswana I drove over a snake in the road and when I stopped to check my staff on the high back of the truck made mighty leaps and ran off into the bush saying the snake would climb up into the vehicle and bite them.

One evening, last year, my wife wanted to bring in a towel that she had left to dry on a rail in our open-air shower at our lodge on a game reserve in Limpopo Province, South Africa. Big windows and a glass door divide the shower enclosure from the bathroom inside. My wife walked up to the door and opened it and, luckily, looked down to see where she was about to step out. Right next to where she would have put her foot, was the head of a 2,5m black mamba, sliding along at the foot of the wall. My wife quickly drew her foot back and closed the door and, with the aid of her flashlight, we watched the big, startled snake, writhe, and thrash about on the smooth shower floor, until it found its way out under a raised door at the back of the enclosure.

Elephants drinking 20 metres from our guest.
bedrooms at our water hole, Limpopo

At the back of our bedroom at the lodge was an old, discarded barbeque on wheels with a 15-cm gap between the floor of the barbeque and the paved area below. I had walked past this most days noticing fallen leaves had accumulated in this gap. One day I noticed a very slight movement and gently moved the barbeque to see what it was. At first, I could see nothing but then saw that the pattern on the back of a large puff adder perfectly matched that of the jumbled leaves in which it was hiding.

These days following a course on how to catch venomous snakes and also treat snake bite by S.A.'s premier herpetologist Johan Marais and having purchased the equipment to catch and store virtually every snake in the book we now catch and relocate all snakes. One piece of advice that he gave that we haven't forgotten "do not under any circumstances try to catch a black mamba bigger than 3 metres!"

Now for something gleaned from his monthly newsletter: Only 10 to 12 people die of snake bite every year in S.A., most of these from mamba or Cape cobra bites. Other major snake bites come from puff adders and Mozambican spitting cobras.

The Bears at the Golden Bear, *by Kerry Knoll*

When the Golden Bear Mine was first built, the operators decided that the eco-friendly way to deal with bears was to live-trap them and release them far away. So, they set up the trap and not long after they had their first black bear. Somebody called the ministry to see what they were should do with it, the government guy asked, "Do you have a trapping license?" Well, no. "Then you got a $1000 fine for illegal trapping." The hapless employee asked what they should have done instead. "Shoot it," the civil servant said.

When we restarted Golden Bear as a heap leach in 1997, the bears really got out of control. Mostly black bears with the occasional grizzly. One old grizzly used to sleep right in the middle of the road, and they had to get the big front-end loader to coax him out of the way. We finally bought four Karelian bear dogs to keep them away and they did a pretty good job until, one by one, the bears got them.

We went back to live trapping, this time with a license. Well, we caught 32 of them the next summer. The ministry required us take them at least 100 km away and release them, but first to get a bucket of paint and a mop and paint the bear's butt white so we could tell if the bear came back to the mine. The bears got really pissed off when their butts were getting painted, so sometimes the paint was all over the place.

Well, it happened that that summer a junior exploration company decided they wanted to use our private road for their program. It was a 150 km access road, complete with 17 bridges, that Homestake and Chevron had built through the mountains. It cost about a million bucks a year to maintain. Our policy was that we would add up the total kilometres driven by us and anyone else who wanted to use it, divide by the maintenance costs, and charge a per kilometre toll to cover maintenance. No charge for the $21 million that was spent building it in the first place.

The guys from the exploration company came up with some obscure policy in the B.C. laws that said they could use our road for free, and they weren't going to pay us. So, we got into a lawsuit with them, which we later won.

The warden came by one day and told us he'd stopped at

the exploration camp along our road and asked them if they had a bear problem too. "You wouldn't believe it," the camp manager told him. "We got all kinds of bears. And they seem to be some kind of strange subspecies, maybe related to that white Spirit Bear, because they all have white butts." The warden was killing himself laughing as he told this.

A Wild Ride on a Moose, *by Dave Rogers*

I borrowed this story from my brother. A newly graduated "Forester" from U.N.B. was their party chief. They were crossing a lake in a motorboat and spotted a large Bull Moose swimming across the lake.

The young forester directed my brother to run the boat up along behind and the side of the Moose. He then jumped out of the boat and onto the Moose's back and grabbing the base of the antlers. Ride 'em cowboy. The Moose was pissed but could not buck him off. Suddenly the water shallowed, and the Moose found his feet in the sand. He just bellowed and took off for the alders and spruce along the shoreline. Gord hollered for the Forester to let go and fall off in the water right away. Oh no! our New Brunswick Forester was going to ride him to shore. Big mistake.

The Moose ran straight into a stand of Alders grading into a bunch of prickly branched spruce trees which became larger. The Moose literally wiped the guy off his back into this prickly mess and kept on going. Needless to say, a geologist would have abandoned ship earlier and avoided a trip to the hospital. The Drs. and Nurses spent hours picking branches out of buddy's body. Oh yes. He survived but it was a painful process.

Now, That was Close! Mountain Sliding B.C. Style, *by* *Peter Hubacheck*

In the field season of 1974, I had just graduated from Haileybury School of Mines and was on my way to Robb Lake, B.C. This was my first job in mineral exploration, and I was hired by Dr. George Mannard, Chief exploration geologist for Texasgulf in Toronto.

I was hired as a prospector / field assistant working with a geological team headed by Bob Gifford and specifically assigned to assist Fran Manns who was working on his PHD on the Robb Lake Lead-Zinc deposit. In early May, we mobbed in from Mackenzie, B.C. in a twin Beechcraft flying through wind-driven mountain passes glistening with cirque bounded glaciers and landed on a 5,000-ft airstrip.

All geologists, assistants, chopper pilot and engineer built our plywood canvas cook tent, sleeping tents and humongous core shack to support the diamond drilling program. My job included cutting spruce logs in the valley floor at elevation 5,500 feet, then hooking up the logs with chokers, so our pilot could drop them off to construct the drill pad log cribs on saddlebacks at elevation 7,500 feet.

One day in in early May, I was with Larry Graham, pilot of our Bell 47 chopper and we spotted a Grizzly bear in a saddle at 5,500 feet, above the treeline. Larry put down the collective and hovered over him then as the Grizzly began to climb the heavy snow-laden north-facing slope. Larry probed him with the stinger a few times. Then the bear galloped straight up a 35-degree slope and reared up and challenged us at the top of the limestone ridgeback. At 7,500 feet! The sheer power of this magnificent animal was awesome to behold.

A week later, I was sent out on two-man prospecting sorties prospecting massive scree piles at the base of cirques. I thought I was well equipped for these high alpine traverses, but little did I know what was in store for me the next day.

After being dropped off by jet ranger chopper on a north facing saddle at 7,000 feet, the snow was crumbly and starting to melt. On that brisk morning, we decided to take a short cut across a frozen snow patch at the top of the cirque to get to an outcrop on the other side.

My Kodiak construction boots began to hydroplane on solid ice and desperately I tried to jam my heels into the snow lying flat on our backs as we were now launched like rockets straight down the mountain. In the twinkling of an eye, both of us landed up to our waists in soft corn snow and amazingly our rock hammers landed right beside us.

Our packsacks still were on our backs. I looked up and immediately realized we had flown over a ledge and were saved by a protected patch of soft snow breaking our fall over a scree slide that was 1,000 feet below to the valley floor.

We carefully picked our way through the heavy limestone scree and waited for our helicopter pilot to arrive. Bruce was a high time 20,000 hr ex-CIA Blackbird pilot and he couldn't believe we had survived this adventure as he had witnessed many calamities in his career. I resolved to get custom-made Buffalo Mountaineering boots which equipped me well over the next 9 years as a Rocky Mountain Geologist in B.C. and the Yukon....and thanks to my guardian angel!

DPR & the Bear, *by Dave Rogers*

We did a lot of shoreline mapping by canoe with short traverses across strike. Halfway through the summer I was climbing up a long, sloping, 65 feet high outcrop on the shoreline. About 20 feet from the top, I glanced up and saw two bear cubs hanging in the top of a small spruce tree. Oh! Oh! Says I and I quickly turned and ran down the sloping outcrop and about 10 feet up I jumped into the bow of the canoe. Grabbed the paddle and power stroked the canoe offshore about 35 feet. Momma Bear was on the shoreline growling at me.

We moved further offshore. I asked the junior did you see me walking into that bear situation. He was a farm boy from southern Ontario and replied. Yes, I wanted to see what the bears would do. Let's face it these idiots come from all walks of life. If we had been on shore with no threatening bears beside us, I would have pushed him in the lake and half drowned him I was so pissed off.

Good or Bad Encounters with Animals, *by Pete Hubacheck*

During the fall of 1977, it was customary for us field geologists working for oil companies based in Calgary to meet at the Four Seasons tavern on Friday afternoons to down a flat of beers with hundreds of other young studs including Rick Mazur, Tom Sills, Bob Maxwell, Locke Bell, ... (8-to-1 male to female ratio)....exchange stories and watch fights.

My friend, Doug Noakes had just returned from an Aquitaine exploration camp north of Great Slave lake. While on a mapping traverse, Doug and his assistant, encountered a barren land grizzly which forced Doug to take evasive action. They managed to run and scale up a rocky knob with the bear circling them menacingly. Doug called in the chopper and the pilot hovered over the bear but to no avail. The chopper went back to camp to pick up the shotgun at camp.

After a few hours, the bear was finally dispatched. The field party decided to get rid of bear by slinging him over a shallow pond and dumped him there. A decision was made to notify the federal wildlife Ministry in Yellowknife. An order came back to the camp to remove the tagged ear from the sunken bear. This was done by Doug's crew, but since the company was domiciled in Calgary, the provincial ministry then made a second request.

Doug's crew had to not only return the ear, but the head had to attached as well. No doubt, this was a difficult exercise to salvage the bear from the lake bottom. This awkward task of severing the head was completed and unceremoniously packaged in plastic garbage bags in a cardboard box and shipped down south. Instead of arriving at the Wildlife office in Calgary, the box landed right on the desk of the main reception floor at Aquitaine's Calgary office. As soon as the receptionist opened the garbage bag inside the box, a massive stampede of people entirely vacated the floor.... We were all howling on the floor as Doug described this event .

THIS AND THAT

The Prospectors All Stars, *by Kerry Knoll*

One day in the mid-1980s when I was editor of The Canadian Mining Journal, geologist Peter Tredger, who was working for Canamax at the time, told me I should come out and play for the Prospectors All Stars, a group that played pickup hockey every Friday night at the Upper Canada College Rink.

There were mining analysts, promoters, geologists, a real mix. Wally Curlook and Graham Farquharson were the senior players on the crew – you knew that because they didn't wear helmets.

One of the highlights of playing with that group was the annual hockey game during the PDAC, where the miners from eastern Canada would suit up against the Vancouver contingent. Jim Priest was our manager, and he would always try to stack our team with ringers. The guys from the west did the same thing. Glen Goldup formerly of the L.A. Kings and Sean Shanahan, who had played under Don Cherry in Boston, were regulars, as were a few former college players.

One year Teck's Norm Keevil, Sr. decided to rent Maple Leaf Gardens for the event, and went all out, hiring a film crew and the real announcers from Hockey Night In Canada. He managed to get superstar Phil Esposito on his side, but Jim was able to counter with Eddie Shack. Our coach was none other than Don Cherry. It was lots of fun, the highlight for me getting hooked violently around the chest in this supposedly non-contact event. I looked around and there was a grinning Esposito. They set up Keevil, who was about 75 at the time, beside the opposition goalpost and finally Espo bounced the puck off of his stick and into the net.

A few weeks later Jim Priest was at a bar somewhere, getting into his cups and bragging about his hockey team to a fellow patron, from the town of Cannington east of Lake Simcoe. The guy said, "Hey, I've got a pretty good hockey team as well, why don't we have a match." Cannington was one of those towns that produced hockey players like Saskatchewan produced wheat.

So it was set that we were going to drive up to the town of Cannington one Saturday night, and play in the town's little arena. But something had gotten badly lost in the translation. Probably something to do with the booze. I drove up with Peter and we arrived at the same time as a number of other players. On the marquee it said:

"CANNINGTON VS THE NHL OLDTIMERS"

WTF? We started lugging our gear to the dressing room and there was a line of kids holding out paper and pens for our autographs. They had peddled tickets for the event and the place was sold out! We got to the dressing room and suited up, wondering what was going to happen next. It turns out they had several former NHLers on their team. Neither of our NHL ringers showed up, and nor did most of our other good players, so it was a disaster. We lost 17-1 (for the record, it is hereby noted that yours truly fired our only goal, but I think it was because their goalie was bored and talking to somebody in the stands when I shot). They had to refund all the money.

Professor Nuffield's Comeuppance, *by Dave Rogers*

Back in the 1960's Prof. Nuffield, a renowned mineralogist, took over as head of the Geology Dept. at the University of Toronto. He made many drastic changes in the name of pure science, upset many Masters and Ph.D. theses in progress and caused strife in the Geology Dept.

He was not popular with neither the students nor most of the faculty. Near the end of his first term, he had called a staff meeting in which he gave a short speech to persuade the members of the geology staff to support him in his quest for a second term. The room was silent.

Prof. F. Gordon Smith, geochemistry, a 5'5" ex-serviceman quietly walked up to stand in front of Nuffield. He bent down and came up from the floor with a closed fist and knocked Nuffield out and flat on his ass. Nothing needed to be said. There were two doors to the meeting room, and everyone quietly stood up and left.

Later someone went looking for Prof. Smith. He was sitting quietly working at his desk in his office. No.... Nuffield did not get appointed to a second term.

Perhaps My Biggest "Miss", *by Dave Rogers*

The fall of 1958 I was visiting my home in Pembroke at the end of a field season. My father, a very successful businessman had earned his MBA (finance) at Harvard following his return from fighting in the First World War. He survived 7 major battles in France.

He asked me if in my short career in geology if I had any good business ideas. I pondered briefly and replied yes. With your money and business experience I suggest we proceed over the next 5 to 10 years to examine, select and acquire as many sand and gravel pits, plus un-exploited deposits in the Ottawa Valley as we can. Over the next 50 years think of the road building, town expansions, new bridges etc. expansion should increase greatly.

A lot of cement with be used and sand & gravel are the necessary ingredients. Long term it should be very lucrative, perhaps better than real estate or bank stocks. He thought about it and agreed it would be something we should pursue.

Of course, I kind of put the project on the back burner because it was pretty dry stuff compared to mineral exploration, and geology around the world. He mentioned it to me every time I came home to visit. BUT.... I just kept putting it off by heading off to a new area, deal or opportunity in the world. The World was my Oyster. My BAD. We never followed through.

A Devoted Partner, *by Chris Jennings*

When about to graduate in late 1956 from Natal University we were visited by virtually every major South African mining company looking to recruit geologists. I was about to marry Jeanne straight after graduation and she had expressed willingness to come into the field under the normal rough camping conditions for the odd six-month plus winter field work season. To my surprise, not a single one of the companies allowed wives into the field. However, the Bechuanaland Geological Survey, part of the British Colonial Service, said wives were most welcome.

The Jennings tent at Lebun Pan, Botswana, 1964

On arriving with my new bride in January 1957, I was assigned almost immediately to a quick field job. To the surprise of the people at the Survey, we found that although most geologists at the survey were married, no wives had ever accompanied their husbands into the field.

So, my statement that my wife would be coming into the field with me caused a major panic at the Survey. For a number of years, we roughed it in the field camping under canvas, drawing our water from 44-gallon drums and cooking on open wooden fires and bathing in tiny folding canvas baths. They later supplied an ugly corrugated iron caravan-like vehicle which we towed everywhere and was quite comfortable on the inside.

Even after our four children were born, they all came into

Caravan near Serowe, Botswana where Seretse and Ruth Khama, later to be President and First Lady, had lunch with the Jennings.

the field from about the age of three months. We regularly heard lions roaring at night, had elephants occasionally walk through our camp at night, and would drive through herds of plains game including springbuck, wildebeest, hartebeest and, in Northern Botswana, Cape buffalo or sable antelope. Sadly, those huge herds are now gone.

Our dogs, Rhodesian ridgebacks, loved to chase the springbuck which would tease them by leaping gracefully into the air arching their backs "pronking" and easily staying out of reach of the dogs. We would also occasionally see a pack of wild dogs with their beautiful multi-coloured coats. On one occasion while sleeping in the open, I heard a leopard coughing quietly as it walked around my cot. It fortunately didn't want to eat me for supper.

Herd of springbok in the Kalahari Desert, Botswana,
one of them pronking

On another occasion our foxhound, inherited from my father-in- law because it refused to hunt the jackals which caused devastation amongst his big flock of merino sheep, chased a threatening leopard when I came upon it unexpectedly while mapping. Leopards were regarded by the early hunters in South Africa as the most dangerous of all wild animals.

The Chainsaw in The Ice Pan, *by Dave Rogers*

An example of Canadian diamond driller's acumen. We had a bad storm the overnight with high winds which cause the huge offshore ice sheet to heave and break up into large pans in places. We had a drill set up closer to an island offshore and a large pan developed and began to rotate. The driller noted it right away.

The casing and drill string were about to be broken off. They opened the back of the drill shack and got out the chainsaw to open a channel for the casing to slide along so it would not break off and we would not lose the drill hole. The ice floe (pan) rotated around the drill casing. When I flew in with the chopper in the morning to check their drilling progress, I noted this long quarter mile plus black line from the back of the drill shack. They explained it to me when I landed. I was impressed and said I will see to it that you both get a bonus for smart thinking.

Random Drib-Drabs, *by Chris Jennings*

It was a great pleasure of being involved in pioneering geophysical surveying for and dating of groundwater. Today, many, many thousands of Batswana are drinking this fresh and potable water. Probably one of the most satisfying things I have done.

Also doing pioneering search for kimberlites with geophysics, using mineral chemistry to predict economic pipes and using new methods for extracting microdiamonds and then predicting grades of kimberlite. Huge excitement in search of kimberlites in Botswana and later the great Canadian diamond staking rush with 300 companies involved. Enjoyed working with Gren Thomas then and again today in North Arrow.

One worry. At the peak of the rush, UTM coordinates were changed from NAD 27 to 83 and millions of dollars were spent drilling wrong coordinates as geologists often were unaware of the change. This change could move a target by as much as 180 metres in one direction and 70 metres in another. Enough to miss a 1.5 hectare-pipe worth US$12 billion!

Unusual Consulting, *by Hamish McGregor*

There have been times when the Canadian Junior Market was extremely strong, money came from everywhere and an endorsement from a Consulting Geologist was about all that one needed to finalize an agreement and lock in the funds.

One such endorsement request to WGM was from a Swiss Bank whose in-house advisor and unknown clients were preparing to back an established Canadian Junior Mining Executive in the acquisition of an up-coming gold mine on which construction of a treatment plant was largely complete.

The call to me requested a quick review and a trip to Switzerland to OK the pending funding. Accepting was routine, but time was short. Even as the job was confirmed and the flight being booked, I headed for the mine site and arranged a trip underground. To my horror, there was only the tiniest trace of mineralization. Next a visit to the treatment plant confirmed that it was essentially being built as expected, but what was it going to process? Reading the available paperwork which I studied quickly, I realized I had a problem.

All of the people involved were considered reputable, and defamatory action by me was simply out of the question. In fact, my only acceptable course of action was to go to Switzerland, meet with and convey the truth to the banker and act further under his instructions.

Our private meeting took place in the morning and the wise banker asked me to attend the public meeting that afternoon as had been previously arranged. I was not party to conversations that the banker had with the others in the remaining time before the meeting, but I was reasonably certain that he would make sure that I would not be embarrassed. The meeting was actually pleasant enough as the absence of reserves or resources was quickly established, and it was clear that any funding would be to the personnel based on their reputations, and not to the intended project. Dinner hosted by the banker was excellent, and we all parted amicably.

I never understood who made the money constructing a treatment plant on a site with no ore, nor do I fully comprehend how a former mayor, in the town where I now live, enabled family to get municipal construction contracts. Seemingly construction can be a profitable and low-risk game.

Another example occurred when my good friend Torr Jensen, also a former member of the Tuesday Club, asked me to extend a consulting trip to South Africa that he knew was about to take place and visit potential diamond mining operations of a Junior American Company (JAC) that was seeking funding from a well-known Canadian financier. The timing was fine and with WGM's approval I completed my assignment at the Newlands Diamond Mine, and then drove to the site of the first of JACs mining developments, which, like Newlands, was on a large farm in the Northern Cape Province.

Construction was underway on what I had been led to believe was the treatment plant for diamondiferous kimberlite to be mined on site. I met the farm owner from whom JAC had optioned (or acquired?) the mining rights, and his brother who had the contract to build the treatment plant, and, while waiting for an employee of JAC to arrive, toured the plant and site.

There was not much to see except a small excavation to bedrock where a very narrow kimberlite dyke was exposed. JAC's employee, a recently hired young geologist, confirmed that there was no drilling or geophysics to provide evidence of an economic deposit. Clearly the construction of a treatment plant was premature.

Before heading home, my new JAC acquaintance and I visited "Pienaar's Pothole", a legendary, alluvial source, formerly mined for diamonds, in the Lichtenberg District of the Transvaal. Perhaps an option, and perhaps remnant gravels could (and can still) be located and mined, I nevertheless could not carry back information to my client that would encourage investment. Not surprisingly, the young geologist accepted my conclusions without dispute, and we departed as friends.

The story did not have a happy ending. On my return to Toronto, I met with the client and advised him not to invest as planned. Later, at home, I received a phone call from the president of JAC, who voiced his disappointment at my client's withdrawal and wanted my explanation. As we talked, I learnt that he had not visited the properties himself – amazing.

A Tale of Two Macs, *by Mac Watson*

In the early 1970s, Lynx-Canada had discovered the Long Lake Zinc deposit north of Kingston, Ontario. Most of our shareholders were from the Ottawa area and were quite vocal. During the exploration drilling, the stock was extremely volatile. A shareholder had contacted the RCMP and inferred the project had no merit and was a pump and dump operation.

Soon, the plainclothes RCMP officers turned up at our office on Adelaide Street in Toronto. After viewing the maps sections and assays, they were satisfied that the project was not a fraud. Years later, I found out that one of the officers was Mac Balkam, now of Eskay Mining. We became good friends over the years, playing golf and visiting Florida. He told me about his visit to the Lynx office, and said, "Mac, I didn't have a clue what you were showing me, but you looked like an honest person."

Real Life Behind the Fiction, *by Richard Hogarth*

I worked for Jack Coghlan from 1955 to 1957 at Bouzan Mines, at their property in the Chibougamau area. He was a rough, tough, gentle and decent character of Irish descent, from Pembroke, Ontario.

The first and last chapters of Arnold Hoffman's book *Free Gold* are about a fictitious character, namely him.

He came to visit, staying at the Wacanichi Hotel. At the bar, he pulled out of his pocket a well-worn cheque from Noranda Mines for $1,000,000, representing 500,000 shares at $2.00, and said "What do you think of that Hogarth".

Editor's Note: That $1 million would be about $10 million in today's dollars.

A Feast of "Spruce Partridge" (The 'Fool Hen'), *by Dave Rogers*

August 30th, 1955. We had finished our traverse and heading back to camp. Suddenly I realize I am surrounded by about 2 dozen spruce partridge. Big smile. Ray we are going to have good fresh 'bush chicken' suppers tonight and tomorrow night. Succulent, fat thighs and breasts. After three celibate months what more could we ask for.

I quietly backed up, selected and trimmed a long thin, lightweight alder trunk. Reached into my back right pocket for my trusty coil of fine copper wire and prepared the noose. I then, clucking quietly to the birds, commenced to slip a noose over the first one's neck. A sharp tug and the headless bird was flopping on the ground. The others just perched around and watched. It took me about 30 minutes to work my way through the entire two flocks. The final hen was perched about six inches above my reach.

I kept moving the noose slowly up and down directly below it and clucking softly. After about 10 minutes and the limit of my patience it finally reached down and put its head in the noose. Snap- Gotcha. Score 100%. Another 20 minutes and I had them all skinned, and the thighs and breasts wrapped up and in my bull bag ready for the trip back to camp. Everyone was satiated after dinner and even more appreciative of DPR's Ottawa Valley wilderness expertise.

Note: The Spruce Partridge are supposedly not good for eating. They taste like spruce needles. Not true May through November. It is only in the winter months when they tend to feed more on the spruce tree.

Mining & the Tech Boom, *by Kerry Knoll*

It was the year 2000 and the tech boom was in high gear. Couriers in elevators were talking about their portfolios. Barbers were speculating with the clients on the next big thing. The young immigrant woman who did my wife's nails was talking about the small fortune she made investing in Amazon. Meanwhile, mining companies were in a severe bear market, with gold at $275 and no money was available. Droves of juniors were making the transformation to tech.

Our Wheaton River was doing fine, but my other company, Glencairn, was on hold, trading at a dime when it traded at all. Luckily, we were sitting with a couple of million dollars in the bank. Two days didn't pass without somebody with a tech concept knocking on the door to grab our "shell". But the proposals were all crap, at least the ones I understood. Most of them were nothing more than ideas. "What value do you put on your concept," I'd ask. Twenty million wasn't an uncommon reply, always with a straight face. In the middle of all of this, a guy from the Alberta Stock Exchange calls.

"So, do you have any plans to get into the Internet business?" he asked. "Many of our listings are doing this and we are encouraging it." I answered that we had looked at dozens of ideas but none of them made any business sense.

"So," he replied. "You're looking at tech. I think you need to put that in a press release." I explained patiently that we weren't close on anything and we may wind up staying with mining. But he was insistent, and so we drafted up a release, and put it out the next day.

The release was like fireworks on the market, the stock opened at 40 cents and within a day went through a dollar on heavy volume. Ian and I looked at each other said "what the fuck?" and sold 100,000 shares each. Thirteen years after founding the company those were the first shares I had sold. I bought my wife a new car. A few months later the shares went back to 10 cents. We stuck with mining and seven years later Glencairn had three operating mines and 1200 employees. If any of those tech ideas we looked at ever saw the light of day, I never heard about it.

The Root of a Problem, *by Dave Rogers*

Dr. George Mannard was Texas Gulf senior geologist-International. He later became President of the company for one year before he was tragically diagnosed with a melanoma cancer at age 50. George was an excellent geologist and a good person. We were good friends.

He and I had been discussing and arguing, strongly at times, over the geology I had mapped regarding new VMS targets. He just did not understand or believe the geology I was trying to demonstrate to him.

I went to bed that night very disappointed that I had not gotten through to him. During the morning drive down to the office it hit me. I walked straight down to his office and without even a 'good morning George', I smiled and said George are you colour blind by any chance?

He looked at me smiling and said yes Dave everyone knows that. I see everything in shades of green. Ouch—our problem was solved. I pulled out the map and sections again and went over the rock types and my colouring scheme. We had our differences solved in minutes and George said yes to my project.

It's the RCMP Calling, *by Mac Watson*

In 1972 while working with Lynx-Canada, I was in my office at 25 Adelaide Street East in Toronto, when I received a call from the RCMP. The officer calling asked me if I knew a Mr. Armstrong. "Yes," I said. "He's an old prospector who works with us." "No, that's not him," he replied. "but we have a Karl Armstrong in custody who had your business card in his wallet. Can we come over to your office and discuss this matter?" I agreed, and they arrive shortly afterwards.

They grilled me, wanting to know why this Karl Armstrong had my business card, then explained that he was one of the major suspects in the University of Wisconsin Madison Campus bombing that destroyed Sterling Hall and killed a researcher. The man was on the FBI's 10 most wanted list.

During the early 70's, it was not uncommon for young people to hitchhike across Canada. I explained to the RCMP officers that I was working in the Beardmore and Dryden areas of northwest Ontario and was driving between job locations. I often picked up hitchhikers with my pickup and had given this man, Karl Armstrong, a ride from Thunder Bay to Ignace.

While we drove, I asked him where he was from and he said the U.S., and that he had crossed the border through Maine into New Brunswick. He was a very pleasant soft-spoken man, with a beard.

In our conversation, I mentioned that a mine was being built north of Ignace and that he could probably get a job there. I gave him my card when I dropped him off in Ignace. The RCMP were satisfied that I had no other connection with Armstrong.

Leaving the Corporate World, *by Dave Rogers*

I formed the David P. Rogers Grubstake to finance a start up in the overburden drilling business. I had designed, built and perfected the equipment while with Texas Gulf but they were not interested in following up on it and gave me the equipment when I left their employ.

It was called Drift Prospecting using a 1.5-inch diameter, dual walled, lightweight aluminum rods I had designed. We simply pumped high pressure water with a wajax fire pump down the outer annulus of lightweight dual walled aluminum rods. The sediment/overburden/till etc. we were drilling (hand power washing) through came back up the inner rod and fell onto a 10-mesh screen where we could give the material a quick evaluation and look for signs of sulphides, gold and/or kimberlite mineralization etc.

We collected the basal sample. The total sample was passed over a shaking table in our lab. The various concentrates would be examined under the binocular microscope in detail. A very effective and cheap and fast way to get a preliminary evaluation of the types of mineralization along the miles of continuous electromagnetic anomalies produced by airborne surveying. But more importantly it was used to target the specific, isolated EM anomalies that might be indicative of a VMS deposit.

While still at TGS I needed to persuade Holyk of its usefulness I drilled two holes down ice from the Kidd Creek Cu-Zn deposit. I pulled up a pail full of chalcopyrite, sphalerite and sulphides from the basal till in both holes. I took both pails to Toronto and showed him. He was surprised, amazed and pleased. Ok Dave you get your budget. A nice fast way to determine if the EM anomaly is barren or contains minerals of economic interest.

Unfettered Optimism, *by Kerry Knoll*

Gold miners are nothing if not optimists. I was at the annual BMO mining conference in early 1997 when it was still held in California. Three hundred people in attendance, including the presidents of the top mining companies and the best precious metals funds in the business. The last day a questionnaire went around. For a case of very good wine, predict the gold price on the first day of the next year's conference. The price then was about $375. Shoot ahead a year later, and at the opening dinner, this U.S. fund manager gets the case of wine for predicting $325. The actual price of gold was $275.

Handing out the price, the MC mentioned that of the 300 votes, only ONE predicted it would go down, everybody else was predicting higher. I went up to the winner afterwards and asked, "how did you know gold was going down when nobody else did?" His answer was, "I thought it was going up too, but I realized that with everybody voting that way, the only chance I had to win the wine was to go contrarian." Not one of the best minds in the gold business was able to predict the price or even the direction!

The following spring, I was at the Canaccord annual golf tournament and they did the same kind of contest. Gold had just had a dead cat bounce into the low $300s and optimism was the order of the day. The ballots were handed out around the tables after dinner, and taking a cue from fund manager, I wrote down $270. Once everybody's estimate was in, the guesses were compiled and passed around. From the other side of the room somebody bellowed "Who the FUCK is Kerry Knoll?" I stood up and waved. It was Clive Johnson, president of Bema (now running B2, with its cool $7 billion market cap). "Explain why the fuck gold is going down," he shouted. He'd written $450 or something.

Predicting the gold price is a mugs game. Do it often enough and you'll be right once in a while. The next year, I went home with the case of wine.

Let's Finish This Off Right, *by Dave Rogers*

I would be negligent if I did not finish this off with what I consider to be one of the best Newfie stories.

      Billy and Bobby were best of friends and they decided to spend the weekend at Billy's cabin trout fishing and drinking a few beers. Sunday evening over the last two beers in the case they reminisced that it was not a bad weekend. Caught 'tousands of trouts'.... kept a few and ate a few and the rest we trew back. Billy screws up his face and says to Bobby. Bobby me son...if your wife was to have my baby ...would that mean we'd be related? ... A long pause and then Bobby says....Billy me son....I don't know if we'd be related or not. But I can assure you that we would be even.

APPENDIX: AND SO THIS IS CHRISTMAS

The Annual Christmas Party

The big event each year for the Prospect and Tuesday clubs was the annual Christmas party with the obligatory photo op. Some of these photos survive. The photographers' names have been lost to the mists of time. The parties have apparently become tamer over the years. Below, one of the early parties probably mid-1970s. Sitting left to right Orval Leigh, David Rae, Jack Tindale, John Austin, Leon La Prairie. Standing Len Bednarz, Al Hutchinson, Bob Van Ingham, John Cook.

Back Row:
Richard Hogarth, Hamish McGregor, George Kent, Ross Lawrence, Philip Day, Michael Bryden

Front Row:
Tor Jensen, Stan Charteris, Bill James, Leon La Prairie, Peter Howe, Durham Sims

TUESDAY CLUB MEMBERS
CHRISTMAS LUNCHEON
DECEMBER 15, 2009

Tor Jenson, George Kent, Ross Lawrence, Nick Tintor, Hamish McGregor, Phil Day, Dick Hogarth

Durham Sims, Peter Howe, Bill James, Leon La Prairie, Stan Charteris, Howard Stockford

Manufactured by Amazon.ca
Bolton, ON